**WEST
EME**

JESSE H. CHOPER
Professor of Law and Dean Emeritus
University of California, Berkeley

YALE KAMISAR
Professor of Law Emeritus, University of San Diego
Professor of Law Emeritus, University of Michigan

MARY KAY KANE
Professor of Law, Chancellor and Dean Emeritus
University of California, Hastings College of the Law

LARRY D. KRAMER
President, William and Flora Hewlett Foundation

JAMES J. WHITE
Robert A. Sullivan Professor of Law Emeritus
University of Michigan

WEST ACADEMIC PUBLISHING'S LAW SCHOOL ADVISORY BOARD

JOSHUA DRESSLER
Distinguished University Professor Emeritus
Michael E. Moritz College of Law, The Ohio State University

MEREDITH J. DUNCAN
Professor of Law
University of Houston Law Center

RENÉE McDONALD HUTCHINS
Dean and Joseph L. Rauh, Jr. Chair of Public Interest Law
University of the District of Columbia David A. Clarke School of Law

RENEE KNAKE JEFFERSON
Joanne and Larry Doherty Chair in Legal Ethics &
Professor of Law, University of Houston Law Center

ORIN S. KERR
Professor of Law
University of California, Berkeley

JONATHAN R. MACEY
Professor of Law,
Yale Law School

DEBORAH JONES MERRITT
Distinguished University Professor,
John Deaver Drinko/Baker & Hostetler Chair in Law
Michael E. Moritz College of Law, The Ohio State University

ARTHUR R. MILLER
University Professor, New York University
Formerly Bruce Bromley Professor of Law, Harvard University

GRANT S. NELSON
Professor of Law Emeritus, Pepperdine University
Professor of Law Emeritus, University of California, Los Angeles

A. BENJAMIN SPENCER
Dean & Chancellor Professor of Law
William & Mary Law School

CONSUMER PROTECTION LAW

IN A NUTSHELL®

FIFTH EDITION

DEE PRIDGEN
Emeritus Professor of Law
University of Wyoming College of Law

WEST ACADEMIC PUBLISHING

The publisher is not engaged in rendering legal or other professional advice, and this publication is not a substitute for the advice of an attorney. If you require legal or other expert advice, you should seek the services of a competent attorney or other professional.

Nutshell Series, In a Nutshell and the Nutshell Logo are trademarks registered in the U.S. Patent and Trademark Office.

COPYRIGHT © 1976, 1981 WEST PUBLISHING CO.
COPYRIGHT © 1999 By WEST GROUP
© 2016 LEG, Inc. d/b/a West Academic
© 2020 LEG, Inc. d/b/a West Academic
     444 Cedar Street, Suite 700
     St. Paul, MN 55101
     1-877-888-1330

West, West Academic Publishing, and West Academic are trademarks of West Publishing Corporation, used under license.

Printed in the United States of America

ISBN: 978-1-68467-477-0

TO MY HUSBAND, KEN AND MY DAUGHTERS KEIKO AND EM

Dee Pridgen

PREFACE TO THE FIFTH EDITION

In the four years that have passed since the fourth edition of this Nutshell was published in 2016, the path of consumer protection law has not been smooth, nor has it been straightforward. No major consumer legislation emerged, with the exception of a comprehensive California privacy law. Some new federal regulations have been promulgated, while others have been rejected or put on hold. A Consumer Financial Protection Bureau (CFPB) regulation that would have limited consumer arbitration clauses was vetoed by Congress, and the main provisions of a regulation governing fringe lenders were revoked at the agency level.

The U.S. Supreme Court issued several major cases in this field, most of which represent retractions in the law. For instance, the Court ruled in 2017 that debt buyers who collect debts they own are not "debt collectors" covered by the Fair Debt Collection Practices Act, thus carving a major exemption out of the debt collection industry. The Court held in 2016 that plaintiffs in statutory consumer law cases tried in federal courts must demonstrate Article III standing, specifically "injury in fact." This requirement created a preliminary hurdle for most consumer plaintiffs in federal court. In 2020, the Court held that the law setting up the CFPB Director as serving a five-year term, removable only for cause, was an unconstitutional undermining of the Article II executive authority of the President. The offending provision was deemed "severable," however, so that the agency can go forward with a Director serving at the pleasure of the President. Also in 2020, the Court struck down a provision of the Telephone Consumer Protection Act that had previously exempted certain federally-related debt collectors from the general ban on "robo calls" to mobile phones.

New technological developments affecting consumer protection have emerged, including online Internet-based small lenders ("Fintech"), and new payment methods (*e.g.,* prepaid accounts, peer-to-peer digital payments, mobile wallets, and cryptocurrency). The CFPB issued amendments to existing Electronic Fund Transfer Act regulations to cover prepaid accounts, among other things. Other payment methods and the Fintech industry are still in flux and consumer protections are evolving. New communication methods that emerged since the passage of the Fair Debt Collection Practices Act in the late 1970s, such as email, text messages and social media, led the CFPB in 2019 to propose detailed regulations to update this longstanding law. Meanwhile, many court cases struggled to apply the FDCPA to modern debt collection practices.

Consumer protection laws are only useful if they are effectively enforced. Thus, this volume, like the preceding edition, covers government and private enforcement of both federal and state consumer protection laws. With a change of administration in 2017, however, the federal government's enthusiasm for enforcing consumer laws appears to have waned somewhat. Also, the standing requirement in federal court cases, as well as the continuation unabated of arbitration clauses in consumer contracts, may deter private enforcement as well.

As this book goes to press in the summer of 2020, the United States is suffering from several crises, including the corona virus pandemic, massive unemployment, and nationwide upheavals around race relations. One can only speculate at this point as to how this "year like no other" will affect consumer protection. There are already reports of increased fraud both specific to the pandemic and generally taking advantage of hard times, an unfortunate side effect of many financial crises. Job loss and medical bills are also major factors in consumer debt defaults. Thus, due in part to the national turmoil, there may be an increase in debt collection, perhaps with a concomitant increase in debt collection abuse. It remains to be seen whether there might be a legislative response to help protect consumers from exploitation, as occurred after the 2008–09 subprime mortgage crisis, resulting in the passage of the historic Dodd Frank Act.

As in the 4th edition, some aspects of consumer law, such as international or comparative consumer law, are beyond the scope of this book. Likewise, consumer product safety and products liability cases, are also not included. In the interest of brevity and to avoid becoming dated, this book mainly uses primary sources, such as statutes, regulations, and cases, for its relatively limited citations. Law review articles related to consumer law, while sparingly referenced here, should be explored by those seeking a more comprehensive knowledge of the subject matter. Another resource for those seeking greater detail and depth are two treatises, Consumer Protection and the Law, and Consumer Credit and the Law, with new yearly editions by current coauthors Dee Pridgen, Richard Alderman and Jolina Cuaresma. The National Consumer Law Center also has a library of detailed reference books on consumer law.

This Nutshell intends to provide a concise overview of the law of consumer protection in the United States. It can be used as a supplement to the regular course materials in a consumer law course, as well as a reference for practicing attorneys, judges and/or legislators, both domestic and international, who wish to obtain a "big picture" perspective on American consumer law. Rather than offering an in-depth study, this Nutshell aims to provide a stepping off point or general orientation to help start the reader on a journey into the fascinating world of consumer protection law.

I wish to again thank Gene Marsh, author of the 3d edition and coauthor of the 4th edition, for providing the foundation upon which this 5th edition has been built. Without his contribution, as well as the work of the authors of the other prior editions, this book would have been much more difficult to construct. I would also like to thank Professors Jeff Sovern of St. John's University School of Law, and Christopher Peterson, University of Utah, S.J. Quinney College of Law, who joined with me in producing a Fifth Edition of Consumer Law: Cases and Materials, published in 2020. The research done to produce the new edition of the casebook proved to be an excellent resource for this book. Finally, and not least of all, I would like to thank the editorial staff of West Academic, including Mac Soto, for their help, encouragement, and technical support in the creation of the 5th edition.

> DEE PRIDGEN
> Emeritus Professor of Law
> University of Wyoming
> College of Law

July, 2020

PREFACE TO THE FOURTH EDITION

The evolution of consumer protection law in the United States has continued apace since the 3rd edition of this Nutshell was published in 1999. The rise of the Internet and online transactions described in the prior edition resulted in a wave of federal legislation and a new concern for consumer privacy that came to the forefront around the time of the first decade of the 21st century. For instance, Congress passed the Children's Online Privacy Protection Act in 1998 and the Gramm-Leach-Bliley (financial privacy) Act in 1999. The Federal Trade Commission (FTC) expanded the Telemarketing Sales Rule in 2003 to include the hugely popular Do-Not-Call Registry, based on the consumer's interest in protecting the privacy of their home from annoying and often fraudulent intrusions by telemarketers. This was soon followed by the CAN-SPAM Act, meant to curb the onslaught of unsolicited commercial emails, or "spam" as it has come to be known. Since 2000, the FTC has used its general authority to police unfair and deceptive trade practices to promote the use of reasonable cyber security practices by companies that handle consumers' personal financial or other information. The Fair and Accurate Credit Transactions Act of 2003, amending the Fair Credit Reporting Act, was also aimed at protecting consumers from identity theft, one of the major consumer scourges of the era. Based on these developments, this edition of the Nutshell has an entire new chapter on consumer privacy, as well as significant updating of the material on credit reporting.

The rise of the subprime credit market, including the use of exotic and sometimes toxic mortgage loans, and the expansion of the credit card industry along with increased fees and hidden penalties for consumers, led in part to the collapse of the housing market and the Great Recession of 2008. Responding to the financial crisis, Congress passed the Dodd-Frank Act in 2010, which created the Consumer Financial Protection Bureau, a major new federal consumer protection agency charged with regulating consumer finance service providers. The Dodd-Frank Act also contained the Mortgage Reform and Anti-Predatory Lending Act, which mandates many substantive and other protections for consumers in the residential real estate finance arena. The CFPB's activities, including new and proposed regulations on mortgage loans, mortgage servicing, fringe lending, and arbitration clauses, are covered in the expanded Truth in Lending chapters featured in this edition. Congress also passed the Credit CARD Act of 2009, which enhanced credit card holders' substantive protections, as well as improving disclosures. Developments regarding credit, debit and stored value cards are covered in a new, separate chapter on modern consumer payment systems.

Consumer law is not only based on legislation and regulations. Consumer-related case law has also seen significant new developments since the publication of the 3rd edition of this Nutshell. For instance, in the landmark 2011 case of *AT&T v. Concepcion*, the United States Supreme Court continued a series of cases in which it upheld standard form mandatory arbitration clauses, including class action waivers, in consumer contracts, based on the supremacy of the Federal Arbitration Act. The CFPB in 2016, after conducting a major study of arbitration clauses in consumer contracts, proposed a regulation that would ban the use of class action waivers in such contracts. Arbitration clauses, as well as other unwelcome clauses, often appear in online contracts contained in hyperlinks or in scroll-down text, next to the click "I agree" button. Many common law contracts cases have enforced such clauses under the legal fiction that consumers have exercised meaningful assent, as long as they have any sort of opportunity to read the terms and conditions and indicate their agreement.

Consumer protection laws are only useful if they are effectively enforced. Thus, this volume covers federal and state government enforcement, as well as private enforcement, of both federal and state consumer protection laws, including state unfair and deceptive trade practices acts and the federal Truth in Lending Act. In addition, the Federal Trade Commission's advertising substantiation doctrine is a major enforcement tool in the advertising area. In a 2015 D.C. Circuit Court case against a dietary supplement maker, the FTC established that when a food or beverage product claims to have disease-related properties, the marketer must have some random, clinical tests to back up such claims.

Other aspects of consumer law, such as international or comparative consumer law, unfortunately are beyond the scope of this book. Likewise, consumer product safety and products liability cases, are also not included. Mainly in the interest of brevity and to avoid becoming dated, this book mainly uses primary sources, such as statutes, regulations and cases, for its relatively limited citations. Law review articles related to consumer law, while not referenced here, should be explored by those seeking a more comprehensive knowledge of the subject matter.

The limitations of scope, as well as the summary nature of the coverage within this book, are premised on the basic purpose of this Nutshell, which is to provide a concise overview of the law of consumer protection in the United States. The book is intended for use as a supplement to the regular course materials in a consumer law course, as well as a reference for practicing attorneys, judges and/or legislators, both domestic and international, who wish to obtain a "big picture" perspective on American consumer law. Any in-depth study of the topics covered here should go well beyond this volume. Nonetheless, it is a goal of this Nutshell to provide a stepping off point or general orientation to help start the reader on a journey into the fascinating world of consumer protection law.

Author Dee Pridgen wishes to thank Gene Marsh, author of the 3rd edition, for providing the foundation upon which the 4th edition has been built. Without his contribution, as well as the work of the authors of the other prior editions, this book would have been much more difficult to construct. I would also like to thank Professor Jeff Sovern of St. John's University, for his helpful review of and comments on several draft chapters of this work. Thanks also to Chris Hoofnagle of the University of California, Berkeley, for his review of the chapter on consumer privacy. I am also grateful to my research assistant, Susan Manown, a law student at the University of Wyoming College of Law, for her assistance in proofreading/reviewing the manuscript as well as constructing the index. I am also indebted to the late Carl M. Williams, who set up the Carl Williams faculty research fund, which helped support this effort. Finally, and not least of all, I would like to thank the editorial staff of West Academic, including Mac Soto, for their help, encouragement and technical support in the creation of the 4th edition. I was delighted to accept the invitation to work on this project, which I view as a natural offspring of my many years of teaching and scholarship in the area of consumer protection law.

> DEE PRIDGEN
> Carl M. Williams
> Professor of Law &
> Social Responsibility
> University of Wyoming
> College of Law

July 2016

PREFACE TO THE THIRD EDITION

Consumer protection laws today reflect fundamental changes in the way individuals obtain credit, pay their bills and make purchases. In the past, consumers purchased most goods and services through local merchants in face-to-face transactions, and borrowed money in established relationships with local depositary institutions. People were more conservative in their use of credit and lenders often required significant down payments, strong credit records and an established history of employment. Consumers paid in cash, occasionally wrote checks, and dealt in a paper world of bank notes and credit sales contracts.

Much has changed. Consumers continue to trade with local merchants, but they also make purchases from telemarketers, catalog sellers and companies marketing their products over the internet. Many cars are leased and some appliances are rented. The "paper world" in consumer credit and payment systems is still with us, but individuals now pay some of their bills electronically. They use credit cards, debit cards, stored-value cards and they access cash through an ATM rather than a teller.

Credit is now available to consumers who have shaky credit records, although the price of the credit may be high. Usury laws no longer exist in some places. And although depositary institutions such as banks, credit unions and a variety of mortgage lenders remain dominant, there are many nondepositary subprime lenders serving individuals who have a history of slow payments and default. The supply of credit to the subprime market has been bolstered through the bundling and securitization of subprime loans, attracting investors in search of higher returns.

Consumers pay more bills electronically, but they also receive payments by means other than the transfer of paper. The federal government is sending Social Security and other federal benefit checks electronically, and a growing number of people have their payroll checks deposited directly in their checking accounts. However, the storage and transfer of information electronically raises concerns about unauthorized access to consumer accounts, credit reports and other personal information.

This Nutshell treats the traditional areas in consumer protection, but also introduces new state and federal laws that reflect the changes noted above. Although there was little activity from Congress in the 1980s in enacting new consumer protection laws, there was a resurgence of activity in the 1990s. The new laws reflect a change in the political climate and the need to provide some procedural protections and additional disclosures, as prices were deregulated in a number of markets. This Nutshell explores the development of the subprime credit market, dealer-arranged financing and the explosion in the use of open-end credit by consumers. The "fringe banks," such as pawnshops, payday lenders and rent-to-own operations are also discussed. Arbitration and class actions in consumer disputes are also discussed, although more complete coverage of these subjects must be found elsewhere.

The author acknowledges the excellent research assistance provided by law students Beth Bosquet, Gregg Curry and Hope Stewart. Typing and technical help were provided by Wanda Elliott. The author also appreciates the research support provided by The University of Alabama Law School Foundation and the George M. and Mary C. Akers Fund. Finally, the author acknowledges the excellent work of Professor David Epstein and Professor Steve Nickles, whose 1981 second edition of this Nutshell stood the test of time and was appreciated by many law students and professors who explored this area of the law.

PROFESSOR GENE A. MARSH

1999

OUTLINE

Preface to the Fifth Edition V

Preface to the Fourth Edition XI

Preface to the Third Edition XVII

Table of Cases XXXI

Chapter One. Introduction to Consumer Protection Law 1
A. What Is a Consumer Transaction? 1
B. What Is Consumer Law? 3
C. Coverage of This Volume 11

Chapter Two. Public and Private Actions to Regulate Consumer Markets 17
A. Overview 17
B. The Federal Trade Commission: A Brief History and Overview 17
C. The Consumer Financial Protection Bureau 26
D. State Agency Enforcement 30
E. Private Actions Using State UDAP Laws 33
    1. General 33
    2. Who May Sue? 34
    3. Who Can Be Sued? 35
    4. Procedural Obstacles to Suit 36
    5. Statutory Damages 37
    6. Attorney's Fees Under State Statutes 38
F. RICO as a Civil Suit Option for Consumers ... 40

XXI

G.	Class Actions..42	
	1. Overview..42	
	2. Basic Requirements for Certification......44	
	3. Potential for Abuse in Class Actions.......46	
H.	Arbitration 49	

Chapter Three. Inducing Consumer Transactions: Advertising and Marketing 57

A.	Advertising..57	
	1. Common Law Actions.............................57	
	2. Federal Trade Commission's Regulation of Advertising..60	
	3. Specific FTC Concerns 64	
	4. Applying State UDAP Statutes to Advertising..67	
	5. Credit Advertising Provisions 69	
B.	Other Sales Practices..75	
	1. Door-to-Door Sales..................................75	
	2. Telephone Sales......................................77	
	3. Mail, Internet and Telephone Order Sales 81	
	4. Unordered Goods & Negative Option Plans...82	
	5. Referral Sales & Pyramid Schemes 84	
	6. Unsolicited Commercial E-Mails (Spam) 86	
C.	Online Sales and Hidden Contract Terms......87	

Chapter Four. Consumer Privacy.....................93

A.	Scope and Overview...93	
B.	Common Law Privacy Torts 95	
C.	Online Consumer Privacy 98	

D.	Children's Online Privacy	105
E.	Data Security	108
F.	Financial Privacy & the Gramm-Leach-Bliley Act	114

Chapter Five. Credit Reports, Identity Theft, and Equal Access to Credit ... 119

- A. Credit Reports 119
  - 1. Use 119
  - 2. Common Law Protection 121
  - 3. Fair Credit Reporting Act 123
    - a. Scope 123
    - b. Requirements for Consumer Reporting Agencies 128
    - c. Requirements for Users of Consumer Reports 132
    - d. Requirements for Furnishers of Information 135
    - e. Rights of Consumers 137
    - f. Identity Theft Protections 142
    - g. Administrative Remedies 145
    - h. Civil Liability 146
  - 4. State Laws 148
- B. Credit Repair Organizations Act 149
- C. Discrimination in Access to Credit 153
  - 1. Scope of Equal Credit Opportunity Act 153
  - 2. Discrimination in Obtaining Information and Signatures in Credit Applications 154
  - 3. Proving Illegal Discrimination in Credit Transactions 155
  - 4. Notification 159

	5.	Effect of Equal Credit Opportunity Act on State Law 161
	6.	Remedies 161

Chapter Six. Credit Disclosures: Truth in Lending Overview and Closed-End Transactions 163

A. Need for Disclosure Legislation and History of TILA 163
B. Truth in Lending Act—Overview 168
    1. Introduction 168
    2. Regulation Z and Official Staff Commentary 168
    3. Scope of Application of TILA 170
        a. Amount of Credit 170
        b. Purpose of Credit 171
        c. Status of Debtor 173
        d. Status of Creditor 173
    4. Organization of TILA and Regulation Z 175
    5. General Disclosure Requirements 177
C. Closed-End Credit Disclosures 180
    1. Time for Disclosure 180
    2. Disclosure of the Finance Charge 183
        a. In General 183
        b. Credit Insurance 189
        c. Hidden Finance Charges 192
    3. Annual Percentage Rate 198
    4. Other Closed-End Credit Disclosure Requirements 200
        a. In General 200
        b. Security Interests 203
        c. Private Education Loans 204

		d.	Location of Disclosures 207

Chapter Seven. Credit Disclosures: Open-End Credit and Real Estate Secured Transactions 209
A. Introduction 209
B. Open-End Credit.. 210
    1. Overview... 210
    2. Scope of Open-End Credit 212
    3. Disclosures with Solicitations and Applications... 213
    4. Account-Opening Disclosures................ 218
    5. Periodic Statements 219
    6. Home Equity Lines of Credit (HELOC).. 223
C. Real Estate Secured Transactions................ 226
    1. Overview... 226
    2. Special Timing Rules............................. 229
    3. Specific Real Estate Disclosure Rules... 233
    4. High-Cost (HOEPA) Loans.................... 236
    5. Substantive Limits on All Home-Secured Credit Transactions................. 242
    6. Reverse Mortgages 249

Chapter Eight. Truth in Lending Enforcement and Related Statutes............ 253
A. Introduction 253
B. Federal Enforcement of TILA........................ 253
C. Consumer Remedies 256
    1. Private Actions—Overview 256
    2. Standing to Bring Claims for Damages... 257
    3. Statutory Damages................................ 259

	4.	Actual Damages 262
	5.	Creditor Defenses................................... 264
		a. Assignee Liability 264
		b. Statute of Limitations................... 266
		c. Creditor Error 268
	6.	Attorney's Fees...................................... 270
	7.	Class Actions and Arbitrations 270
D.	Right of Rescission... 273
E.	Related Statutes 278
	1.	Truth in Savings Act 278
	2.	Consumer Leasing Act 280
	3.	Interstate Land Sales Full Disclosure Act 283
	4.	Real Estate Settlement Procedures Act 286

Chapter Nine. Regulating the Cost of Credit 291
A. History of Rate Regulation 291
B. Should There Be Rate Ceilings? 294
C. Problems in Proving Usury............................ 296
   1. Intent... 297
   2. Should Loans and Credit Sales Receive Different Treatment?.............................. 298
   3. Has the Maximum Legal Rate Been Exceeded?... 299
D. Federal Preemption 299
E. Types of Lenders and Credit Covered by Rate Regulation 304

Chapter Ten. Holder in Due Course and Warranties 311
A. The Holder in Due Course Doctrine 311
   1. Introduction 311
   2. The Loss of Holder in Due Course Status in Certain Consumer Lending ... 315
   3. Should the FTC Rule Limit Affirmative Recovery? 318
   4. Limitations on the FTC Holder Rule's Coverage 321
   5. Special Cases of Third-Party Creditor Liability—Credit Cards 322
B. Warranties 326
   1. Uniform Commercial Code—Article Two 326
   2. The Magnuson-Moss Warranty Act 332
     a. Overview 332
     b. Disclosure Requirements 334
     c. Substantive Requirements and Provisions 337
     d. Informal Dispute Resolution and Arbitration Under the MMWA 339
   3. Lemon Laws 342
   4. Home Warranties 348

Chapter Eleven. Default and Debt Collection 353
A. Limits on Default Provisions in Consumer Credit Contracts 353
   1. Introduction 353
   2. Prohibited Practices 354
     a. Cosigner Provision 354
     b. Pyramiding Late Charges 356

		c.	Confession of Judgment.................. 356
		d.	Non-Purchase Money Security Interests in Certain Household Goods... 357
		e.	Waiver of Exemptions..................... 359
		f.	Assignment of Wages...................... 360
B.	Informal Debt Collection................................ 361
	1.	Introduction.. 361
	2.	Common Law Actions............................. 363
	3.	Fair Debt Collection Practices Act 366
		a.	Introduction 366
		b.	Transactions and Persons Covered 367
		c.	Validation of Debts 372
		d.	False or Misleading Information ... 376
		e.	Collection of Time-Barred Debts.... 379
		f.	Harassment or Abuse 381
		g.	Unfair or Unconscionable Practices... 382
		h.	Additional Restrictions on Communications with the Consumer and with Third Parties.. 385
		i.	Government Enforcement, Civil Liability and Bona Fide Error Defense.. 388
C.	Debt Collection Within the Judicial System 390
	1.	Garnishment and Seizure of Property... 391
	2.	Obtaining Judgments............................. 396
	3.	Special Rights of Lien Creditors............ 397
		a.	Repossession in General 397

| | b. Actions Under UCC Article 9......... 397
| | c. Limitations on Deficiency Judgments 398

Chapter Twelve. Credit and Debit Cards and Other Modern Consumer Payments 403
A. Special Protections for Credit Card Consumers 403
   1. Introduction... 403
   2. Limits on Rates and Fees...................... 404
   3. Credit Cards and Young Consumers..... 407
   4. Unauthorized Use 409
   5. Billing Errors 415
   6. Billing Periods and Payments............... 418
B. Debit Cards and Other Electronic Fund Transfers.. 421
   1. Overview.. 421
   2. Unauthorized Use 425
   3. Billing errors 428
   4. Overdraft Protection and Debit Card/ATM Transactions................................. 431
   5. Preauthorized EFT................................ 434
   6. Civil and Criminal Liability 438
C. Gift Cards, Stored Value/Prepaid Cards and International Remittances..................... 438
   1. Gift Cards.. 439
   2. Stored Value/Prepaid Cards.................. 440
   3. International Remittances 445
D. Internet, Mobile Payments, and Cryptocurrency 446
   1. Internet-Based and Mobile Device Payments... 447

2. Crypto- and Virtual Currency 448

INDEX 451

TABLE OF CASES

References are to Pages

Abele v. Mid-Penn Consumer Discount, 261
Adiel v. Chase Federal Sav. & Loan Ass'n, 271
Allied-Bruce Terminix Companies v. Dodson, 51
American Bar Assoc. v. FTC, 115
American Express Co. v. Italian Colors Restaurant, 52
Anderson v. United Finance Co., 154
Andrews v. TRW, Inc., 129
Anglin v. Tower Loan of Mississippi, Inc., 146
Apple, Inc., In re, 108
AT&T Mobility LLC v. Concepcion, 48, 52, 272
Attias v. Carefirst, Inc., 113
Baker v. Sunny Chevrolet, Inc., 269
Bankwest, Inc. v. Baker, 307
Barash v. Gale Employees Credit Union, 258
Barbato v. Greystone Alliance, LLC, 370
Barnes v. Chase Home Finance, LLC, 275
Barr v. American Ass'n of Political Consultants, 78, 371
Basset v. ABM Parking Servs., Inc., 147
Beach v. Ocwen Federal Bank, 277
Beck v. McDonald, 113
Benion v. Bank One, 212
Berkson v. Gogo, LLC, 90
BJ's Wholesale Club, Inc., In re, 109
Bose v. Interclick, Inc., 103
Boyd v. Wexler, 378
Bradley v. Franklin Collection Service, Inc., 384
Britton v. Bill Anselmi Pontiac-Buick-GMC, Inc., 343
Brophy v. Chase Manhattan Mort. Co., 230
Brown v. Payday Check Advance, Inc., 262
Bryant v. Mortgage Capital Resource Corp., 266
Buchholz v. Meyer Njus Tanick, PA, 390
Burrell v. DFS Services, LLC, 140
Campbell-Ewald Co. v. Jose Gomez, 48, 78
Caputo v. Professional Recovery Services, Inc., 365
Castano v. American Tobacco Co., 45

TABLE OF CASES

Central Hudson Gas & Electric Corp. v. Public Service Commission of New York, 69
CFPB v. All Financial Services, LLC, 251
CFPB v. Capitol One, 74
CFPB v. Commercial Credit Consultants, 152
CFPB v. Navient Corp., 28
CFPB v. Park View Law, Inc., 152
CFPB v. TCF National Bank, 434
Cherry v. Amoco, 158
Citibank (South Dakota) v. Mincks, 171, 325, 417
Clark v. Absolute Collection Service, Inc., 375
Cliffdale Associates, Inc., In re, 19
Clomon v. Jackson, 376
Cohen v. Rosicki, Rosicki & Assoc., Inc., 390
CompuCredit Corp. v. Greenwood, 151
Consumers Union of U.S., Inc. v. FTC, 25
Crestar Bank, N.A. v. Cheevers, 417
Cripe v. Leiter, 36
Cruz v. International Collection Corp., 386
Davis v. Southern Energy Homes, Inc., 341
De La Torre v. CashCall, 295
Deer Creek Construction Co. v. Peterson, 39
Dennis v. Handley, 260
Doctor's Associates, Inc. v. Casarotto, 52
Douglass v. Convergent Outsourcing, 383
DSW, Inc., In re, 109
Dwolla, Inc., In re, 112
Dwyer v. American Express Co., 96
Eachen v. Scott Housing Systems, 319
Edwards v. Niagara Credit Solutions, Inc., 387
Ellis v. General Motors Acceptance Corp., 265
Engl v. National Grocers by Vitamin Cottage, Inc., 113
Evon v. Law Offices of Sidney Mickell, 386
Expressions Hair Design v. Schneiderman, 196
Facebook, Inc., United States v., 100
Feinstein v. Firestone Tire & Rubber Co., 339
Fero v. Excellus Health Plan, Inc., 114
Fischl v. General Motors Acceptance Corp., 160
Flurish, Inc., d/b/a LendUp, In re, 75
Ford Motor Co. v. FTC, 70, 164
Ford Motor Credit Co. v. Morgan, 320
Foreign Commerce v. Tonn, 297

TABLE OF CASES *XXXIII*

Forrest v. Verizon Communications, Inc., 90
Freyermuth v. Credit Bureau Services, Inc., 380
FTC v. Credit Bureau Center, LLC, 23, 63, 84
FTC v. Gill, 152
FTC v. H.N. Singer, Inc., 23
FTC v. Herbalife Internat'l of America, Inc., 86
FTC v. LeadClick Media, LLC, 66
FTC v. LifeLock, Inc., 110
FTC v. Pantron I Corp., 65
FTC v. QT, Inc., 62
FTC v. Seismic Entertainment Productions, Inc., 101
FTC v. Southwest Sunsites, Inc., 22
FTC v. Volkswagen Group of America, Inc., 63
FTC v. Wyndham Worldwide Corp., 111
FTC v. Xtel Marketing, Inc., Stipulated Permanent Injunction, 117
Galaria v. Nationwide Mutual Insurance Co., 113
Gallegos v. Stokes, 171
Gammon v. GC Services Ltd. Partnership, 376
General Motors Corp. v. FTC, 164
Geocities, In re, 99
Goldstein v. Hutton, Ingram, Yuzek, Gainen, Carroll & Bertolotti, 370
Google Inc. Cookie Placement Consumer Privacy Litigation, In re, 103
Gray v. American Express Co., 416
Green Tree Financial Corp.-Alabama v. Randolph, 52, 272
Greenlee v. Steering Wheel, Inc., 265
Guitierrez v. Wells Fargo Bank, N.A., 433
Gulley v. Markoff & Krasny, 368
Hamilton v. Ford Motor Credit Co., 365
Heintz v. Jenkins, 370
Henson v. Santander Consumer USA, Inc., 369
Hill v. Gateway 2000, Inc., 89
Holzman v. Malcolm S. Gerald & Assoc., Inc., 380
Home Savings Ass'n v. Guerra, 319
Hyland v. First USA Bank, 324
Hyundai Motor America, Inc. v. Goodin, 329
Irby-Greene v. M.O.R., Inc., 320
Izraelewitz v. Manufacturers Hanover Trust Co., 324
James v. Wadas, 370
Javins v. First National Realty Corp., 350

Jerman v. Carlisle, McNellie, Rini, Kramer & Ulrich LPA, 389
JetBlue Airways Corp. Privacy Litigation, In re, 100
Johnson v. MBNA America Bank, 140
Jones v. Experian Information Solutions, Inc., 139
Jones v. Federated Financial Reserve Corp., 135
Jones v. U.S. Child Support Recovery, 364
Kidd v. Thomson Reuters Corp., 127
King v. Capital One Bank, 152
Klocek v. Gateway, Inc., 89
Koropoulos v. Credit Bureau, Inc., 130
Kraft, Inc. v. FTC, 21, 61, 68
Krautsack v. Anderson, 40
Krieger v. Bank of America, N.A., 414, 416
Kruser v. Bank of America, 427
Kuhn v. Account Control Technology, Inc., 382
Kurz v. Chase Manhattan Bank USA, NA., 270
Ladick v. Van Gemert, 368
Lafferty v. Wells Fargo Bank, N.A., 321
Lewert v. P.F. Chang's China Bistro, Inc., 113
Ly v. Nystrom, 34
Lymburner v. U.S. Financial Funds, Inc., 271
Mabe v. G.C. Services Ltd. Partnership, 368
MacDonald v. Thomas M. Cooley Law School, 58
Madden v. Midland Funding, LLC, 308
Maddox v. St. Joe Papermakers Federal Credit Union, 258
Mainstream Marketing Services v. FTC, 80
Markham v. Colonial Mortg. Service Co., Associates, Inc., 155
Maronda Homes, Inc. v. Lakeview Reserve Homeowners Association, Inc., 349
Marquette National Bank v. First of Omaha, 296, 299
McAdory v. M.N.S. & Associates, LLC, 370
Meade v. Avant of Colorado, LLC, 307
Meade v. Marlette Funding, LLC, 307
Melvin, In re, 180
Messineo v. Ocwen Loan Servicing, LLC, 269
Midland Funding, LLC v. Johnson, 380
Miller v. American Exp. Co., 155
Miller v. Nissan Motor Acceptance Corp., 283
Mims v. Arrow Financial Services, LLC, 78

TABLE OF CASES

Minskoff v. American Express Travel Related Services Co., 413
Moore v. Wells Fargo Bank, N.A., 289
Mount v. Pulsepoint, Inc., 103
Musical.ly Corp., United States v., 107
Myers v. First Tennessee Bank, 213
Najarro v. SASI Int'l, Ltd., 297
National Financial Services, Inc., United States v., 377
National Petroleum Refiners Ass'n v. FTC, 24
Nguyen v. Barnes & Noble, Inc., 91
Novartis Corp. v. FTC, 64
Obduskey v. McCarthy & Holthus, LLP, 372
Ognibene v. Citibank, N.A., 428
PayPal, Inc., In re, 111
Peart v. Shippie, 136
Perino v. Mercury Finance, 194
Perry v. First Nat'l Bank, 126, 406
Peter v. GC Services L.P., 375
Peters v. Jim Lupient Oldsmobile Co., 262
Peterson v. Volkswagen of America, Inc., 333
Petroff-Kline, United States v., 262
Pollard v. Law Office of Mandy L. Spaulding, 375
POM Wonderful v. FTC, 62
Premera Blue Cross Customers Data Security Breach Litigation, In re, 114
Price v. Berman's Automotive, Inc., 263
ProCD, Inc. v. Zeidenberg, 89
Ramadan v. Chase Manhattan Corp., 265
Regions Bank, In re, 434
Richardson v. Citibank, 300
Richardson v. Fleet Bank, 130
Robins v. Spokeo, Inc., 148
Rodash v. AIB Mortgage Co., 259
Rossman v. Fleet Bank, 217
Royster v. Toyota Motor Sales, U.S.A., Inc., 344
Russell, In re, 263
Ryan v. American Honda Motor Co., Inc., 333
Safeco Ins. Co. of America v. Burr, 134, 146
Santander Bank, In re, 434
Sarver v. Experian Information Solutions, 130
Schreiber v. Ally Financial, Inc., 43
Schroyer v. Frankel, 371

Schwartz v. HSBC Bank USA, N.A., 259, 268
Sears Holdings Management Corp., In re, 101
Seila Law, LLC v. CFPB, 10, 26
Semar v. Platte Valley Fed. Sav. & Loan Ass'n, 172
Sheriff v. Gillie, 378
Shibley v. Time, Inc., 96
Shuler v. Ingram & Associates, 382
Simpson v. Termplan of Georgia, Inc., 261
Singer v. Chase Manhattan Bank, 324
Smiley v. Citibank (South Dakota), N.A., 300
Smith v. Cotton Brothers Baking Co., Inc., 395
Smith, In re, 262
Snapchat, Inc., In re, 110
Snow v. Jesse L. Riddle, P.C., 368
Sorchaga v. Ride Auto, LLC, 331
Soundboard Association v. FTC, 80
Spearman v. Tom Wood Pontiac-GMC, Inc., 181
Specht v. Netscape Communications Corp., 91
Spiegel, Inc. v. FTC, 396
Spokeo, Inc. v. Robins, 147, 258, 389
Starke v. SquareTrade, Inc., 91
Stenberg, State ex rel. v. Consumer's Choice Foods, Inc., 320
Sterling Drug, Inc. v. FTC, 62
Stewart v. Travelers Corp., 395
Stieger v. Chevy Chase Sav. Bank, 412
Stout v. FreeScore, 151
Strubel v. Comenity Bank, 259
Suesz v. Med-1 Solutions, LLC, 385
Syed v. M-1, LLC, 146
Sykes v. Mel S. Harris and Associates LLC, 389, 396
Tashof v. FTC, 65
Tavares v. Horstman, 349
TaxSlayer, LLC, In re, 116
Taylor v. Quality Hyundai, Inc., 265
Teflon Prods. Liab. Litig., In re, 45
Telebrands Corp. v. FTC, 21
Thomka v. A.Z. Chevrolet, Inc., 269
Thompson Medical Co., In re, 61
Tucker v. Chase Bank USA, N.A., 178
Twitter, Inc., In re, 109
Unico v. Owen, 314

United States Finance Co. v. Jones, 314
Vallies v. Sky Bank, 262
Van Jackson v. Check 'N Go of Illinois, Inc., 204
Virachack v. University Ford, 195
Virginia State Board of Pharmacy v. Virginia Citizens
    Consumer Council, Inc., 68
Voelker v. Porsche Cars N. Am., Inc., 338
Walker Bank & Trust Co. v. Jones, 413
Walker v. Wallace Auto Sales, 194
Walsh v. Ford Motor Co., 45
Walton v. Rose Mobile Homes LLC, 55, 341
Warner-Lambert Co. v. FTC, 63
Watters v. Wachovia Bank, 302
Weinberger v. Great Northern Nekoosa Corp., 46
Wetherby v. Retail Credit Co., 122
Whalen v. Michaels Stores, Inc., 113
Whitaker v. Spiegel, Inc., 298
Williams v. American Honda Finance Corp., 400
Zortman v. J.C. Christensen & Associates, Inc., 387

CONSUMER PROTECTION LAW
IN A NUTSHELL®

FIFTH EDITION

CHAPTER ONE
INTRODUCTION TO CONSUMER PROTECTION LAW

A. WHAT IS A CONSUMER TRANSACTION?

A consumer transaction occurs when a person obtains goods, real property, credit, or services for personal, family, or household purposes. Examples include:

(1) An elderly couple, Art and Alma, contact a mortgage broker about financing a home remodeling project. Their house is worth $200,000 and has a $60,000 mortgage balance. They wish to refinance their mortgage to obtain $100,000 for the home remodel as well as some medical expenses. Their income is not sufficient to make the payments on the new loan so their broker submits falsified documents regarding their income. The loan also permits the borrowers to pay the interest only for some payments, which will result in negative amortization. When housing prices in their area fall, Art and Alma find they cannot resell their house for enough to pay off the mortgage and they are now facing foreclosure.

(2) Nick Haley purchased a tablet computer online for his personal use. He clicked the "I agree" button to accept the terms and conditions of the sale specified in the

manufacturer's standard form contract, available on a website hyperlink near the "I agree" button. Nick did not read the terms and conditions. When he received the tablet he found it did not function as advertised and sought to get a refund or repair from the seller. He was told that (a) the tablet contained a disclaimer of all warranties, and (b) that the terms and conditions he had agreed to required him to submit all disputes to binding arbitration.

(3) Cassie Berry needs $200 cash, but has no relationship with a bank or traditional lender. In order to raise the money she obtains a "car title" loan, which allows her to continue to drive the vehicle but gives the lender a security interest in the car. Although the state usury law sets the maximum permissible rates on $200 consumer loans at 20 percent, the title lender charges Cassie 300 percent interest on the transaction. When Cassie later defaults on the loan, the lender repossesses the car, which she needed to get to her job, and resells it to cover her outstanding balance, which is now over $500 due to the accumulation of fees and finance charges.

In each circumstance, the ordinary rules of contract law apply. However, since each is also a "consumer transaction," special consumer protection statutes and rules may be in play as well. In the case of Art and Alma, there is a federal law that requires lenders to verify that borrowers have the ability to repay a home-secured loan, and certain practices are prohibited, such as negative amortization and so-called "no-doc" loans.[1] As to Nick, unfortunately disclaimers of warranty and arbitration clauses may be permitted if the terms he agreed to were adequately disclosed online.[2] Cassie may be protected by a state usury law, but federal regulation of payday and car title loans has been revoked in substantial part.[3] Consumer protection statutes typically attempt to provide some advantages to the consumer in what is presumed to be a one-sided bargain that favors the merchant or financial service provider. Thus, in every area covered in this volume, it is critical to be aware of the boundaries of the legal protections discussed, because these protections may not be applicable outside of the consumer transaction context.

B. WHAT IS CONSUMER LAW?

Consumer law emerged as a separate area of law in the 1960s and 1970s when many consumer

---

[1] These mortgage related provisions are covered in Chapter 7, Part C, *infra*.

[2] Online contracts are covered in Chapter 3, Section C, *infra*. Arbitration clauses are covered in Chapter 2, Section H, *infra*. The Magnuson-Moss Warranty Act may void the disclaimer of implied warranties or limit it to the duration of the written warranty. The MMWA also provides for informal dispute resolution more favorable to consumers than private arbitration, but the arbitration clause may be enforced. *See* discussion in Chapter 10, Section B, *infra*.

[3] Regulating the cost of credit is the subject of Chapter 9, *infra*.

protection statutes were enacted at the state and federal level. Prior to that time most consumer transactions were governed by the ancient rule of caveat emptor or "let the buyer beware." There was a common law cause of action for fraud, but the elements of proof, including justifiable reliance and intent to defraud, were difficult for consumer plaintiffs to meet. Also, the cost of litigation for relatively small consumer claims was a barrier to obtaining any type of legal remedy for merchant deception. Problems encountered by plaintiffs attempting to use a fraud theory in false advertising cases will be discussed more thoroughly in Chapter Three.

In addition to the common law, the Federal Trade Commission also existed prior to the main body of consumer legislation discussed here, and it had a statutory mandate to police unfair and deceptive trade practices, but the FTC did not have sufficient resources to protect all the consumers who may have been harmed in the marketplace. Nonetheless, the FTC emerged as the nation's leading consumer protection agency, and its work will also be discussed in this volume. Finally, after World War II, the availability and use of consumer credit exploded and consumers were buying goods, services, and real estate pursuant to credit contracts and credit marketing that defied understanding by the average person. All these factors led to the creation of what we now view as "consumer protection law."

The body of law called "Consumer Law" refers to the collection of statutes, regulations, agency cases and court cases that proliferated in response to the consumer movement which was on the rise in the late 1960s and early 1970s. The statutes were both federal and state level and most of the statutes passed during this era remain with us today although they are frequently amended to address new issues in the consumer marketplace as they evolve over time.

At the state level, there was a wave of state "unfair and deceptive acts and practices" laws, or UDAP statutes, that were eventually passed by all fifty state legislatures. The FTC, the Council of State Governments and the Commissioners on Uniform State Laws recommended that the states enact these UDAP statutes out of a belief that effective regulation of unfair and deceptive acts could not occur without state aid and private lawsuits. The types of statutes and the particulars of the statutes vary considerably from state to state, and an extensive body of case law has emerged to interpret the reach of the various statutes. The aim of these statutes, most of which date back to the 1970s, was to expand the consumer protection mission of the FTC out to the state government and individual consumer level. In addition, the Uniform Consumer Credit Code was promulgated by the National Conference of Commissioners on Uniform State Laws in 1968, and amended in 1974, but was not passed by many states. However, most states do have some type of consumer credit code that operates alongside the federal legislation.

The 1970s saw an outpouring of major consumer protection legislation from the U.S. Congress. First, there was the passage of the major consumer credit laws, including the Truth in Lending Act, the Fair Credit Reporting Act, the Equal Credit Opportunity Act, the Electronic Funds Transfer Act, and the Fair Debt Collection Practices Act. These federal laws provide the bulwark of consumer protection in the credit area and were built on the idea that consumers need information about the costs of credit, as well as some substantive protections against discrimination and unfair or deceptive practices. The Magnuson-Moss Warranty Act was also passed by Congress in 1975 aimed at providing information and some substantive protections for consumers vis-à-vis consumer product warranties. Another important federal statute passed in the 1970s is the Real Estate Settlement Procedures Act, which protects buyers and sellers of residential real estate from unreasonably high settlement costs by requiring advance disclosure and outlawing certain "kickbacks."

In the 1980s, the federal government prioritized the free market and did not initiate much new legislation, but the pre-existing statutes remained in place. In 1980, the Truth in Lending Simplification Act revamped the disclosure requirements of that law, and improved the readability and formatting of the disclosures. In 1988, Congress also improved disclosures for credit card solicitations, and passed legislation requiring specific disclosures for new forms of consumer credit, including Home Equity Lines of Credit (HELOCs) (open end credit secured by the consumer's dwelling), and Adjustable Rate Mortgages (ARMs). The 1980s also saw the passage in almost every state of so-called "lemon laws" that aimed to protect new car buyers who complained of inadequate warranty protection.

In the 1994, Congress amended TILA to add special protections for consumers taking out high cost loans secured by their homes, in a law called the Home Owners Equity Protection Act (HOEPA). Congress also amended the Fair Credit Reporting Act during this decade to extend the Act's duties beyond the major credit reporting agencies to also include entities that furnish information about consumers. Also, in response to abusive marketing practices involving the use of the telephone, in 1994 Congress passed the Federal Telephone Consumer Protection Act (FTCPA) which regulates junk faxes and "robo" calls. The Telemarketing and Consumer Fraud and Abuse Prevention Act (TCFAPA) of 1994 was enacted to provide some substantive protections, addressing deceptive telemarketing in the sale of goods and services, as well as contests and prizes. This Act authorized the FTC to promulgate the Telemarketing Sales Rule, which later led to the popular "Do-Not-Call" registry, which allows consumers to stop telemarketing calls by registering their phone numbers.

At the end of the 1990s and beginning of the 2000s, email marketing in the form of unsolicited commercial emails, or "spam," clogged consumers' email inboxes with unwanted messages, pornography and malicious attachments. In response, Congress passed the CAN-SPAM Act in 2003. Also, during this period, consumers became concerned about their privacy vis-à-vis internet marketers. Congress passed the Children's Online Privacy Protection Act (COPPA) in 1998, which requires privacy policies and parental permission for websites that collect personal information from children under the age of 13. The Gramm-Leach-Bliley Act of 1999 also requires privacy disclosures by financial institutions and an "opt-out" provision for consumers who do not wish to have their financial information shared. There is still no comprehensive federal online privacy legislation in the U.S., but the FTC has been active in this area, using their general "unfair and deceptive trade practices" authority. The state of California passed a broad privacy statute in 2019, the first of its kind in the nation. Since California is often a bellwether jurisdiction in consumer law, its approach may be taken up by other states or even the federal government in the future.

By the mid-2000s, there was an uptick in subprime lending, especially in real estate, followed by a financial crisis, a crash in housing prices, and a rise in foreclosures and unemployment. The Great Recession of 2008 led to some major developments in consumer protection legislation. In 2009, Congress passed the Credit CARD Act, which amended TILA to provide better disclosures and substantive protections for consumers with regard to credit cards. Even more monumental for consumer protection law was the passage in 2010 of the Dodd Frank Wall Street Reform and Consumer Protection Act. This law contained within it the Mortgage Reform and

Anti-Predatory Lending Act, which mandated a ground-breaking reform of mortgage lending disclosures, as well as requiring that creditors make sure that their consumers have an "ability to repay" their loans.

The Dodd Frank Act also established the Consumer Financial Protection Bureau in 2011, which ushered in a new era of consumer protection law in the United States. This new agency consolidated the consumer protection functions of the Federal Reserve Board and other bank regulatory agencies into one agency that supervises and regulates all providers of consumer financial services, from very large banks to fringe lenders. The CFPB works side by side with the FTC to protect consumers in all sectors of the economy.

The CFPB has both regulatory and adjudicatory powers, and has been active in all aspects of consumer finance. It promulgated unified disclosures for home mortgage loans ("know before you owe"), as well as regulating real estate appraisers and servicers. It issued a regulation on stored value/prepaid payment cards and issued proposed regulations under the Fair Debt Collection Practices Act. In its first four years, the CFPB attained $11 billion in customer refunds, forgiven debts, and financial penalties. With a change in administration after the 2016 election, however, the CFPB's enforcement activities were greatly reduced, its payday loan regulation was cut back substantially, and its rule banning class action waivers in arbitration clauses was vetoed by Congress in 2017.

In 2020, the agency barely survived an existential threat. The U.S. Supreme Court ruled that the structure of the agency (single director with five-year term removable only for cause) was an unconstitutional infringement on the executive authority of the President. *Seila Law LLC v. CFPB*, 140 S. Ct. 2183 (2020). The Court also held that this particular provision was severable from the rest of the statute that created the agency, so that it can continue to exist going forward with a Director who can be removed at will by the President.

Consumer transactions (and scams) now play out on a global level, due to the expansion of world trade and the ability for consumers everywhere to engage in Internet-based purchases. Although this Nutshell does not examine consumer protection policies outside of the United States, there is a growing consensus of international opinion on what good consumer laws and practices should be. In 1985 the United Nations adopted *The United Nations Guidelines for Consumer Protection*. The UN Guidelines have had a significant influence on consumer policy actions undertaken by governments and consumer groups, across many cultures. There is a growing body of literature on consumer law and consumer protection activities across the globe.[4]

---

[4] For a thorough treatment of consumer protection in transnational and emerging markets, *see Consumer Law In The Global Economy: National and International Dimensions* (Ian Ramsay, ed. 1997); and for a comparative study of U.S. and European Union law, *see* William T. Vukowich, *Consumer Protection in the 21st Century: A Global Perspective* (2002).

Consumer product safety laws could also legitimately be considered as part of consumer law. A federal agency, the Consumer Product Safety Commission, was set up in the 1970s to protect the public from dangerous products. In addition, there is a huge body of products liability tort law that also deals with the same subject. This aspect of consumer law is also beyond the scope of this Nutshell.

C. COVERAGE OF THIS VOLUME

This Nutshell provides a comprehensive but concise overview of the law of consumer protection. As noted in the prior section, there are a myriad of federal and state statutes involved, and the breadth of the topics covered has only grown over the decades since consumer law came into its own. In this volume, we try to present this topic in an organized fashion that will make it accessible to law students, lawyers, judges, legislators and others as well.

Chapter Two begins with a presentation of the basic players in the field of consumer protection, along with their legal authorities and prerogatives. The federal agencies include the 100-year old Federal Trade Commission, and the relatively new agency, the Consumer Financial Protection Bureau. State agencies are next and finally, the private bar. Of course, the marketplace as a whole, including both consumers and businesses, provide the basic raw materials upon which this body of law is based.

After the initial two chapters, the book proceeds in roughly chronological fashion from the beginning to the end of a consumer transaction. Thus, Chapter

Three deals with the advertising and marketing practices that induce consumer transactions. Here the law includes common law, FTC and CFPB actions, state statutes, and other specific laws and regulations concerning marketing practices from door-to-door sales, to telemarketing, to spam emailing. Online sales with their hidden contract terms are also covered in this chapter.

With the coming of age of the Internet, online marketing became commonplace, and with this came more advanced methods of tracking and storing mountains of personal information about consumers. Thus, this Nutshell features for the first time a separate chapter, Chapter Four, on Consumer Privacy. This chapter begins with an overview of common law privacy torts, and then goes on to cover laws relating to online consumer privacy, for both adults and children, data security and financial privacy. Both federal and state law is covered, including a ground-breaking California privacy law that became effective in 2020. Note that this volume deals only with privacy regarding commercial access to consumers' personal information and does not address citizens' privacy rights vis-à-vis the government.

For most consumers, having access to credit is a necessary prerequisite to their ability to purchase goods and services. To obtain credit they usually will need to grant a creditor access to their credit report. This industry has been under federal regulation by the Fair Credit Reporting Act since the mid-1970s. This law is covered in Chapter Five, as well as the related topic of consumer protections and remedies for identity-theft. There is also a federal law, the Equal Credit Opportunity Act, which prohibits discrimination on the basis of race, gender, and marital status, among other things, and which is also covered in this chapter.

Another preliminary step in most consumer credit transactions, is the process by which consumers determine which type of credit and which credit offeror they will use to obtain goods or services in the marketplace. Providing consumers with a uniform measure of the cost of credit to enable comparison shopping for credit was the premise of the Truth in Lending Act, a cornerstone of American consumer protection law. The TILA disclosures have evolved over time and are also specific to different types of credit offerings, and thus require three chapters to be fully covered. Chapter Six starts with an overview of TILA provisions that are generally applicable and then proceeds to discuss the disclosures for "closed-end" credit transactions. This type of credit transaction is exemplified by an installment contract to finance a relatively expensive product such as an automobile. These closed end installment loans were prevalent when TILA was first passed and so these provisions form a type of foundation for the rest of TILA. Chapter Seven covers open-end credit disclosures, which includes both credit cards and home-secured open-end credit or Home Equity Lines of Credit. Open end credit is becoming more prevalent and has a more complex disclosure scheme than closed end due to the ongoing nature of the relationship between consumer and creditor. Real estate secured credit transactions, *i.e.*, home mortgage loans, are usually more high stakes for consumers and have complicated multiple disclosures. Both credit cards and real estate-secured loans were the subject of legislation in 2009–2010 which added some substantive protections to the pre-existing disclosure provisions. Chapter Eight covers TILA enforcement, including the right of rescission for certain real estate secured transactions. It also covers some other federal statutes that are related to TILA, such as the Truth in Savings Act and the Consumer Leasing Act.

Chapter Nine covers regulation of the cost of credit, otherwise known as credit ceilings or usury laws. This type of regulation was drastically cut back due to judicial and legislative developments in the 1980s, especially on the federal level. Some states still regulate consumer credit costs for certain types of fringe lenders, such as payday lenders. There is also a question about how the relatively new Internet-based "Fintech" lenders will or will not be regulated under these state laws.

Chapter Ten looks at issues that are more likely to come up after the transaction has concluded, rather than before. The Holder in Due Course doctrine is a reference to a legal doctrine that provided protection to certain types of creditors from any claims or defenses that the debtor could have raised against the initial seller. This doctrine has been all but eliminated in consumer transactions but cannot be completely ignored. After the sale, a consumer may also look to the product warranties if there is a

SEC. C   COVERAGE OF THIS VOLUME   15

breach. Chapter Ten features brief coverage of the Uniform Commercial Code's handling of warranties and warranty enforcement, as well as the federal Magnuson-Moss Warranty Act. Lemon laws, which deal with new car warranties, as well as home warranties for new homes, are also covered in this chapter.

Chapter Eleven deals with the post-transaction issues of default and debt collection, including the FTC's Credit Practices Rule as well as the federal Fair Debt Collection Practices Act. The FDCPA is a long-standing federal law that deals with informal debt collection by third party debt collectors and contains a host of very specific provisions. Violations are subject to both government and private actions. In 2019, the CFPB issued a detailed proposed regulation implementing the provisions of the FDCPA, as they were empowered to do under the 2010 Dodd Frank Act.[5] Debt collection by private entities within the judicial system is also covered.

Finally, Chapter Twelve covers credit, debit and other modern consumer payment systems. When consumers pay with either a credit or debit card and later review their statement, they may discover unauthorized use, a billing error, or unexpected fees or charges. Two federal laws deal with these issues, TILA for credit cards and the Electronic Funds Transfer Act for debit cards. Finally, consumers who are not bank customers may use other types of cards

---

[5] Note that as of this writing, the CFPB's debt collection regulations have not been finalized. Thus, there may be some changes in the final version when it is promulgated.

to pay for consumer transactions, such as prepaid or stored value cards. These payment systems were brought under the protection of the pre-existing Regulation E by the CFPB in 2019. Other Internet-based or mobile-phone-based payment systems and the consumer protection laws that apply are also discussed in Chapter Twelve.

CHAPTER TWO
PUBLIC AND PRIVATE ACTIONS TO REGULATE CONSUMER MARKETS

A. OVERVIEW

The emergence of public agencies as the primary enforcers of consumer rights in the consumer transaction arena was, in part, due to problems with private enforcement of consumer protection at common law. In the modern era of consumer transactions, various state and federal agencies have a wide array of responsibilities. Part B of this chapter will provide a brief overview of enforcement by the Federal Trade Commission. Part C will discuss the creation of the Consumer Financial Protection Bureau under the 2010 Dodd-Frank Act, and its role in enforcing consumer protection laws in the financial sector. Part D will discuss state enforcement of both state and federal consumer protection laws. The rest of this chapter focuses on the private enforcement of consumer protection statutes, both state and federal, including class actions and arbitration.

B. THE FEDERAL TRADE COMMISSION: A BRIEF HISTORY AND OVERVIEW

The Federal Trade Commission Act of 1914 led to the formation of the FTC in 1915. Five Commissioners are appointed by the President to sit for terms of seven years each. Under the Act, no more than three Commissioners may be members of the same political party.

Section 5 of the FTC Act confers consumer protection responsibilities on the FTC. As originally passed, section 5 prohibited only unfair methods of competition. This section was amended in 1938 to add coverage of "unfair or deceptive acts or practices in commerce," which clarified that the FTC had a specific consumer protection mission in addition to its competition mission. FTC Act § 5(a)(1), 15 U.S.C. § 45(a)(1).

The FTC can enforce the prohibition on unfair or deceptive acts or practices in almost every business sector of the economy, except banks, railroads and trucking companies, meat packers, airlines, the insurance industry and nonprofit organizations. The FTC has overlapping jurisdiction with the Food and Drug Administration (FDA) over the food and drug industries. The FTC's jurisdiction also overlaps to some extent with the Consumer Financial Protection Bureau in regard to financial products and services affecting consumers, with the FTC limited to non-bank entities. The FTC's enforcement authority reaches all the statutorily prohibited practices, local or national, as long as they are "in or affecting commerce."

But, what is an "unfair or deceptive act or practice"? In the early years of the FTC's consumer protection mission, these critical statutory words were defined on a case-by-case basis by virtue of the body of FTC cases and "industry guides" as well as trade regulation rules. In the early 1980s, in response

to criticism in Congress
regulation to curtail com
children's television, the
statement defining the term "
This was intended in part to fe
the FTC's general grant of stat
policy statement, at first embo
Congress, and later codified in t
states that an unfair practice is one at "causes or is likely to cause substantial injury to consumers which is not reasonably avoidable by consumers themselves and not outweighed by countervailing benefits to consumers or to competition." 15 U.S.C. § 45(n). Prior to the issuance of the 1980 policy statement, the FTC had used a definition of unfairness that was based on public policy, morality and consumer injury.

The FTC issued a separate policy statement in 1983, which defined a deceptive act or practice as a "representation, omission, or practice that is likely to mislead the consumer acting reasonably under the circumstances as to a material fact." *Cliffdale Associates, Inc.*, 103 F.T.C. 110, 174 (1984) (appendix). Prior to this, the FTC had looked at whether a practice had a "tendency or capacity" to deceive consumers, including the ignorant and the unwary. Despite some initial controversy, both of these policy statements continue to represent the FTC's stance on the meaning of unfair and deceptive acts or practices.

The FTC has an array of enforcement tools at its disposal to police unfair and deceptive trade practices, including cease and desist orders issued

...gh administrative proceedings, injunctive actions taken in federal court, industry guides and trade regulation rules, and policy statements, such as the unfairness and deception statements described above.

Before 1973, the only enforcement option under section 5(a) of the FTC Act was the cease and desist order. Under this procedure, if the FTC believes that a person is violating section 5(a) and if the FTC determines that action would serve the public interest, then it can give the party involved an opportunity to either "consent" to a formal cease and desist order or to agree informally to discontinue the prohibited practice. "Consent," in this context, refers only to future practices and does not imply an admission of past violations. If a case is not settled by a "consent" order or an informal agreement, the FTC can then issue a complaint and notice of a hearing. After the complaint is filed against the "respondent," a public hearing is held before an administrative law judge of the FTC. This trial type hearing has all the safeguards provided for in the administrative procedure provisions of 5 U.S.C. §§ 556–557.

After hearing testimony, the administrative law judge drafts an initial decision for the full Commission, consisting of the five Commissioners. If the Commission then determines the act violates section 5(a) it can issue a cease and desist order. The Commission can also issue its own formal opinion, similar to an appellate court opinion. The FTC order can encompass similar albeit not identical behavior or products to those charged in the case, under so-called "fencing-in" orders. *See, e.g., Kraft, Inc. v. F.T.C.*, 970 F.2d 311 (7th Cir. 1992); *Telebrands Corp. v. F.T.C.*, 457 F.3d 354 (4th Cir. 2006). The respondent then has sixty days to file a petition for review with the appropriate U.S. Court of Appeals. 15 U.S.C. § 45(g)(2). If review is sought and granted, the FTC order only becomes final after the order is affirmed by the Court of Appeals and/or by the U.S. Supreme Court, if taken to that court for review. A case may therefore take years from the filing of the original complaint before the cease and desist order becomes final. According to FTC policy, most orders will "sunset" (automatically expire) 20 years after the initial issuance, unless there have been subsequent complaints.

The FTC can also go to federal district court and seek civil penalties of up to $10,000 per violation if the respondent later violates a cease and desist order. 15 U.S.C. § 45(*l*). The FTC can also obtain civil penalties for violations of orders issued against third parties, if that party can be shown to have "actual knowledge" that the act or practice in question was unfair or deceptive. 15 U.S.C. § 45(m)(1)(B).

In the mid-1970s, Congress significantly increased the remedies available to the FTC, going well beyond the cease and desist order pursuant to an administrative proceeding. This development may well have been in response to the rise of the consumer movement during this period, and a pair of reports critical of the FTC's timidity in pursuing its consumer protection mission. In 1969, Ralph Nader's "Raiders" published a report criticizing the FTC for pursuing trivial cases involving such things as the sale of chinchilla farms, while overlooking more serious forms of consumer fraud. Soon thereafter, a special American Bar Association Committee studied the FTC and rendered a report which generally supported the Nader findings. Both reports urged additional statutory authority to allow the FTC broader consumer protection powers.

In response to these recommendations, Congress in 1973 empowered the FTC to obtain restraining orders and preliminary injunctions in federal district court against violators or those who threatened to violate *any provision* administered by the Commission. Trans Alaska Pipeline Authorization Act § 408(f), adding FTC Act § 13(b), 15 U.S.C. § 53(b). Since obtaining this authority, the FTC has been very active in pursuing injunctions, and courts have been willing to use their general equitable powers to impose a wide range of penalties in these "13(b)" injunction cases. See *F.T.C. v. Southwest Sunsites, Inc.*, 665 F.2d 711 (5th Cir. 1982). These injunctive remedies have included asset freezes, required posting of performance bonds, restrictions and/or preventive requirements, lifetime bans on engaging in certain types of activities, as well as monetary penalties and consumer redress. Thus, the § 13(b) injunction has become a staple in the FTC's armory against fraudulent practices.

As part of the 1975 FTC Improvements Act, Congress also authorized the FTC to seek consumer redress in court for violations of rules or orders. FTC Act § 19, 15 U.S.C. § 57b. In order to obtain consumer redress under this section, the FTC must prove that "the act or practice to which the cease and desist order relates is one which a reasonable man would have known under the circumstances was dishonest or fraudulent." *Id*. This relatively difficult standard of proof has resulted in a dearth of cases filed under this section by the FTC. Instead, the Commission now routinely seeks consumer redress as part of the equitable remedies available under an injunction case filed under § 13(b). This approach was judicially approved in *F.T.C. v. H.N. Singer, Inc.*, 668 F.2d 1107 (9th Cir. 1982), and has been used successfully by the FTC ever since. In a 2019 Seventh Circuit case, however, the court held that the FTC did not have the statutory authority to order restitution in a § 13(b) case, based on a plain language reading of the statute. *FTC v. Credit Bureau Center*, LLC, 937 F.3d 764 (7th Cir. 2019). It remains to be seen whether other courts will follow this minority ruling.

The FTC has long issued interpretive "industry guides" to describe acts or practices in a particular industry which the FTC considers unfair or deceptive. However, these industry guides do not have the force and effect of law. Thus, in 1962, the FTC started to enact "trade regulation rules" to specify practices which the Commission deemed to violate the Act. These rules are delineated in the Code of Federal Regulations, Title 16, Subchapter D. Unlike the industry guides, which are merely interpretive, violations of the trade regulation rules are considered violations of the statute from which the regulation is derived. In other words, for a violation of a trade regulation rule, the FTC would not have to prove that the act or omission constituted an unfair or deceptive act, but would only have to prove that a particular rule provision had been violated. However, if the FTC only issues an industry guide, any action by the FTC would have to show that an action contrary to the guide is an unfair or deceptive act in violation of Section 5. Alleging a violation of the industry guide alone would simply not be sufficient.

The FTC's power to issue trade regulation rules was upheld in *National Petroleum Refiners Ass'n v. FTC*, 482 F.2d 672 (D.C. Cir.1973). Nonetheless, just a few years later, Congress formalized the FTC's trade regulation rule authority in the Magnuson Moss FTC Improvement Act of 1975. FTC Act § 18, 15 U.S.C. § 57a. During the initial period after the passage of this statute, the FTC proposed some twenty trade regulation rules. The "Magnuson-Moss" rules were constrained by a specific type of rulemaking process, however, which provided more safeguards than would be applied under the Administrative Procedure Act (APA), yet a bit less than what would occur in an adjudicative hearing. Due to these relatively burdensome procedures, as well as some judicial and political pushback, most of the initial Magnuson Moss rules were abandoned by the mid-1980s. The most controversial of these proposed rules was the Children's Television Advertising rule, which provoked Congress to temporarily remove the FTC's funding to issue advertising regulations based on unfairness theory. The controversial rules proposed during this period also led to the 1980 FTC Improvements Act, featuring a legislative veto provision which was later overturned in court. *Consumers Union of U.S., Inc. v. F.T.C.*, 691 F.2d 575 (D.C. Cir. 1982), *aff'd* 463 U.S. 1216 (1983). As mentioned above, it was also during this era that the FTC issued policy statements on unfairness and deception, which apparently succeeded in fending off any further Congressional efforts to cut back the FTC's statutory powers.

In the succeeding decades, the FTC became relatively inactive in promulgating Magnuson Moss trade regulation rules. Instead, the Commission has issued rules using APA notice and comment procedure when so ordered by Congress in specific areas. For instance, when Congress passed the Telemarketing Act in 1994, this statute contained a legislative mandate for the FTC to implement rules that bypassed the Magnuson Moss rulemaking process. These rules now contain the highly popular "Do-Not-Call" registry. 16 C.F.R. Part 310. The FTC has also returned to the practice of issuing non-binding "industry guides," such as the Environmental Marketing Guides, and the Guides concerning Endorsements and Testimonials in Advertising.

The FTC Act has never featured a private right or action, nor a state government right of enforcement. As will be discussed below, however, the FTC successfully urged the states to pass their own "little FTC acts," that used the language of the FTC Act but provided for state and private enforcement, thus indirectly expanding the enforcement of the FTC Act itself, at least as far as its consumer protection mission is concerned. Also, prior to the passage of the Dodd-Frank Act in 2010 and the creation of the Consumer Financial Protection Bureau, the FTC shared regulatory and enforcement authority under the federal consumer credit protection statutes with the Federal Reserve Board and various bank regulatory agencies.

C. THE CONSUMER FINANCIAL PROTECTION BUREAU

In one of the most important developments in consumer protection in nearly a century, Congress in 2010 created a second federal consumer protection agency, the Consumer Financial Protection Bureau (CFPB). 12 U.S.C. §§ 5481–5552. This agency is housed within the Federal Reserve Board but is mostly self-sufficient. In contrast to the FTC, the CFPB has a single director, appointed by the President for a five-year term, rather than a multi-member commission. It is also self-funding out of Federal Reserve banking fees, rather than being dependent on Congress for its yearly budget. Its jurisdiction is limited to consumer financial products or services, but does include banks as well as non-bank providers of such products or services.

This basic structure of the CFPB, especially the provision for a single director removable for cause only, has been controversial. The U.S. Supreme Court in *Seila Law, LLC v. CFPB*, 140 S. Ct. 2183 (2020), held that the single director with limited removal by the President, was in fact an unconstitutional infringement on the authority of the chief executive. Nonetheless, the Court ruled that under the severability clause of the Consumer Financial Protection Act, it could simply strike down the director provision and make the CFPB Director serve at the discretion of the President, while otherwise retaining the agency as it stands.

Prior to the creation of the CFPB, consumer financial protection at the federal level was shared by the Federal Reserve Board, and other bank regulatory agencies, such as the Comptroller of the Currency, the Office of Thrift Supervision, and the National Credit Union Administration, as well as the FTC for non-bank creditors. The Consumer Financial Protection Act (CFPA), by housing the responsibility for consumer financial protection within one agency, was meant to reduce "capture" of the bank regulatory agencies who relied on the regulated entities' fees to finance their own budgets. With the new structure, there is no incentive for the regulated entities to seek to change their charters to obtain a better regulatory deal since they must all deal with the same agency.

The CFPB now holds the authority to issue or amend regulations under the federal consumer credit statutes, as well as to enforce those statutes through litigation and/or through the bank examination process. The 2010 legislation also lessened federal preemption of state consumer financial protection laws, making the federal law a floor or minimum, with the states free to enact laws that are more protective of consumers. 12 U.S.C. § 5551(a)(1), (2).

In addition to enforcing the pre-existing consumer credit statutes, the CFPB has the authority to take action to prevent "unfair, deceptive and abusive practices" within the consumer financial sector. The unfairness standard is identical to the FTC standard, and the definition of a "deceptive" practice, while not set forth in the statute, is being applied by the CFPB in a manner that defers to the pre-existing FTC policy. 12 U.S.C. § 5531(c). The CFPB also has the authority under its statute to curb "abusive" practices, which are specifically defined to include practices that interfere with the consumer's ability to understand terms and conditions, or that take unreasonable advantage of the consumer's lack of understanding or inability to protect their own interests. 12 U.S.C. § 5531(d). For example, using the authority to curb "abusive" financial practices, the CFPB sued a leading student loan servicer, Navient, for steering student loan borrowers into disadvantageous loan programs. CFPB v. Navient Corp., 2017 WL 3380530 (M.D. Pa. 2017).

The CFPB has general rulemaking authority to regulate "unfair, deceptive and abusive" practices using standard federal rulemaking procedures, as contained in the Administrative Procedure Act's notice and comment provisions. This contrasts with the more cumbersome "Magnuson Moss" rulemaking that must be used by the FTC when exercising their general rulemaking authority. The CFPB was also specifically directed by Congress to issue certain regulations, especially in the area of residential mortgage credit. One of these mandated regulations combined the previously separate disclosures required by the Truth in Lending Act and the Real Estate Settlement Procedures Act rules. 78 Fed. Reg.

79730 (Dec. 31, 2013) (dubbed "Know Before You Owe"). The agency also issued a mortgage servicer regulation and an appraiser independence regulation. A final rule that would have curbed mandatory arbitration provisions containing class action waivers was vetoed by Congress in 2017. Using its discretionary rulemaking power, the CFPB issued a rule in late 2017 that would have made it an unfair and abusive practice for a lender to make payday or vehicle title loans without reasonably determining that consumers would have the ability to repay the loan. 82. Fed. Reg. 54472 (Nov. 17, 2017). Since that time, however, the agency under a new director changed course, and in 2020 finalized amendments that effectively eliminate most of the substantive aspects of the rule. In 2016, the CFPB amended Regulation E to extend the Electronic Funds Transfer Act to protect holders of "prepaid" or "stored value" accounts. In 2019, it also proposed regulations implementing the Fair Debt Collection Practices Act.

The CFPB also has the authority to go to federal court to enforce its statutory mandate, as well as to engage in formal bank examinations to check for compliance. This authority, like the regulatory authority, encompasses both the general statutory prohibition on unfair, deceptive and abusive financial practices, as well as the specific statutes under the umbrella Consumer Credit Protection Act, including the Truth in Lending Act, the Fair Credit Reporting Act, the Equal Credit Opportunity Act, the Fair Debt Collection Practices Act, and the Electronic Funds Transfer Act. These enforcement activities of the

CFPB, as well as those of the FTC, will be covered as relevant to specific subject areas covered in this volume.

As with the FTC Act, there is no private right of action to enforce the general provisions of the Consumer Financial Protection Act. There is some limited enforcement authority that could be used by state attorneys general. In addition, there remains a private right of action to enforce the specific consumer credit protection statutes mentioned above.

D. STATE AGENCY ENFORCEMENT

There are a number of state agencies which regulate consumer transactions. Within any state, the attorney general and agencies such as the state banking department and state insurance department may be charged with the responsibility to license and regulate businesses within their respective industries.

As is true at the federal level, some state legislatures enact laws, but grant the authority to the appropriate state agency to promulgate regulations, license the businesses and hire examiners to conduct audits and investigate consumer complaints. Across the country, state regulation is often uneven, based on legislative authority, budgetary constraints and the politics of the state.

All fifty states and the District of Columbia have enacted general consumer protection statutes which for the most part are modeled on the Federal Trade

Commission Act. Since these statutes prohibit "unfair or deceptive acts or practices," they are commonly called UDAP statutes. All of the statutes provide for both state and private enforcement. Most states have also enacted consumer credit laws which parallel and supplement the federal consumer credit laws.

State UDAP statutes are typically enforced by the state attorneys general. In some states, especially if the attorney general post is an elected rather than an appointed office, the attorney general takes on a high profile in consumer regulation, and is expected to serve as a guardian for the public. The state UDAP statutes were initially passed in the late 1960s and early 1970s, and state enforcement started out independently under each state's own authority. Beginning in the 1990s with the state AG litigation against tobacco companies, however, states began to join together in multistate litigation on behalf of consumers. This trend has continued with some coordination and support provided by the National Association of Attorneys General (NAAG). The use of multistate litigation can increase the clout of the state AGs vis-à-vis large corporate defendants, and can also spread the benefits of any consumer redress or injunctive relief obtained to states that might not otherwise have the resources to fund such litigation on their own. States may also hire private counsel to represent them on a contingency fee basis, which can also serve to ameliorate issues with enforcement budgets. Not surprisingly, these developments have been criticized as promoting the use of class plaintiff attorneys as "guns for hire" and for pressuring defendants to settle unmeritorious cases.

The state attorney general's office and departments that regulate industries such as consumer credit or insurance, may have the authority to issue injunctions or cease and desist orders against unlawful business practices, and also to collect consumer redress or civil penalties from violators. In some cases, consumer hotlines are established to help mediate positive outcomes for consumers who have a complaint with a business. In other states, agencies refer cases to private attorneys in a collaborative effort to represent the interests of consumers.

In states where effective and aggressive state regulatory enforcement is rare, the void can be filled by federal agencies such as the Federal Trade Commission and the Consumer Financial Protection Bureau. However, real teeth in the enforcement of consumer protection is usually found in private litigation, where plaintiffs use state and federal laws, as well as class actions, to seek redress for fraudulent practices and statutory violations found in the marketplace. Indeed, many state and federal laws empower consumers to act as "private attorneys general" in the policing of markets and enforcement of consumer protection laws. This is particularly true where the statutes provide for attorneys' fees and costs, in addition to damages for the harm caused by the illegal business practice.

E. PRIVATE ACTIONS USING STATE UDAP LAWS

1. GENERAL

Every state now has at least one statute aimed at protecting consumers against unscrupulous or misleading trade practices. However, these statutes vary widely in the types of relief they offer to injured consumers. Because these laws regulate a whole array of "unfair or deceptive acts or practices," they are commonly called "UDAP statutes."[1] Because they are modeled for the most part on the FTC Act, these laws are also called "little FTC Acts." Most of the state UDAP statutes contain a proviso that courts should be guided by FTC precedents in interpreting the state law. When the FTC changed its deceptive practices policy in 1980 to focus on practices likely to mislead consumers acting reasonably under the circumstances, however, the question arose whether the states should change their policies in tandem with the FTC, or stay with their original standard of tendency or capacity to deceive. Most states have shifted their policies to accord with the FTC, but some have not.

All of the states have statutes which expressly or as interpreted by the courts, allow consumers to sue

---

[1] For a thorough background on the history, scope and remedies available under UDAP statutes, including a state-by-state analysis of the laws, *see* DEE PRIDGEN, RICHARD M. ALDERMAN & JOLINA CUARESMA, CONSUMER PROTECTION AND THE LAW, Chapters 2–7 (2019–2020 ed.); and NATIONAL CONSUMER LAW CENTER, UNFAIR AND DECEPTIVE ACTS AND PRACTICES (9th ed. 2016).

those engaged in prohibited practices for damages or to obtain other relief. These statutes frequently allow rescission of proscribed transactions, and most allow the prevailing consumer an award of attorney's fees. The attorney's fees provision encourages enforcement of the statute by helping consumers attract competent counsel and encouraging them to protect their rights. Attorney's fees are discussed more fully in Section E.6, *infra*. All the state statutes which allow a private cause of action allow recovery of actual damages. While some statutes allow only recovery of actual damages, others allow recovery of multiple damages. Remedies are discussed in Section E.5, *infra*.

2. WHO MAY SUE?

Not all purchasers of goods may sue under state UDAP statutes. For instance, most states exclude business plaintiffs from the statutory coverage. Some states allow only "natural persons" to sue, thereby excluding corporations and associations. Due to the enhanced remedies and lower burden of proof of most state UDAP laws, businesses will often seek to use these statutes to resolve contract or tort disputes with other businesses. A few states allow retailers or "business buyers" a private remedy as "consumers." This is especially true if the business buyer happens to be a small business owner. *See, e.g., Ly v. Nystrom*, 615 N.W.2d 302 (Minn. 2000). Coverage of purely business-to-business disputes, however, could be viewed as contrary to the original goal of the state UDAPs, which was to provide consumers with better and more equal access to justice for marketplace injuries.

Persons suffering purely physical injuries from defective products may also be excluded from suing under state UDAP laws, especially if recovery under the statute is limited to injuries to business or property or other types of "economic loss." This type of exclusion tends to eliminate products liability tort cases. There are states that do allow recovery under state UDAPs for physical and mental injuries, however.

3. WHO CAN BE SUED?

Nearly all UDAP statutes exclude from their coverage some class or classes of defendants. Almost all exempt mass media advertisers who merely publish claims made by others. Several states specifically exclude categories of service providers, particularly professionals such as architects, real estate brokers, accountants, attorneys, clergy, and doctors. Some only exclude one or two professions, while others speak of professional service providers in general in their exemption clause. Most states exclude certain regulated industries, such as banks, public utilities, securities and investment companies and insurance companies.

The applicability of a UDAP statute to lawyers or doctors may be limited by a statutory exemption. Even where there is no express exemption, some courts have been reluctant to apply UDAP statutes to a professional practice. The rationale is that it would diminish the professional status of the practice of law or medicine if such services are viewed merely as one more element of "trade or commerce." *See, e.g., Cripe v. Leiter,* 703 N.E.2d 100 (Ill.1998). Courts in most states, however, either view the activities of lawyers and other professionals dealing with consumers to be covered outright, or they will cover such professionals to the extent of the business-oriented aspects of their activities, such as advertising and billing. Some states exempt actions involving the actual practice of the profession, since those aspects are covered by malpractice claims or by state professional and/or ethical codes.

4. PROCEDURAL OBSTACLES TO SUIT

The state UDAP statutes have various procedural prerequisites or other requirements applicable to private suits, including notice requirements, proof of ascertainable loss, and a public interest requirement.

A few states require the complaining consumer to give notice of the complaint or to give the defendant a demand letter before actually filing the complaint with the court. The defendant is then allowed a certain number of days to make a settlement offer. Should the consumer nevertheless elect to go to court, multiple damages and attorney's fees may be denied if the consumer is not awarded damages *substantially in excess of the settlement offer*. The apparent purpose of such a procedural requirement is to further judicial efficiency by denying large damage awards to plaintiffs who make no attempt to settle.

Many states require consumer plaintiffs to allege they have suffered an "ascertainable loss" in order to have standing to sue. This does not necessarily mean actual out-of-pocket loss, but can cover hard-to-quantify injuries, such as the loss of time or foregoing of other opportunities involved in a deceptive bait-and-switch advertising scheme. The point of this prerequisite is to limit UDAP plaintiffs to persons who have a stake in the outcome, and who are not simply filing lawsuits for the sake of the statutory damages.

A few states require consumer plaintiffs to show that the litigation of their particular disputes would be in the "public interest," or that their particular complaint would be capable of repetition. This type of requirement is meant to eliminate from the statutory coverage private contractual disputes that could be resolved without resort to the UDAP statutes. The public interest requirement also reflects the idea that private UDAP plaintiffs are actually functioning as "private attorneys general" in that they are suing and thereby deterring a merchant who might otherwise harm other members of the public.

5. STATUTORY DAMAGES

The state UDAP statutes provide a range of approaches to the award of statutory damages.[2] From the point of view of the consumer-plaintiff, the best

---

[2] For a state by state summary of these remedies, *see* DEE PRIDGEN, RICHARD M. ALDERMAN & JOLINA CUARESMA, CONSUMER PROTECTION AND THE LAW, §§ 6:10–6:16, Appendix 6A (2019–2020 ed.).

statute requires an award of treble damages to a successful plaintiff without requiring proof that the violation was knowing or willful. Such liberal relief is available under the applicable statute in Alaska, Hawaii, New Jersey and North Carolina. Eleven state statutes allow the recovery of multiple damages if the plaintiff proves the defendant willfully engaged in an unfair act or practice. A less attractive statute to the consumer, adopted in several states, leaves the award of multiple damages to the court's discretion. Nine consumer protection statutes specifically authorize the award of punitive damages, typically based on the same type of showing needed for common law fraud, *i.e.,* willful and knowing violation. Twenty states provide successful consumer plaintiffs with the right to recover a minimum amount of damages, ranging from $25 to $15,000. These damages are awarded even if the consumer cannot prove the amount of the actual loss. The least desirable statute provides only for recovery of actual damages, which can be relatively small in consumer cases, and indeed would often not cover the cost of litigation. Fifteen states have taken this approach.

6. ATTORNEY'S FEES UNDER STATE STATUTES

The consumer who wishes to bring suit under a state UDAP statute will, as a practical matter, do so only if the statute provides for recovery of attorney's fees. Once again, each state's statute varies significantly.[3] In twenty-five states, a prevailing plaintiff will always receive attorney's fees. In a few states, the successful plaintiff may need to show that the defendant willfully violated the statute before attorney's fees will be awarded. The rest of the states allow for attorney's fees to the prevailing consumer plaintiff at the discretion of the court. Fifteen states allow a prevailing *defendant* to receive attorney's fees if he or she shows that the lawsuit was frivolous. Four states simply allow recovery of attorney's fees to the *prevailing party*, whether plaintiff or defendant.

Clearly, the statutes which allow recovery of attorney's fees only to successful plaintiffs are the most attractive to would-be consumer litigants. Conversely, statutes allowing attorney's fees to prevailing defendants are much more likely to chill consumer utilization of the statutory cause of action. For instance, in *Deer Creek Construction Co. v. Peterson*, 412 So.2d 1169 (Miss.1982), a home buyer sued a builder, asserting both a breach of contract and false advertising under the UDAP statute. While she prevailed on the contract claim, receiving a $3450 damages award, she lost the consumer claim. As a result, she had to pay the defendant's attorney's fees for that part of the suit, for a net loss to her of $484. In Illinois, the state Supreme Court construed the UDAP statute allowing attorneys' fees for the prevailing defendant to be limited to cases in which

---

[3] *See generally* DEE PRIDGEN, RICHARD M. ALDERMAN & JOLINA CUARESMA, CONSUMER PROTECTION AND THE LAW, §§ 6:17–6:22 (2019–2020 ed.).

the defendant could show that the suit was brought in bad faith. *Krautsack v. Anderson*, 861 N.E.2d 633 (Ill. 2006). As the majority stated:

> Limiting a consumer fraud defendant's ability to recover fees to instances where the plaintiff acted in bad faith is consistent with the purpose of the Act. If this limitation did not exist, a prevailing defendant could be awarded fees simply because the plaintiff, although having a legitimate claim and proceeding in good faith, lost at trial on the proofs. The potential for such a penalty would act as a deterrent to the filing of valid consumer fraud claims. *Id.* at 646.

Obviously, whether a statute allows for attorney's fee recovery (and *which party* the statute allows to recover) will often determine whether the consumer will bring a UDAP claim.

F. RICO AS A CIVIL SUIT OPTION FOR CONSUMERS

In 1970, Congress enacted the Racketeer Influenced and Corrupt Organizations Act (RICO), codified at 18 U.S.C. §§ 1961–1968. The purpose of the Act was "to seek the eradication of organized crime in the United States by strengthening the legal tools in the evidence-gathering process, by establishing new penal prohibitions, and by providing enhanced sanctions and new remedies to deal with the unlawful activities of those engaged in organized crime." Pub.L.No. 91–452, 84 Stat. 922, 923 (Congressional Statement of Findings and Purpose).

The Act opened the door to the use of state and federal fraud statutes to pursue violators. Furthermore, the law allowed private litigants to recover treble damages, costs and attorney's fees if they established that the form of fraud amounted to "a pattern of racketeering activity."

In the years after its initial passage, RICO remedies were sought and achieved in cases where no direct link to "organized crime" (at least in the classic "Mafia" sense) was proven. Thus, the potential use of the statute in more conventional commercial litigation is vast and offers a defrauded consumer a remedy in some ways more attractive than that traditionally provided for in tort or contract law, or even in the state little FTC Acts. For instance, if a plaintiff shows a pattern of statutory fraud (*e.g.*, repeated fraudulent claims made in a national sales campaign), he or she may choose to bring a claim under RICO. RICO claims are also possible for claims of repeated payday or other fringe lending activity in violation of the state usury laws. By bringing a RICO claim, a plaintiff, who lives in a state with a UDAP statute which awards attorney's fees to the "prevailing party," avoids the risk of paying such fees while retaining a cause of action with favorable provisions for prevailing plaintiffs.

The use of RICO by civil plaintiffs who allege violations of fraud statutes to meet the statutory "predicate acts" requirement has generated criticism. The critics claim, among other things, that (1) RICO was intended to be used to prevent the infiltration of legitimate business by organized crime, not ordinary commercial fraud and (2) that the threat of treble damages forces many defendants to settle questionable or unmeritorious claims out of court. Proponents of the widespread use of RICO counter by arguing that (1) Congress intended the use of the statute against any criminal "enterprise," not merely organized crime and (2) that out of court settlements are evidence of RICO's merit in filling gaps left in statutory and common law remedies against fraud.

So far, efforts to neutralize or remove RICO's fraud provisions have been unsuccessful. In the 1990s, RICO claims were particularly common in consumer credit cases, including disputes involving credit insurance products, loan brokers, mortgage escrow accounts, loan flipping (frequent loan renewals), documentation fees and charges to consumers who pay off loan balances before the loan matures. The future trend for civil RICO in consumer cases is unclear. While the remedies favor the prevailing plaintiff, there are some problems of proof. At least one study has found that civil RICO cases appear to have peaked in the mid-2000s.

G. CLASS ACTIONS

1. OVERVIEW

Class actions play an important part in the enforcement of consumer protection laws. In cases where individual consumer claims would produce a small award of damages, a class-based effort may provide the appropriate incentives to bring the action. Attorney's fees may also be available and may be substantially higher in a class action than in an individual case or in individual joined actions, due to economies of scale.

Class actions may also be more effective than individual claims in forcing defendants to modify their behavior. A company may be willing to risk continuing a predatory business practice if the odds are that only infrequent individual claims will be filed. However, the filing of a statewide or national class generally raises both the stakes and the publicity surrounding the business practice. Class actions make it possible for individual consumers with relatively small claims, who would otherwise be out-resourced, to join together and take on economically powerful interests.[4] For instance, in a 2018 case a class action settlement provided a total of nearly $20 million in reimbursements to class members who had paid an average of $238 in undisclosed purchase option fees to an auto leasing company. *Schreiber v. Ally Financial, Inc.,* Order Approving Class Settlement No. 1:14-cv-22069 (S.D. Fla. Oct. 11, 2018).[5] However, pursuing a class action can be both time consuming and expensive, and will require an analysis of the merits of the case, the costs

---

[4] For a comprehensive treatment of class actions for consumer claims, *see* NATIONAL CONSUMER LAW CENTER, CONSUMER CLASS ACTIONS (10th ed. 2020).

[5] Note the settlement came after a federal court of appeals ruled that the mandatory arbitration clause was not binding on the lessors. 634 Fed. Appx. 263 (11th Cir. 2015). As noted below, such clauses are often obstacles to pursuing consumer class actions.

and the scope of the case (nationwide or statewide class) before proceeding.

2. BASIC REQUIREMENTS FOR CERTIFICATION

Many consumer laws provide specifically for class actions. Such statutory provisions normally specify prerequisites, procedures and safeguards against abuse. Otherwise, consumer class actions will be governed by the state's general rules on class action, which in turn are typically modeled on the federal rules. Rule 23 of the Federal Rules of Civil Procedure provides the prerequisites for certification of class actions in federal court. Rule 23 provides:

(a) **Prerequisite to a Class Action.** One or more members of a class may sue or be sued as representative parties on behalf of all only if (1) the class is so numerous that joinder of all members is impracticable, (2) there are questions of law or fact common to the class, (3) the claims or defenses of the representative parties are typical of the claims or defenses of the class, and (4) the representative parties will fairly and adequately protect the interests of the class.

Other requirements noted in Rule 23(b) depend on the type of class action being brought. These requirements include that questions of law or fact common to the members of the class predominate over questions affecting only individual members, that a class action is superior to other available methods of adjudication, and that the case is manageable as a class action.

An in-depth analysis of the procedural hurdles to class certification will not be undertaken here. However, note that the Rule 23(a) prerequisites of numerosity, commonality, typicality and adequacy must be met, as well as at least one of the requirements under Rule 23(b).

Variations in state law often present a difficult hurdle for plaintiffs whose claims may be based on a claim such as fraudulent misrepresentations or fraudulent suppression. In determining whether class treatment is appropriate, courts "must consider how variations in state law affect predominance and superiority." *Castano v. American Tobacco Co.*, 84 F.3d 734, 741 (5th Cir.1996). Defendants may be able to defeat class certification by showing that state law variations present "insuperable obstacles" to a purported nationwide class. *Walsh v. Ford Motor Co.*, 807 F.2d 1000 (D.C. Cir.1986). Some courts have implied a requirement that class members be "ascertainable," in order to prevent compensation from going to uninjured consumers. *In re Teflon Prods. Liab. Litig.*, 254 F.R.D. 354, 370 (S.D. Iowa 2008). This may involve a demand for "proof of purchase," within a specified period of time, which could be difficult for classes composed of large numbers of purchasers of relatively inexpensive retail products.

3. POTENTIAL FOR ABUSE IN CLASS ACTIONS

Although class actions provide a powerful tool for consumers, there has been criticism of class actions where attorneys come away with multi-million dollar fees, while consumers are left with nothing or little as a class member. One court stated the problem precisely, noting that "the [class] lawyers might urge a class settlement at a low figure or on a less-than-optimal basis in exchange for red-carpet treatment for fees." *Weinberger v. Great Northern Nekoosa Corp.,* 925 F.2d 518, 524 (1st Cir.1991).

Some judges have refused to approve settlements where the defendant offers the class little, while offering the class counsel a large amount in fees. This is particularly true in cases where a proposal was made that class members should receive coupon settlements, while class attorneys would receive millions of dollars in fees. Often the coupon could only be used at the very establishment that was cited as having injured the consumer, and in some cases the terms for use of the coupon made redemption unlikely. Thus, the consumer became victimized by both the business and the attorneys, both in the initial consumer transaction and in the "friendly" settlement.

In response to several abusive class action settlements, in 1997 the National Association of Consumer Advocates (NACA) developed and published a set of guidelines to protect consumers. *The National Association of Consumer Advocates' Standards and Guidelines for Litigating and Settling*

Class Actions, published at 176 Federal Rules Decisions, addresses ten topics in class action practice, including coupon settlements, attorneys fees and the legitimacy of "settlement classes." NACA is an organization of more than 350 individuals who represent plaintiffs in individual litigation and class actions. The NACA guidelines should provide good guidance to courts and counsel in considering class outcomes that will be fair to consumers who have been harmed by illegal business practices.

Another response to perceived abuses in class action was the federal Class Action Fairness Act (CAFA) of 2005. This Act both expanded federal jurisdiction over most class actions and placed significant restrictions on class action settlements in federal courts. Based on the perception that consumer class action plaintiffs were forum-shopping for favorable state court venues, CAFA confers federal jurisdiction over any class action in which the aggregated claims of all the plaintiffs exceeds $5 million and at least one plaintiff is diverse from one defendant. 28 U.S.C. § 1332(d). Federal courts have proved to be rather hostile toward multi-state consumer class actions based on state law and have denied numerous class certifications due to differences in applicable law. Thus, the expansion of federal jurisdiction over these consumer class actions will likely put the brakes on this consumer protection tool. CAFA also deals with so-called "coupon" settlements, in which class members receive coupons good for future purchases from the defendant, in lieu of a cash recovery, while the attorneys received a large cash contingent fee. CAFA requires judges to scrutinize coupon settlements and mandates that the attorney's fees be based on the value of coupons actually redeemed, as opposed to the total of coupons available to class members. 28 U.S.C. § 1712(d). This restriction will likely make coupon settlement far less popular.

At times class action defendants attempt to "pick off" a named class representative through an individual settlement. Once the class representative has settled, the defendant may be able to avoid the greater class liability unless another class representative can be found. If the class representative rejects the settlement offer, however, the case cannot be dismissed for mootness, according to a 2016 Supreme Court case, because "an unaccepted settlement offer has no force." *Campbell-Ewald Co. v. Jose Gomez*, 136 S. Ct. 663 (2016).

Many consumer contracts now contain mandatory arbitration clauses. Such clauses are often paired with waiver of class action clauses. Despite the fact that some courts had found such clauses to be unconscionable, the U.S. Supreme Court categorically upheld class action waivers in *AT&T Mobility LLC v. Concepcion*, 563 U.S. 333 (2011). This makes it more likely that class actions and class arbitrations will be eliminated through the widespread use of these waiver clauses in consumer contracts. The adverse effect of mandatory arbitration clauses on consumers' access to court is discussed next.

H. ARBITRATION

The widespread use and enforcement of mandatory, pre-dispute arbitration agreements in consumer contracts is probably the most controversial and potentially the most detrimental development in 21st century consumer law. Retailers, lenders, credit card issuers, as well as cable, internet and mobile phone providers and many others increasingly are requiring consumers to sign arbitration agreements at the time of contracting. In some cases, businesses attempted to add arbitration provisions to the contract through "bill stuffer" provisions included in a monthly statement, where the original contract lacked an arbitration provision. Today, most consumers who purchase anything online will encounter scroll down or hyperlinked terms and conditions to which they must agree prior to completing the purchase. Many of these online boilerplate agreements also contain arbitration clauses.

In its purest form, arbitration is a procedure employed by parties who choose to have a dispute determined by an arbitrator of their own selection and at their own expense. Each party presents evidence to the arbitrator in writing or through witnesses. Arbitration proceedings are generally more informal than court proceedings and adherence to the rules of evidence is usually not required. The arbitrator's award may or may not be binding on the parties, depending on the terms of the arbitration agreement. Binding arbitration awards are usually not published, and the right to appeal is quite limited.

Arbitration is often confused with mediation. In mediation, the mediator does not make a decision. The mediator works with both parties and their representatives in the attempt to reach a voluntary agreement. The essence of successful mediation is compromise. On the other hand, in arbitration, the arbitrator reaches a decision that is usually binding.

The concept of arbitration is ancient and is mentioned in writings dating back to ancient Greece. Arbitration has been used in the United States since the 18th century. Congress passed the Federal Arbitration Act (FAA) in 1925 as a way to endorse cheaper and faster alternatives to court proceedings, and to overcome judicial hostility toward arbitration. This law states in relevant part that "[a]n agreement in writing to submit to arbitration . . . shall be valid, irrevocable, and enforceable, save upon such grounds as exist at law or in equity for the revocation of any contract." 9 U.S.C. § 2. The issue of arbitration clauses in consumer contracts did not emerge until the mid-1990s, when arbitration clauses began to become more common in consumer contracts.

As these clauses became more prevalent, consumer advocates and some courts became increasingly critical of mandatory arbitration provisions incorporated in consumer contracts, where the businesses will not deal with the consumer unless the arbitration provision is included.[6] Consumers have no real choice in those situations, particularly where the arbitration provision has swept the industry through the work of a trade association, such as a state automobile dealer association. In some cases, the automobile dealer representatives fail to describe the concept of arbitration and present it as a "take-it-or-leave-us" choice. This is at odds with the notion that arbitration is a process chosen by the parties to resolve their disputes. Scholars have also pointed out that consumers typically do not understand what the arbitration clause means or why it is significant even if they read it,[7] thus undermining the precept that these clauses should be binding because of freedom of contract.

Beginning in this period, the United States Supreme Court issued several important decisions supportive of arbitration. In *Allied-Bruce Terminix Companies v. Dodson*, 513 U.S. 265 (1995), the Court held that the Federal Arbitration Act requires state courts to enforce an arbitration provision if the contract involves or affects interstate commerce. The test for "affects interstate commerce" is as broad as it is in cases of constitutional law and federal jurisdiction. The Court has also held that the FAA preempts most state statutes that seek to place limits

---

[6] *See* Mark E. Budnitz, *Arbitration of Disputes Between Consumers and Financial Institutions: A Serious Threat to Consumer Protection*, 10 OHIO ST. J. ON DISP. RESOL 267 (1995).

[7] Jeff Sovern, Elayne E. Greenberg, Paul F. Kirgis, Yuxiang Liu, *"Whimsy Little Contracts" with Unexpected Consequences: An Empirical Analysis of Consumer Understanding of Arbitration Agreements*, 75 MD. L. REV. 1 (2015).

on the enforceability of arbitration clauses. *See Doctor's Associates, Inc. v. Casarotto*, 517 U.S. 681 (1996). The Court has also refused to set aside arbitration clauses in cases where consumers sought to litigate rights under federal or state consumer protection statutes, thus depriving consumers of most of the remedial provisions of those statutes, such as attorney's fees and statutory damages. *See Green Tree Financial Corp.-Alabama v. Randolph*, 531 U.S. 79 (2000). While many state and some federal courts sought to curb the effects of arbitration clauses in one-sided contracts of adhesion, typically through the application of the unconscionability doctrine, the Supreme Court has swept aside most of these objections to the enforcement of arbitration clauses.

In 2011, the Supreme Court decided *AT&T Mobility LLC v. Concepcion*, 563 U.S. 333 (2011). In this case, a consumer class action challenged AT&T's marketing practices but the class action was kept out of court due to an arbitration clause, despite the fact that the California Supreme Court had deemed such clauses under certain circumstances to be unconscionable. The Supreme Court held that the FAA preempted the California unconscionability doctrine. As a result, the Court held that not only was the arbitration clause itself enforceable, but that its companion class arbitration waiver was also enforceable, portending an uphill battle for consumer class actions post-*Concepcion*. Another class action waiver was upheld in *American Express Co. v. Italian Colors Restaurant*, 570 U.S. 228 (2013), in a case involving an antitrust challenge brought by participating merchants against a card issuer.

Given the clear intransigence of the Supreme Court in applying the FAA to consumer and most other arbitration clauses, the harsh effects have been ameliorated through means other than court challenges. For instance, in May of 1998 the American Arbitration Association published the *Consumer Due Process Protocol for Mediation and Arbitration of Consumer Disputes.*

Principle 11 of the *Protocol* provides:

Consumers should be given:

(a) clear and adequate notice of the arbitration provision and its consequences, including a statement of its mandatory or optional character;

(b) reasonable access to information regarding the arbitration process, including basic distinctions between arbitration and court proceedings, related costs, and advice as to where they may obtain more complete information regarding arbitration procedures and arbitrator rosters;

(c) notice of the option to make use of applicable small claims court procedures as an alternative to binding arbitration in appropriate cases; and,

(d) a clear statement of the means by which the Consumer may exercise the option (if any) to submit disputes to arbitration or to court process.

There are fifteen principles in the *Protocol* that draw attention to the concerns of consumers in the arbitration process. The principles were developed to establish clear benchmarks for conflict resolution processes involving consumers.

In 2008, the National Arbitration Forum announced that it was no longer taking consumer arbitration cases, after being challenged by the Minnesota Attorney General for conducting biased arbitration proceedings.

Informal alternatives to court proceedings to settle consumer disputes, if done with appropriate safeguards for consumers, can actually be helpful. Note that the Magnuson-Moss Warranty Act of 1975, tried to encourage the use of informal dispute resolutions by consumer product warrantors and required consumers to exhaust such procedures, if offered, prior to going to court under that statute and related state "lemon laws." *See infra* Chapter Ten. The FTC issued regulations under the Act specifying that consumers who used the informal dispute resolution process would always have a right to go to court to press their statutory or breach of warranty cases, and that the informal procedures would be offered at no cost to them and under a specific timeframe. 16 C.F.R. Part 700. When certain consumer product warrantors, notably mobile home manufacturers, started inserting mandatory arbitration provisions into their consumer contracts, however, most courts held that the arbitration clause "trumped" the MMWA informal dispute resolution process. *See, e.g., Walton v. Rose Mobile Homes LLC*, 298 F.3d 470 (5th Cir. 2002). Thus, consumers are losing the benefit of this important option and will be bound to resolve their disputes under more formal and less favorable types of private arbitration if so provided in their contracts.

The Federal Arbitration Act appears to be the driving force behind the Supreme Court jurisprudence upholding arbitration clauses. Since the FAA is a Congressional statute and not a Constitutional provision, however, the Congress or its duly empowered regulatory agencies could alter the landscape. This process has already begun. Some groups have won exemptions from mandatory pre-dispute arbitration, including automobile dealers and poultry and livestock farmers. Congress in 2006 passed a law that, among other things, voids arbitration clauses in payday loan contracts with military service members or their dependents. 10 U.S.C. § 987(e)(3), (f)(4). Also, as part of the Dodd-Frank Wall Street Reform and Consumer Protection Act of 2010, Congress prohibited the use of arbitration clauses in residential mortgage loans. 15 U.S.C. § 1639c(e)(1). In the same legislation, Congress directed the newly created federal Consumer Financial Protection Bureau to conduct a study of pre-dispute arbitration in consumer finance contracts and also gave the agency the authority to issue regulations limiting the use of such contracts. 12 U.S.C. § 5518. The CFPB completed its study in 2015, and in 2017 promulgated a regulation that banned class action waivers in consumer arbitration contracts within its jurisdiction. This regulation was vetoed by Congress at the end of 2017, and thus never went into effect.

CHAPTER THREE
INDUCING CONSUMER TRANSACTIONS: ADVERTISING AND MARKETING

A. ADVERTISING

1. COMMON LAW ACTIONS

An action for fraud is one common law cause of action that provides a potential remedy for the injured consumer. The first and most common fraud claims are tort-based claims for deceit or false and misleading advertising. A buyer may bring an action in deceit against a seller for falsely advertising a product if he can prove all of the following elements: (1) that the seller made a false representation of a material fact; (2) that the seller had knowledge or belief that the representation was not based on known information or that the seller had a reckless disregard for known facts; (3) that the seller intended for the buyer to rely on the representation made; (4) that the buyer justifiably relied on the representation and (5) that the buyer suffered damages because of the reliance.

The most difficult element to prove in a fraud action is that a representation is one of fact, and not one of opinion. This is because advertisements usually consist of exaggerated claims used to boost the sale of a product. Therefore, a common, and often successful, defense asserted by sellers is the "puffing" exception defense. The "puffing" defense exempts a harmless exaggeration of opinion which is not intended to deceive the consumer from being considered as a fraudulent misrepresentation. Courts generally look to several factors to determine whether a representation can be considered as "puffing," including: (1) how specific the representation is; (2) whether the advertisement describes virtues about the product that do not exist; (3) whether it is common practice in the industry to make such assertions and (4) how knowledgeable the buyer is about the product. Generally, a representation made with very specific details regarding the product will be considered as a representation of fact rather than opinion. Justifiable reliance and damages may also be stumbling blocks for consumers especially in cases of mass advertising rather than one-to-one transactions.

Justifiable reliance is also a difficult element of common law fraud for consumer plaintiffs to prove. For instance, when some recent law school graduates sought to sue their law school for common law fraud based on the dissemination of false employment statistics used to attract applicants, their claim was dismissed because the court found they were not justified in relying on statistics that were internally contradicted in the school's materials. *MacDonald v. Thomas M. Cooley Law School*, 724 F.3d 654 (6th Cir. 2013).

A cause of action alleging false advertising may also be asserted as a breach of warranty claim. A seller has made an express warranty if he makes "[a]ny affirmation of fact or promise . . . to the buyer which relates to the goods and becomes part of the basis of the bargain ... " UCC § 2–313(1)(a). If the goods do not conform to the affirmation or promise, then the buyer may have a claim for breach of warranty. Since a breach of warranty action requires the plaintiff to show that the defendant made an affirmation of fact or promise, like an action on deceit, the "puffing" exception is available as a defense. Unlike an action on deceit, however, the buyer does not have to prove that the seller intended to deceive him. What is required is proof that the seller's representation was part of the basis of the bargain. In cases of mass media advertising by a manufacturer who sells through retail outlets, however, the lack of privity between the distant warrantor and the consumer may be a problem in breach of warranty cases.

Although common law actions may be difficult to prove because of the strict element requirements, common law actions have several advantages for the consumer. First, most fraud actions allow the consumer to seek punitive damages which may be unavailable under other statutory remedies. Secondly, the common law element requirements are less strict in those states which have liberalized and broadened the scope of the intent and factual requirements when the case involves consumers. On the other hand, most consumer cases, especially if litigated individually rather than as a class action, involve such small damages that they may not be economically feasible to pursue in court. The state UDAP statutes discussed in the preceding chapter were meant in part to address this issue.

2. FEDERAL TRADE COMMISSION'S REGULATION OF ADVERTISING

The FTC has been a bastion for the protection of consumers against false or misleading advertising since its inception in the early 20th century. The FTC has many tools at its disposal in this regard, including specific statutory provisions, its general authority under Section 5, Policy Statements, the advertising substantiation doctrine, FTC rules and guides, as well as actions for consumer redress, injunctions, cease and desist orders, and disclosure requirements (including corrective advertising). Each of these aspects of the FTC's policing of advertising will be discussed below.

Section 12 of the FTC Act expressly prohibits certain categories of false advertising. Section 12 makes unlawful the dissemination of false advertising by mail or other means that directly or indirectly induce consumers to purchase food, drugs, services or cosmetics. 15 U.S.C. § 52. This provision expressly brings false advertising under the provisions of section 5, so that a false advertisement is automatically considered as an unfair or deceptive practice. Section 15 defines the term "false advertisement" as an advertisement that is materially misleading. Although the term "misleading" is not defined, section 15 provides that:

> "in determining whether any advertisement is misleading, there shall be taken into account (among other things) not only representations made or suggested by statement, word, design, device, sound, or any combination thereof, but

also the extent to which the advertisement fails to reveal facts material in the light of such representations or material with respect to the consequences which may result from the use of the commodity to which the advertisement relates under the conditions prescribed in the advertisement, or under such conditions as are customary or usual."

15 U.S.C. § 55.

The FTC Policy Statements on unfair and deceptive practices discussed in the previous chapter provide substantive guidance for the FTC's efforts in the advertising arena. When interpreting claims being made in any particular advertisement, the FTC uses its "net impression" to pinpoint the express and implied claims made by express representations, by half-truth or innuendo, by visual aspects or by omission of material facts. *Kraft, Inc. v. FTC*, 970 F.2d 311 (7th Cir. 1992). While the FTC often relies on "extrinsic evidence" (e.g., consumer surveys or expert testimony) to interpret advertising, courts have said such evidence is not necessary for the FTC to act.

Since the 1970s, the FTC has used its "advertising substantiation" doctrine to require that all advertisers have in their possession, prior to dissemination, a reasonable basis for all material claims made in their advertisements. *See* FTC Policy Statement Regarding Advertising Substantiation, appended to *Thompson Medical Co.*, 104 F.T.C. 648, 839 (1984). This doctrine has the effect of placing the burden on the advertiser to have prior substantiation, rather than for the FTC to affirmatively prove that the claims in the advertisement are deceptive. The rationale for this doctrine is that an advertisement lacking a reasonable basis deceives the public which assumes that all advertisements do have such a reasonable basis for their claims. The level of substantiation required will vary according to the type of claim being made. The highest level of substantiation, two well-controlled clinical studies or the equivalent competent and reliable scientific evidence, is applicable to over-the-counter drugs making claims that their benefits have been scientifically established. *Sterling Drug, Inc. v. FTC*, 741 F.2d 1146 (9th Cir. 1984). Limited substantiation is required for advertisements that specify a particular type of substantiation in the advertisement itself, and no substantiation is required for claims deemed to be "puffing." "Reasonable basis" is the default standard applicable to most advertising claims.

For products making therapeutic claims, such as pain relief, studies showing the product may have a "placebo" effect do not constitute sufficient substantiation. *See FTC v. QT, Inc.*, 512 F.3d 858 (7th Cir. 2008). Also, a dietary supplement, such as pomegranate juice or pills, whose advertising makes specific disease prevention or cure claims, should have at least one randomized clinical trial to support such claims. *See POM Wonderful v. FTC*, 777 F.3d 478 (D.C. Cir. 2015).

The FTC has used informal guides and reports to advise businesses as to what claims they can make or what substantiation they will need in their advertising. The FTC actively litigates and provides guidance regarding the advertising of weight loss products as well as dietary supplements, an area where it shares jurisdiction with the FDA. The FTC has also issued detailed guides for advertising of products claimed to have environmental benefits. 16 C.F.R. Part 260, originally issued in 1992 and updated in 2012.

The FTC's remedies for deceptive advertising include cease and desist orders, injunctions, and consumer redress, typically as part of a § 13(b) injunction or as part of a § 5 settlement. For instance, in a case involving Volkswagen's alleged disabling of the pollution detection devices on its diesel vehicles to avoid detection of its excessive emissions, VW settled FTC charges by offering consumers a buyback and lease termination deal worth up to $10 billion in consumer compensation. *FTC v. Volkswagen Group of America, Inc.*, Case 3:16-01534, Stipulated Judgment (N.C. Cal. 2016), available at ftc.gov. In a 2019 case, however, the Seventh Circuit Court of Appeals held that the FTC does not have statutory authority to obtain restitution in a Section 13(b) proceeding. *FTC v. Credit Bureau Center, LLC*, 937 F.3d 764 (7th Cir. 2019). It remains to be seen whether other courts will follow this unprecedented holding.

Corrective advertising is also an important remedy for certain types of false or deceptive advertising. This statutorily implied remedy was recognized in *Warner-Lambert Co. v. FTC*, 562 F.2d 749 (D.C.

Cir.1977). In that case, the court held that the FTC has the authority to require a violator to affirmatively disclose in future advertisements unfavorable facts regarding the product to remedy the lingering deceptive effects of previous misleading advertisements and to prevent future deception. *See also Novartis Corp. v. FTC*, 223 F.3d 783 (D.C. Cir. 2000).

3. SPECIFIC FTC CONCERNS

The FTC exercises its regulatory powers over deceptive advertisements in many areas. One major source of regulation concerns bait-and-switch sales. The FTC's "Guides against Bait Advertising" set out the scope and definitions of bait-and-switch advertising. *See* 16 C.F.R. § 238. Bait advertising is defined as:

> an alluring but insincere offer to sell a product or service which the advertiser in truth does not intend or want to sell. Its purpose is to switch consumers from buying the advertised merchandise, in order to sell something else, usually at a high price or on a basis more advantageous to the advertiser. The primary aim of a bait advertisement is to obtain leads as to persons interested in buying merchandise of the type so advertised.

16 C.F.R. § 238.0.

In essence, the "bait" is a bogus offer to sell a product at a favorable price. Whether an advertisement is a bogus offer or a bona fide offer depends on certain factors such as: (1) the disparagement of the advertised product; (2) the showing of a defective or an unusable product; (3) an insufficient supply of the advertised product, compared to anticipated demand or (4) the method of compensation or penalty given to salespersons as an incentive or disincentive to sell the higher priced product versus the advertised product. 16 C.F.R. § 238.3. For example, in *Tashof v. FTC*, 437 F.2d 707 (D.C. Cir.1970), the FTC found that a seller had engaged in deceptive practices when it was shown that out of fourteen hundred total pairs of eyeglasses sold, less than ten pairs were sold at the advertised price.

FTC advertising enforcement has also addressed the lengthy product commercials commonly known as "infomercials." Infomercials are usually five to thirty minute television commercials that are designed to appear like reporting programs or talk shows. The deception caused by the infomercials occurs because the commercial is portrayed in a form that appears to be an objective description of the advertised product. Uninformed consumers are unaware that the representations made in the commercials are really biased, persuasive and promotional, rather than factual. For example, in *FTC v. Pantron I Corp.*, 33 F.3d 1088 (9th Cir.1994), the court found that a seller had engaged in deceptive practices by representing in its infomercials that scientific studies supported the corporation's claim that the product's formula promoted new hair growth in balding persons.

"Native advertising" is the latest form of marketing that tends to blur the lines between objective news or articles and sponsored content, which could potentially lead consumers to give the advertising unwarranted credibility. This type of advertising is similar to "infomercials" but is more prevalent in modern social media settings. The FTC's 2016 "Enforcement Policy Statement on Deceptively Formatted Advertisements" attempts to provide guidelines on when sponsored content might be considered deceptive, and when it is legal. 81 Fed. Reg. 22596 (April 18, 2016). The use of deceptive means to attract customers to an online marketer, such as posting "fake news" stories, has been successfully challenged by the FTC. *FTC v. LeadClick Media, LLC*, 838 F.3d 158 (2d Cir. 2016).

A third major category of advertising controversy, and one to which every person has had some exposure, is celebrity endorsements and consumer testimonials. The product's credibility is boosted by being associated with and directly linked to the reputation of a favorite celebrity. Also, consumers are likely to believe that a consumer testimonial as to, for example, a weight loss product, is describing results that would be achievable by the average consumer.

Under the FTC Guides, originally promulgated in 1980 and updated in 2009, a misleading endorsement is a deceptive act or false advertisement if an endorser makes a false or misleading representation in the advertisement, whether knowingly or unknowingly. *See* 16 C.F.R. § 255. The Guides require that (1) the advertisement reflect the present opinion of the endorser; (2) the endorser be a bona fide user of the product at the time of the advertisement and (3) required disclosures be given to consumers if the celebrity has a direct financial interest in the sale of the product beyond the reasonable expectations of the consumer. Consumer testimonials must also reflect the experience of the average consumer. Disclosures such as "results are not typical" are not sufficient. The updated version of these Guides also provides examples of compliant and noncompliant endorsements made in blogs or social media.

The latest version of consumer endorsements is the widespread use of consumer reviews in online marketing. Obviously, planting false positive reviews of one's own products (or phony negative ones for a competitor's offerings) would be deceptive or unfair. In another twist, some companies had attempted to penalize consumers who posted negative reviews, through the enforcement of boilerplate clauses in online consumer contracts. Congress stepped in to stop this practice by passing the Consumer Review Fairness Act, that bans the use of non-disparagement clauses restricting negative, yet truthful, reviews of products and services by consumers. 15 U.S.C. § 45b.

4. APPLYING STATE UDAP STATUTES TO ADVERTISING

All the states have adopted legislation to regulate deceptive or misleading trade practices, including advertising, under state UDAP statutes, as discussed in Chapter 2 of this nutshell. In discussing the application of advertising regulation, it is important to keep in mind the major variations of UDAP statutes adopted among the states: (1) states that model the FTC Act and broadly prohibit unfair or deceptive acts; and (2) states that provide a per se laundry list of prohibited conduct that may or may not include a catchall provision. Among those states that have adopted a per se variation, many expressly include misleading advertising within the laundry list of prohibited acts.

Most UDAP statutes expressly exclude from liability parties that are responsible for distributing advertising materials within a particular media. For example, printers, publishers, magazines, newspapers and television stations are generally held not liable for deceptive advertising contained within a printed or televised advertisement.

A common defense under both UDAP statutes and the FTC Act is the right to freedom of speech under the First Amendment. The Supreme Court has spoken on this issue in detail and has held that commercial speech is afforded some protection under the Constitution. *Virginia State Board of Pharmacy v. Virginia Citizens Consumer Council, Inc.*, 425 U.S. 748 (1976). The protection, however, is limited and is less than that afforded to noncommercial speech. Lower courts have repeatedly held that the FTC may freely regulate commercial speech that is misleading because false and misleading advertisements are not protected by the First Amendment. *See, e.g., Kraft, Inc. v. F.T.C.*, 970 F.2d 311 (7th Cir. 1992). The Supreme Court has also held that regulations of truthful commercial speech, although protected by the First Amendment, can nonetheless be regulated if the following three-pronged test is met: (1) the government must have a substantial interest in the regulation; (2) the limitations on commercial speech must directly advance that interest and (3) the regulation must be narrowly drawn. *Central Hudson Gas & Electric Corp. v. Public Service Commission of New York*, 447 U.S. 557 (1980).

5. CREDIT ADVERTISING PROVISIONS

The advertising of consumer credit and other consumer financial services or products is subject to special advertising provisions under federal law. These include the Truth in Lending Act (TILA) and Regulation Z, as well as the general prohibitions against unfair, deceptive or abusive practices under the Consumer Financial Protection Act, and the FTC ban on deceptive or unfair practices.

The Truth in Lending Act's required disclosure of the cost of credit using uniform measurements was based in part on the desire of Congress to eliminate consumer confusion caused by the advertising of consumer credit. Prior to the passage of TILA, creditors touted add-on, discount, and other rates that were not comparable to the more familiar simple interest rate applied to a declining balance. For example, the automobile finance industry advertised a six percent add-on rate for car financing that consumers might have believed was comparable to a simple interest rate, but was in fact equivalent to an eleven percent simple interest rate. The FTC pursued such cases under their general authority over unfair or deceptive trade practices. *See, e.g., Ford Motor Co. v. FTC*, 120 F.2d 175 (6th Cir. 1941).

TILA not only requires uniform disclosures of the cost of credit, as discussed *infra* Chapters Six and Seven, but also imposes some specific requirements on the advertising of credit. The credit advertising disclosure requirements are not the same as the more detailed disclosures required prior to consummation of closed-end credit transactions or at various points of open-end credit plans, due to the desire not to overburden credit advertising that could actually be useful to consumers. Thus, the credit advertising requirements took a "triggered" disclosure approach, which was meant to discourage the emphasis in advertisements on the "good news" about a low down payment or low introductory rate, for example, without also disclosing the other pertinent terms of the deal within the advertisement itself.

To address the issue of advertising noncomparable financing rates, the law now requires that if an advertisement mentions a rate it must be expressed as an annual percentage rate. 12 C.F.R. § 1026.24(c). Also, if the advertisement mentions any of the so-called triggering terms, i.e., the amount or percentage of any down payment, the number of payments or period of repayment, the amount of any payment or the amount of any finance charge, then it must also state all of the triggered terms, which are the amount or percentage of any down payment, the terms of repayment applicable over the full term of the loan, including any balloon payment, and the annual percentage rate and whether that rate may be increased after consummation. 12 C.F.R. § 1026.24(d).

The regulation of open-end credit advertising, mainly credit cards or home equity lines of credit, takes a similar trigger/disclosure approach. If a triggering term is mentioned in such an advertisement, then the following must also be disclosed: any minimum, fixed, transaction or other similar charge that could be imposed; any periodic rate that may be applied; and any membership or participation fee. 12 C.F.R. § 1026.16(b). Solicitations for credit cards must contain a table of specific disclosures subject to formatting requirements. 12 C.F.R. § 1026.60, discussed *infra* Chapter Seven. In order to avoid "bait" advertising of credit products, the advertisement must include only those terms that are actually being offered or will be arranged. 12 C.F.R. §§ 1026.16(a) and 1026.24(a).

Beginning in the 1990s, leasing became an increasingly popular alternative to credit sales of automobiles. The advertising of lease terms was perceived to be subject to the same types of issues as other forms of credit advertising, namely that the advertiser would highlight the favorable terms of the lease without disclosing the unfavorable ones. The federal Consumer Leasing Act and its accompanying Regulation M take a trigger/disclosure approach just as the credit advertising regulations do. For lease advertisements, the triggering terms are: (1) the amount of any payment or (2) a statement of any capitalized cost reduction or other payment. If any of the triggering terms are mentioned in an advertisement, then the triggered terms must be disclosed, which include: (1) that the advertised transaction is a lease; (2) the total amount due at consummation or delivery; (3) the number, amounts, due dates or periods of scheduled payments; (4) a statement of whether or not a security deposit is required; and (5) a statement that an extra charge may be imposed at the end of the lease term, if applicable. 12 C.F.R. § 1013.7(d).

During the 2007–2009 period, the country was experiencing a financial crisis, part of which was manifested in a rise in foreclosures of home mortgages which had originated in the subprime market. These loans often featured low teaser rates and/or payment plans that had built-in rate hikes that the borrowers ultimately could not afford. Since the advertisements for these types of mortgages had emphasized the immediately attractive features without adequately disclosing the risks, the regulation of home mortgage loan marketing was strengthened. First the Federal Reserve Board amended Regulation Z to provide some additional requirements specifically relating to mortgage loan advertisements. 12 C.F.R. § 1026.24(f) & (i). The regulations now provide for disclosures of all applicable rates if any rate is mentioned, so that so-called "teaser" rates do not have more prominence than the other applicable rates. The regulation also requires the disclosure of all payment levels that will apply over the term of the loan, including any balloon payment, and the period of time during which each payment will apply, if the advertisement chooses to mention a payment amount. The required advertising disclosures must be equally prominent to any payment or rate that is a triggering term. This advertising regulation also lists seven specifically prohibited practices, including misleading use of terms like "fixed" rate or payments, misleading comparisons, misrepresentations about government endorsement, misleading use of the current lender's name, misleading claims of debt elimination, misleading use of the term "counselor," and misleading foreign language advertisements.

During this same time period, the FTC also issued a regulation on mortgage advertising, Regulation N, that covers entities subject to FTC jurisdiction. 12 C.F.R. § 1014 (now under the purview of the CFPB but enforced jointly with the FTC). This rule applies to nonbank mortgage lenders, mortgage brokers, mortgage servicers and real estate brokers who may advertise home mortgage products. The rule contains prohibitions against various misleading representations but does not contain any affirmative disclosure requirements.

Home equity lines of credit (HELOCs) are also subject to advertising regulations that are somewhat more stringent than the regulations applicable to other open-end credit advertisements. As with the closed-end home mortgage advertisements discussed above, these requirements were enhanced during the financial crisis of the late 2000s, and generally take a triggered disclosure approach. 12 C.F.R. § 1026.16(d).

While most of TILA's provisions are subject to private enforcement, the credit advertising sections are not. Nor is there any allowance for direct state enforcement of TILA's credit advertising restrictions. Thus, these detailed regulations are enforced mainly by the Federal Trade Commission, and as of 2011, by the Consumer Financial Protection Bureau (CFPB). The FTC has been active in policing credit advertising for many years, and has focused on entities within its jurisdiction, such as retail stores, car dealers, payday lenders, and home builders. The Federal Reserve Board originally had the authority to promulgate and issue regulations and staff commentary on the credit advertising provisions of TILA, but that task has been handled by the CFPB since 2011.

The CFPB has also been active in bringing deceptive and unfair advertising and marketing cases in the credit and financial services sector, using its general authority to police "unfair, deceptive and abusive" practices. For instance, the CFPB's first enforcement action in 2012 charged Capitol One with deceptive marketing of credit card "add-on" products. It settled the case for $140 million in refunds for consumers. CFPB v. Capitol One, available at consumerfinance.gov. The CFPB has also brought suits alleging deceptive advertising of data security procedures, deceptive and unfair marketing to Navajo Nation customers of high interest tax refund anticipation loans, and unfair and abusive practices by companies that attempted to steer students into taking out disadvantageous student loans, or opting into unfavorable loan repayment programs. In a 2016 case, the CFPB took action against an online consumer lender called LendUp, charging the company with deceptive and illegal practices, including misleading advertising to consumers about the benefits of using their loans to progress up to larger loans with better terms, misstating the actual price of the loans, and failing to report information to credit reporting agencies to improve the consumers' credit record, as promised. The company agreed to end their unlawful practices, and to pay $1.83 million in redress to victims, as well as a $1.83 civil penalty. In re Flurish, Inc., d/b/a LendUp, available at consumerfinance.gov.

B. OTHER SALES PRACTICES

1. DOOR-TO-DOOR SALES

Most people are familiar with the traditional method of door-to-door sales. Up until telemarketing and internet sales began to take off, a variety of products were promoted through door-to-door sales, from vacuums to aluminum siding to insurance. The risk of deception in door-to-door sales is great because of the nature of the sale itself. First, the salesperson typically approaches a consumer at his home, a place where he is vulnerable and cannot easily leave. Secondly, the salesperson generally uses high pressure tactics to induce the consumer to purchase the goods or a service. Third, the consumer, who is usually not psychologically prepared for a sales pitch, will feel compelled to purchase something just to end the encounter. Therefore, because of the history of door-to-door sales and the abundant opportunities to deceive consumers, the FTC issued the Cooling-Off Period Rule in 1974. 16 C.F.R. Part 429.

The Cooling-Off Period gives the consumer the right to cancel any sale resulting from a home solicitation within three days after the sale. In addition, the seller must provide the buyer with a written copy of the sales contract and attach to the contract two copies of a notice of the buyer's right to cancel. The Rule requires that the contract include the same terms as used to make the sale. An oral disclosure of the right to cancel must also be given. A consumer cannot waive this right to cancel and the seller must not misrepresent this right. There is a limited provision for the consumer to waive the three-day cooling-off period if there is a "bona fide immediate personal emergency." A home solicitation includes any personal contact from a sales representative at a person's home or other locations outside the home such as a motel room, but excludes a place of business. The Cooling-Off rule does not include mail or telephone solicitations. There are some concurrent state home solicitation statutes, however, that do include a cooling-off period for telephone sales.

The Truth in Lending Act also provides a three day cooling-off period or "right to rescind" certain credit transactions secured by the consumer's principal dwelling. 15 U.S.C. § 1635, 12 C.F.R. §§ 1026.23 & .15. This TILA right of rescission is limited to "second" mortgages. It does not include the purchase money mortgage. While the TILA right to rescind is not limited to door to door sales, it so happens that unscrupulous actors have used home solicitations to convince homeowners to sign a credit contract for home repairs secured by a mortgage. The three-day cooling-off period is meant to provide the consumer the opportunity to reconsider any transaction which would have the serious consequence of putting the title to his home at risk. A more detailed discussion of the TILA right of rescission can be found in Chapter Eight, *infra*.

2. TELEPHONE SALES

Historically, the promotion or sale of a product by telephone was a primary source of fraud. Typically, telephone scams take the form of (1) a phony business investment or work-at-home opportunity that promises unrealistic returns in exchange for relatively high costs; (2) prizes or awards promised in return for a fee or (3) "recovery room" scams that target victims of scams and promise to recover the lost prize or investment in return for a fee. Victims usually possess some vulnerable characteristic, such as being poor, financially unsophisticated or elderly. The constant ringing of the telephone on behalf of marketers was also considered a nuisance at best or a serious invasion of privacy at worst. The profitability of telemarketing has been reduced, however, by the popular "do-not-call" rule and the advent of mobile phones and internet sales. This industry is confined by strict federal and state regulations dating back to the 1990s.

First, the Telephone Consumer Protection Act (TCPA), 47 U.S.C. § 227, is a federal law passed in 1991 that bans (1) the use of artificial or prerecorded voice messages ("robo calls") to residential telephone lines without prior consent, (2) the use of automatic dialing systems or robo calls without prior consent to any emergency telephone line, hospital patient, pager, cellular telephone or other service for which the recipient is charged, and (3) sending unsolicited advertisements to fax machines ("junk faxes"). A text message to a cellular telephone qualifies as a "call" under the TCPA. Campbell-Ewald Co. v. Gomez, 136 S. Ct. 663 (2016). The Act requires that phone calls be made only between 8 a.m. and 9 p.m. local time of the person called. Additionally, the Act allows consumers to bring private actions in state courts for violations and makes available treble damages for willful conduct or injunctions for losses greater than $500. In 2012, the U.S. Supreme Court held that private actions alleging violations of the TCPA may also be brought in federal court. *Mims v. Arrow Financial Services, LLC*, 565 U.S. 368 (2012). In 2020, the Court upheld the TCPA's general ban on robo calls to mobile phones, but struck down an exemption that had been added in 2015, for persons collecting debts either owed to or guaranteed by the federal government. The Court found the exemption to be a violation of the First Amendment because it was content-based and singled out a group of persons for special treatment. *Barr v. American Ass'n of Political Consultants*, 140 S. Ct. 2335 (2020).

A second source of regulation is the Telemarketing and Consumer Fraud and Abuse Prevention Act of

SEC. B OTHER SALES PRACTICES 79

1994 (TCFAPA), 15 U.S.C. § 6101, which placed specific limitations on the time, place and manner of telemarketing calls, among other restrictions. The FTC, as authorized by the TCFAPA, issued regulations that specifically prohibit deceptive and abusive telemarketing acts or practices. Telemarketing Sales Rule (TSR) 16 C.F.R. Part 310. Telemarketing is defined as any plan, program or campaign designed to induce the purchase of a product or service by the use of the telephone. Mandatory disclosures are also required, including the identification of the seller and purpose of the call. The FTC rule requires that an offer of goods or services be accompanied by a description of their nature. If a prize is offered, the seller must inform the consumer that it is not necessary to purchase the good or service to enter the contest and qualify to win a prize. Additionally, all costs, fees, restrictions, limitations, conditions or refund limitations must be disclosed. Coercive means used to induce participation, threats, intimidation and harassment by repeated calls are expressly prohibited. Requesting advance fees for "recovery" services or extensions of easy credit is also prohibited.

The FTC amended its Telemarketing Sales Rule in 2003 to create a national "do-not-call" registry by which individuals could have their phone number listed as being off-limits to telemarketers. 16 C.F.R. § 310.4(b)(1)(3). The rationale was to prevent fraud and protect consumer privacy. The registry proved to be hugely popular with consumers who signed up for the registry in large numbers. The rule has exceptions for marketers who are calling consumers with whom they have a business relationship or who have not signed up for the Do-Not-Call registry. Nonprofit and political calls are also exempted. The rule was challenged in court as an unconstitutional infringement of commercial free speech, but the regulation was upheld. *Mainstream Marketing Services v. FTC*, 358 F.3d 1228 (10th Cir. 2004).

In 2008, the FTC again amended the Telemarketing Sales Rule to prohibit the use of prerecorded or "robo" telemarketing calls without the express written consent of the consumer. 16 C.F.R. § 310.4(b)(1)(v). Such banned robocalls include the use of "soundboard" technology, which is a system that partially automates telemarketing calls. *Soundboard Association v. FTC*, 888 F.3d 1261 (D.C. Cir. 2018).

The use of 900 numbers created another widespread problem during the 1990s, although their use is fading with the availability of the Internet and mobile phones. With 900 or "pay-per-call" numbers, the caller pays an extra charge to an independent information provider, but is billed on his or her regular telephone bill. These 900 numbers lured customers with an endless array of gimmicks, including talk lines, sexual material, games-of-chance and even children's stories, often without adequate disclosure of the charges. As a result, substantial regulation of 900 numbers is in place to prevent and prosecute such fraud. The Telephone Disclosure and Dispute Resolution Act of 1992 (TDDRA), 47 U.S.C. § 228 and 15 U.S.C. § 5711, authorizes the FCC and FTC respectively to enforce the provisions of the Act. The Act and the regulations prohibit phone companies and long distance carriers from disconnecting a customer's service because of unpaid 900 number charges. Phone companies are required to itemize 900 number charges and to provide customers with an option of blocking 900 number access from their phones. The rules also require disclosure of the cost of any advertised pay-per-call service, prohibit advertising directed to children under the age of 12, and require providers to use a billing error procedure.

3. MAIL, INTERNET AND TELEPHONE ORDER SALES

The FTC addresses the issue of late delivery of ordered products under the Mail, Internet or Telephone Order Merchandise Rule, 16 C.F.R. § 435. This Rule protects consumers' expectations regarding the time and delivery of goods and services ordered by mail, internet or telephone. The Rule requires that the delivery of the ordered merchandise be made within thirty days from the date of a properly completed order, which means that the buyer has tendered full or partial payment in the proper amount in the form of cash, check, money order, or authorization to charge an existing account or other payment method. This 30-day time period is only a default period, however. The seller may be bound to comply with a shorter time period if the seller so specifies or promises. The time limit may also be extended beyond the thirty days if the consumer expressly consents to an extension. If the seller cannot meet the thirty-day rule or other deadline, then the consumer must be contacted, at which time, the consumer may either consent to an extension or cancel the order and demand a refund. The FTC Mail Order Rule was originally passed in 1975, was amended to cover telephone sales in 1993, and was extended to internet sales in 2014.

4. UNORDERED GOODS & NEGATIVE OPTION PLANS

Another category related to mail order sales is the attempted sale of unordered goods which are mailed to the consumer without any prior telephone or written contact by the consumer. Although the consumer may assume these goods are free gifts, sellers may try to frame the shipment as an offer to sell. The seller bets on the probability that the consumer will fail to return the goods although such failure, according to the seller, acts as an acceptance and binds the consumer to a financial obligation to pay for the goods. It is very likely that the consumer will not return the goods, considering the expense and associated inconvenience of doing so. Fortunately for consumers, federal law (with some limited exceptions) prohibits the delivery of unordered goods by mail and considers such deliveries as a per se violation of the FTC Act. 39 U.S.C. § 3009. Therefore, the consumer may, in fact, treat any unsolicited goods as a free gift.

A "negative option" plan is one in which the consumer signs up for a plan under which merchandise (such as a book or a CD) is automatically shipped and billed to the consumer

SEC. B OTHER SALES PRACTICES

unless the consumer takes some action to cancel. Like unordered merchandise, the negative option plan takes advantage of the human tendency to procrastinate and do nothing. An FTC regulation, 16 C.F.R. § 425, requires such plans to make adequate disclosures of the need to cancel to avoid being billed, and to promptly credit consumers for returned merchandise. The FTC has also challenged marketing plans using "free trial" offers without adequate disclosure of the need to take affirmative actions to avoid being charged.

In 2010, Congress passed the Restore Online Shoppers' Confidence Act (ROSCA), to deal with various negative option and "free" trial offer abuses in online sales. 15 U.S.C.A. §§ 8401–8405. This statute makes it illegal to charge a consumer for goods or services sold in an internet transaction through any negative option method, unless the marketer clearly and conspicuously discloses all material terms before obtaining a consumer's billing information, obtains the consumer's express informed consent before charging the consumer and provides a simple method for the consumer to stop recurring charges from being placed on their account. ROSCA also addresses offers made by or on behalf of a third party during or just after a transaction with the initial merchant. The FTC is the main government enforcer of this law and has brought many successful cases since its inception. In a notable case against a company selling a credit report service, the company used a marketing affiliate who advertised a fictitious apartment on Craigslist, and then directed interested tenants to sign up for a "free" credit report from the company's website in order to be shown the property. Many customers unwittingly signed up for an expensive monthly credit monitoring service with a very short cancellation window and also learned that there was no apartment to rent. The FTC won summary judgment on the ROSCA count, but the $5 million restitution award was overturned. FTC v. Credit Bureau Center, LLC, 937 F.3d 764 (7th Cir. 2019).

5. REFERRAL SALES & PYRAMID SCHEMES

A referral sales plan is a scheme whereby the seller offers large, often impossible and insincere discounts to consumers on products contingent on some future event. That future event typically requires the consumer to provide the seller with a referral list of other consumers who must also purchase the product for the first consumer to get the discount promised. Referral sales may be a per se violation of UDAP regulations or the FTC Act as a deceptive practice because of the misrepresentation of the ease of getting the discount. To make matters worse, often even if the consumer satisfies the usually difficult contingency, he still does not receive the promised discount. The Uniform Consumer Credit Code, adopted in eleven states, contains a provision banning referral sales. U.C.C.C. § 3.309.

A related scam is the "pyramid" scheme whereby the seller seems to be offering to sell a product at a discounted price when he is actually selling rights to sell new memberships or recruit new salespeople to obtain the discount or some other reward. The sales scheme is named for its "pyramid" effect. The earliest "investors" at the top of the pyramid are the real beneficiaries of the plan because they are the few who reap the largest percentage of profits as more memberships are sold by the members beneath them. The layers of membership increase as each top layer creates new generations of members beneath them. Because profits are distributed from the top down, and because of the shrinking availability of new recruits, however, the members at the lower levels may never recoup their original investment much less achieve the promised returns. These schemes have been around for a long time, and originally were promoted by "revival" style meetings featuring charismatic speakers such as Glenn Turner. Now they are more likely to be found on the Internet and have expanded worldwide.

Many states have specific statutes prohibiting such schemes. The difficulty is defining an illegal pyramid scheme in a way that distinguishes it from a legitimate multi-level marketing (MLM) plan. The FTC has challenged some pyramid/MLM schemes under its general authority to prohibit unfair and deceptive trade practices under FTC Act § 5. For instance, in 2016, the FTC settled charges against Herbalife, which marketed dietary supplements through multi-level marketing. The FTC's case centered on the fact that the company was set up to emphasize and reward recruiting other participants, rather than actually selling the product, so that participants were unable to succeed to the extent promised. The settlement required the company to restructure its sales distribution plan and to pay

$200 million in redress to its distributors. *FTC v. Herbalife Internat'l of America, Inc.*, Case No. LA CV16-05217 BRO(GJXx), stipulated order (C.D. Cal. 2016), available at ftc.gov. The FTC has not as yet attempted to restrain pyramid schemes by regulation. The FTC's Business Opportunity Rule, 16 C.F.R. Part 437, provides that certain disclosures must be made prior to a buyer paying for a "business opportunity," but the Commission declined to write the rule in a way that would include multi-level marketing.

6. UNSOLICITED COMMERCIAL E-MAILS (SPAM)

Unsolicited commercial emails, also known as "spam," have become one of the scourges of the 21st century consumer. This type of sales practice is unique in that it costs more to receive these advertisements than it does to send them. Once a spammer has a list of email addresses, the cost of sending spam is minimal, but the user must deal with a clogged email inbox or pay for a filter. The FTC found that a large percentage of such emails are deceptive, and many contain explicit sexual content which would be offensive to some recipients. In response to these problems, Congress passed the CAN-SPAM Act of 2003, codified at 18 U.S.C. §§ 7701–13.

The CAN-SPAM Act regulates but does not ban spam. It contains some major requirements, such as: no use of false or misleading header information; no use of misleading or deceptive subject lines;

recipients must be given a working opt-out method; the email must be identified as an advertisement and give the sender's physical postal address. The FTC has issued a regulation that defines commercial email for purposes of application of the law and also gives recipients the right to unsubscribe without charge or other requirement. 16 C.F.R. § 316. The FTC declined to initiate a "do-not-spam" registry equivalent to its popular "do-not-call" list for telemarketing, however, saying it would not be feasible until there is a better system to authenticate the origin of email messages. These provisions are enforced by the FTC, as well as by states and internet access providers, but there is no private right of action for individual consumers. The federal law also preempts for the most part the myriad of state laws that had been passed in the period leading up to the passage of CAN-SPAM.

C. ONLINE SALES AND HIDDEN CONTRACT TERMS

One aspect of inducing consumer transactions that demands some attention is the inclusion in the deal of potentially unjust terms that are hidden in standard form contracts. This issue has been exacerbated by the use of the Internet to finalize all sorts of consumer contracts, from the purchase of software, to physical goods, to mobile phone or cable television or internet access services. While standard form contracts existed in paper form prior to the Internet, the use of online contracting means that consumers are induced to simply click "I agree" on a computer screen without paying attention to the often lengthy terms that are involved. Unlike with paper contracts, where the sheer length of the provisions and the requirement to actually sign one's name might give consumers some pause, consumers appear to be even less likely to read online terms than they were to read standard terms on paper. Also, the proliferation of seller-friendly provisions online is in part propelled by the low cost to the vendor of placing all manner of potentially unwanted or one-sided terms on their server without the consumer ever noticing until a dispute actually comes up at a later time. Examples of such terms that have been litigated include mandatory arbitration clauses, waivers of class action, forum selection clauses, bans on unfavorable consumer reviews, and disclaimers of warranties. Thus far the courts have been enforcing these types of contracts as long as the consumer has some opportunity to read and decline the terms, either by not buying the product or service from that vendor, or in some cases by returning the product once the consumer is provided with the terms "in the box."

Online and related consumer contracts can be divided into three types: shrinkwrap (or pay now, terms later, or terms in the box), clickwrap and browsewrap. Each of these types of contracts will be discussed below.

The term "shrinkwrap" comes from the shrinking transparent film used to wrap boxes of software or other products. A shrinkwrap contract refers to one in which the consumer is bound by the terms once he or she "breaks" or opens the shrinkwrap or starts using the product. The leading case on this point is *ProCD, Inc. v. Zeidenberg*, 86 F.3d 1447 (7th Cir. 1996), which held that the terms inside a box of software are binding on the consumer who uses that software after having had an opportunity to read the terms and reject them by not using and returning the product. A similar situation occurs when a consumer orders a product on the telephone or in a store, and the product is shipped out later with the contract terms inside the box. In the influential case of *Hill v. Gateway 2000, Inc.*, 105 F.3d 1147 (7th Cir. 1997), the consumers had ordered a personal computer which came with terms inside the box, including a mandatory arbitration clause. The terms stated they would be binding if the consumer did not return the computer within 30 days. The court in this case held that the arbitration clause was binding because the consumers had an opportunity to read and review the terms and failed to return the product. The fact that the consumers had paid for the product before seeing the relevant contract terms was not determinative provided the consumer had a reasonable right of return. A few post-*Gateway* decisions have refused to enforce terms in the box, or terms revealed after payment, on the basis that these terms should be considered "additional terms" that would require express consumer consent under the Uniform Commercial Code § 2–207. *See, e.g., Klocek v. Gateway, Inc.*, 104 F. Supp. 2d 1332 (D. Kan. 2000). Some consumer advocates have objected to this type of "rolling contract" because it places an undue burden on the consumer to return the merchandise in order to shop for better contract terms.

The term "clickwrap" refers to the practice that commonly occurs in electronic or web-based transactions in which the buyer is asked to assent to the terms and conditions of the contract by clicking an "I agree" button. This button can appear at the end of a scroll-down window that contains the standardized terms or it can be next to a link that if clicked will take the consumer to another part of the website that contains the relevant terms and conditions. In most cases, these types of agreements are enforced by the courts, if the terms are noticeable and accessible to the consumer prior to the "click" that signifies agreement. *See, e.g., Forrest v. Verizon Communications, Inc.*, 805 A.2d 1007 (D.C. App. 2002). This is the prevailing view despite the fact that most consumer research has shown that very few consumers ever read the terms and conditions before indicating assent by clicking "I agree," thus making the element of mutual assent to such contracts a "legal fiction." Courts do at times refuse to enforce clickwrap agreements if the notice of terms and conditions is not sufficiently prominent. In a case in which the consumer could "assent" by clicking a box labeled "sign-in" that was separate from the hyperlink for the "terms of use" and where that link was not readily and obviously available, the court held that the terms in question were not binding. *Berkson v. Gogo, LLC*, 97 F. Supp. 3d 359 (E.D.N.Y. 2015).

The third category of online contract is the "browsewrap" agreement, which is the least likely to be enforced in court. In a browsewrap situation, there is no click on an "I agree" button, but instead the website contains a link to standard terms that are agreed to by simply using the website or by downloading or purchasing something elsewhere on the site. In one of the leading browsewrap cases, *Specht v. Netscape Communications Corp.*, 306 F.3d 17 (2d Cir. 2002), the court held that where a reasonably prudent consumer would not have known of the existence of the contract terms, because the existence of license terms were on a submerged screen below the download button, there was no meaningful assent that would bind the consumer to the terms. Similarly, in *Nguyen v. Barnes & Noble, Inc.*, 763 F.3d 1171 (9th Cir. 2014), the court held that even a conspicuous hyperlink to the terms and conditions on every page of the website is not sufficient to bind the consumer if users are not notified that they will be bound by those terms simply by proceeding with a transaction. Courts appear to be increasingly focused on the "notice" of terms, and will scrupulously examine the website and other notification methods, such as email, to determine whether the notice of terms is adequate, and will strike down terms that don't meet the standard. *Starke v. SquareTrade, Inc.,* 913 F.3d 279 (2d Cir. 2019) (striking down terms included in email after purchase).

Note that the above discussion concerns whether the contract terms are going to be enforced based on the assent of the consumer. Even if the court finds such a binding assent, however, the clauses being challenged could still be struck down due to unconscionability or some other type of illegality. Many of these cases, especially those involving a mandatory arbitration clause in the "wrap" contract, have in the end rejected any substantive objection to such clauses.

The American Law Institute is considering a controversial Restatement of the Law of Consumer Contracts that would provide for adoption of terms where the consumer has reasonable notice and opportunity to review the terms prior to commitment, and manifests assent. The proposed Restatement also includes unconscionability and deception as potential defenses that consumers could use with regard to the adopted terms. Tentative Draft, Restatement of the Law: Consumer Contracts (April 2019) (not yet adopted by the ALI membership as of this writing).

CHAPTER FOUR
CONSUMER PRIVACY

A. SCOPE AND OVERVIEW

Privacy has always been an elusive concept. It includes the "right to be let alone" as well as the right to keep certain aspects of one's life shielded from public view. In the consumer protection context, the right of privacy is focused on the consumer's interest in shielding personal information, financial and otherwise, from being seen and shared by marketers and other commercial entities except with the consumer's consent. The privacy interest of the individual vis-à-vis the government in the criminal and national security contexts are beyond the scope of this volume.

Legal protection of consumer privacy in the United States is widely seen as being "sectoral" in nature. That is to say, there is no overarching law or legal doctrine of consumer privacy, but instead there are a series of laws regarding the protection of consumer privacy each focused on particular business sectors or on particular media or types of communication or solicitation. For instance, the protection of consumer financial information collected and distributed by private consumer reporting agencies is governed by the Fair Credit Reporting Act, a federal law that has been on the books since the early 1970s. That statute is discussed at length in Chapter Five, *infra*. Certain types of commercial solicitations, including door-to-door sales, telemarketing, and spam emails, raise concerns about the individual's right to be left alone in their own homes. The privacy protecting measures that apply to these types of marketing methods were covered in Chapter Three, *supra*. Consumers' personal health information, a topic that is beyond the scope of this volume, is protected by the Health Insurance Portability and Accountability Act or HIPAA, and the disclosure of consumer prescription information is limited under 42 U.S.C. § 17935.

The discussion in this chapter will focus on the remaining aspects of consumer privacy not covered elsewhere in this volume. First, there are some limited tort causes of action that have been used to protect consumer privacy. These common law approaches have not been very successful for consumers. Second, as consumers have flocked to the Internet for shopping, information gathering, and social interactions, the ability of commercial interests to gather and use or resell personal information has also increased dramatically. The Federal Trade Commission has taken the lead in protecting consumers' online privacy, which often involves behavioral profiling and tracking. The FTC has also acted to force companies to stop using intrusive computer software unbeknownst to the consumer. The FTC's actions thus far have been based on its own general authority to police unfair and deceptive trade practices, in the absence of any general federal legislation protecting internet privacy. Note that while the FTC's activities can set norms for consumer privacy, they do not in themselves create any private rights of action for consumers. Third, within the online world, special legal protections do exist to protect children, namely the Children's Online Privacy Protection Act (COPPA). Fourth, consumers entrust various commercial entities with access to their sensitive personal financial information. Such entities are responsible, under FTC law, for establishing reasonable data security measures so that consumers will be protected against data breaches that put them in danger of becoming victims of identity theft. States have also passed legislation to notify consumers of such data breaches. Finally, in 1999 Congress passed the "Gramm-Leach-Bliley Act" or GLBA which requires financial institutions to notify consumers of the private financial information they are collecting and sharing, and to provide consumers with the ability to opt out of such information sharing. Each of these aspects of consumer privacy will be considered below.

B. COMMON LAW PRIVACY TORTS

Consumers have sometimes sought to use common law remedies as a way of protecting themselves from unwanted intrusions by marketers or other commercial entities such as consumer reporting agencies or debt collection agencies. The four basic common law privacy torts are: (1) intrusion upon seclusion; (2) public disclosure of private facts; (3) publicity which portrays the individual in a false light; and (4) appropriation of one's name or likeness for another's advantage. RESTATEMENT 2D OF TORTS § 652. None of these torts have proven to be terribly useful to consumer plaintiffs, however.

Intrusion upon seclusion generally means there has been an unauthorized intrusion or prying into a private area or matter which is offensive to a reasonable person and causes anguish or suffering. Cases that have attempted to apply this tort to the sale of personal buying or other financial information for marketing purposes have failed because typically the consumer has voluntarily relinquished the information in question, and it is usually not considered unreasonably offensive to disclose one's buying habits to a select group of marketers. *See, e.g., Dwyer v. American Express Co.*, 652 N.E.2d 1351 (Ill. App. Ct. 1996). Another early case held that the damages stemming from the sale of magazine subscription lists, i.e., an increase in unwanted junk mail, was minimal and did not constitute an invasion of privacy. *Shibley v. Time, Inc.*, 341 N.E.2d 337 (Ohio Ct. App. 1975).

Public disclosure of private facts is a concept that does not readily apply in the consumer privacy context. Marketers and other commercial actors do not collect such information in order to publicly disclose it, but usually they wish to use the information themselves to make sales or they may sell the information to a defined group of subscribers.

Publicity that portrays an individual in a false light would not typically be applicable to the collection and sale of personal information of consumers because the collectors of the information have an incentive to try to be sure the information is not false. If they were in the habit of portraying individuals in a false light, their "product" would not be so valuable. Also, as noted above, the type of consumer information discussed here is usually not publicized, but instead is considered a valuable commodity that is not freely made available.

Finally, the tort of "appropriation" of one's name or likeness without consent is not typically recognized with respect to the use of an ordinary consumer's name or likeness because, outside of celebrities, the individual's name or likeness in isolation usually has little value. It is only valuable when the information has been collected and placed in categories that may be of interest to the buyers of such information.

As to credit reports, the consumer reporting agencies have enjoyed a "privilege" defense against common law torts, by which courts will require a showing of malice in order for them to be sued under common law. The Fair Credit Reporting Act also contains a section granting immunity from common law causes of action to the CRAs as well as users and furnishers of information in credit reports. 15 U.S.C. § 1681h(e). Credit reports are discussed *infra*, Chapter Five.

Consumers may also seek to assert an invasion of privacy with regard to certain activities of debt collectors, but they have not been very successful due to the extremely high burden of proof needed to prevail on these types of claims. Consumer protection in the debt collection area will be discussed in Chapter Eleven, *infra*.

C. ONLINE CONSUMER PRIVACY

The Internet has proven to be a mixed blessing for many consumers. The convenience of being able to access shopping, information and friends from a multitude of interconnected devices has been tempered by the concurrent wholesale surrender of personal information to the various advertisers and other players who have created and supported the modern applications of the Internet. Consumers' personal information has become a valuable commodity, and although most indeed are grateful for the variety of services provided by the Internet, some are also worried that their personal information may be misused by identity thieves and in other ways.

The Federal Trade Commission has emerged as the main U.S. government agency poised to protect consumer privacy in the online world. There is no comprehensive federal legislation on consumer privacy, and thus the FTC has had the task of promoting consumer privacy through a series of reports, public workshops, calls for legislation, and perhaps most importantly, though a series of enforcement actions under Section Five of the FTC Act, prohibiting unfair and deceptive trade practices. 15 U.S.C. § 45(a). As one comprehensive article has put it, "FTC privacy jurisprudence is the broadest and most influential regulating force on information-privacy in the United States—more so than nearly any privacy statute or common law tort."[1] On the

---

[1] Daniel J. Solove & Woodrow Hartzog, *The FTC and the New Common Law of Privacy*, 114 Colum. L. Rev. 583, 587 (2014).

other hand, the FTC has not undertaken to promulgate a trade regulation rule on consumer privacy based on its general authority over unfair and deceptive trade practices, due in part to the practical and political burdens on the agency of undertaking such rulemaking in the absence of a specific mandate from Congress, which thus far has not been forthcoming.

The FTC began its efforts to protect consumers' online privacy by using a somewhat conservative legal theory, *i.e.,* the law of deceptive trade practices. Almost all commercial websites either voluntarily or as required by state law, contain a so-called "privacy policy," that sets forth the company's policies with respect to the proposed gathering and uses of information submitted by consumers. The FTC reasoned that a company that promises not to share its customers' personal information but then does so without notice or consent, has committed a deceptive trade practice. *See, e.g., In re Geocities,* 127 F.T.C. 94 (1999). The FTC has continued this approach of policing privacy policies and holding companies responsible when they break their own privacy promises without notice or consent. Internet giant Google settled FTC charges in 2011 that it had falsely stated it would not use customer's personal information differently than the purposes for which it was collected, unless the consumer had consented to the variation. *In re Google, Inc.,* C-4336 (Oct. 12, 2011), available at www.ftc.gov. Similarly, Facebook, the social media behemoth, was charged with an FTC violation when it made public certain previously designated private information without notice or consent. *In re Facebook*, C-4365 (Nov. 29, 2011), available at www.ftc.gov. Both companies agreed to keep their promises in the future, and to get consumer consent prior to making privacy policy changes, and also to set up their own comprehensive privacy programs. Despite this, Facebook again faced FTC charges a few years later that it used "privacy settings" that were not as private as consumers were led to believe. Facebook entered an historic $5 billion settlement with the FTC in 2019, in which they agreed to more privacy controls and accountability for consumer privacy. *U.S. v. Facebook, Inc.*, Case No. 19-cv-2184, Stipulated Order (D.D.C. 2018), available at ftc.gov. Over the years, the FTC has chalked up many similar consent orders against other companies after filing charges based on failure to uphold the companies' own privacy statements.

Some courts have recognized that a privacy notice could be considered as a contract and that affected consumers could sue for its breach, although most of these cases also found that the consumers did not have sufficient damages stemming from breach of the privacy policy to pursue a case. *See, e.g., In re JetBlue Airways Corp. Privacy Litigation*, 379 F. Supp. 2d 299 (E.D.N.Y. 2005). This approach could be a double-edged sword for consumers, however, because if a privacy notice is a contract, and it contains provisions allowing the company to share personal information or track consumers online, then consumers who blindly clicked "I accept" to the privacy policy may have unwittingly bound themselves to these terms. The FTC has also challenged companies that disclose a policy involving customer information, but do it in such a way that it subjects the customer to unfair surprise. This approach looks to consumer expectations rather than binding them to whatever they had theoretically agreed to in the fine print, which is quite different from the "notice and choice" approach often favored by the FTC, as discussed below. For instance, Sears, the large retailer, distributed a software program to consumers that tracked their activities on the Internet including secure sessions involving financial or health information. Consumers agreed to this by clicking an "I accept" button online but the full scope of the tracking was buried in a lengthy End User License Agreement. The FTC alleged that this method of disclosure was tantamount to a deceptive omission or unfair surprise. The company settled with the FTC, agreeing that in the future such unexpected tracking of personal information would be more prominently disclosed. *In re Sears Holdings Management Corp.*, C-4264 (Aug. 31, 2009), available at www.ftc.gov. Critics of online privacy policies and licensing agreements such as the one used in the *Sears* case, have pointed out that most of them are lengthy and densely written, thus obscuring the actual plans the company has for using or tracking customers' information, rather than being a true "privacy" policy.

The FTC has also used its "unfairness" authority to police companies that trick consumers into installing so-called "malware" or spyware on their computers, resulting in damage to their devices or unwarranted invasions of privacy. *FTC v. Seismic Entertainment Productions, Inc.*, 2004 WL 2403124

(D.N.H. 2004). Another case involved a major music company, Sony BMG Entertainment, which embedded Digital Rights Management software in all its music CDs without adequately notifying customers. This software restricted the number of times audio files could be copied, prevented the music from being played on non-Sony players and gathered information from users on their listening preferences. The company agreed to disclose these features more prominently and to obtain the customer's express consent in the future. *In re Sony BMG Entertainment*, C-4195 (2007), available on www.ftc.gov. The FTC also challenged and settled with a company that sold software to rent-to-own stores that, unknown to the consumer and without prior consent, reported back the location of rented computers, tracked the consumer's activities on the computer and secretly photographed the consumer by activating the rental computer's webcam. *In re DesignerWare, LLC*, C-4390 (April 15, 2013), available at www.ftc.gov.

Unlike the FTC, private plaintiffs who have tried to sue companies that surreptitiously circumvented the privacy protections against unwanted tracking devices ("cookies") have not met with much success in court. For instance, in a 2016 case, personal computer owners alleged that an online advertising company had circumvented their default browser settings in order to set tracking cookies on their devices, in violation of federal and state law. The court in *Mount v. Pulsepoint, Inc.*, found that the plaintiffs had not alleged sufficient injury to support any of their claims, including a claim under a state

UDAP statute. 2016 WL 5080131 (S.D.N.Y. 2016). Other consumer plaintiffs have been able to at least stave off dismissal with similar claims. *See In re Google Inc. Cookie Placement Consumer Privacy Litigation*, 806 F.3d 125 (3d Cir. 2015) (stated claim under California invasion of privacy claim); *Bose v. Interclick, Inc.*, 2011 WL 4343517 (S.D.N.Y. 2011) (stated claim under New York UDAP statute).

The FTC has at various times pushed for either federal legislation, industry self-regulation and/or a general framework for dealing with consumer privacy issues on the national level. The FTC favors the implementation of "Fair Information Practice Principles," which include Notice, Choice, Access and Security. This "notice and consent" model has been criticized for leading to the proliferation of complex and incomprehensible privacy policies that are more aimed at protecting the information collectors than the consumer. The "notice and consent" approach also burdens the consumer to read notices and take action. In a 2012 report, the FTC encouraged the online information industry to provide better and more consumer-friendly statements disclosing their data collection practices and to allow consumers to control the collection and use of their own information. This report also recommended a "Do-Not-Track" option permitting consumers to opt out of online tracking. "Privacy by Design" is another approach that the FTC has promoted to encourage technology designers to consider privacy protections and ethical principles when creating new products or services, so that privacy protection is built in by default and not necessarily dependent on consumer notice and choice. None of the FTC's recommendations have been enacted into law, however, and the industry self-regulation in this field has been relatively ineffective.

Many multi-national companies deal online with consumers on a global level, and their privacy practices may be influenced by European Union law, which generally is much more protective of consumer privacy than American law. In 2000, the U.S. Department of Commerce negotiated the "US-EU Safe Harbor Privacy Principles," a self-certification program enforced by the FTC, which basically seeks to assist U.S. companies who wish to sell to European consumers. In the end, it is possible that American consumers dealing with such companies may indirectly benefit from the implementation of European privacy principles.[2]

In 2018, the state of California stepped into the void created by the lack of comprehensive federal consumer privacy legislation, and passed the sweeping California Consumer Privacy Act. Cal. Civ. Code §§ 1798.100–.199. Effective in 2020, this law requires businesses to provide requesting consumers with the information being collected about them, and to disclose whether such information is being sold or disclosed to third parties. It also requires businesses to allow consumers to opt out of such information collection, and to delete information if the consumer so requests. Only certain large businesses are

---

[2] *See* CHRIS JAY HOOFNAGLE, FEDERAL TRADE COMMISSION: PRIVACY LAW AND POLICY, 319–326 (Cambridge University Press 2016).

covered, if they do business in California. The state Attorney General is tasked with issuing regulations and with enforcement of the law. Given the need to comply with California law for businesses that have customers in that state, this law could have far-reaching effects. Also, other states are considering enacting or have enacted similar statutes. *See, e.g.,* Nev. Rev. Statutes Chapter 603A.

D. CHILDREN'S ONLINE PRIVACY

In response to concerns about the possible exploitation of unsupervised children providing personal information on the Internet, the FTC filed some early cases against companies targeting websites to children and teens. Congress also acted in 1998, passing the Children's Online Privacy Protection Act (COPPA), which set forth certain safeguards for children interacting with companies online. COPPA also set up the FTC as the main enforcer of the law. 15 U.S.C. §§ 6501–6506. The FTC implemented rules under the Act, which became effective in 2000 and were updated effective 2013. 16 C.F.R. Part 312.

COPPA regulates the collection of personal information from children under the age of thirteen by websites or other online service providers, broadly defined to include mobile apps and website plug-ins. To trigger COPPA duties, the website or online service must be directed to children or the provider must have actual knowledge that they are collecting personal information from children.

Websites that are covered by COPPA are obliged to take the following actions:

- Post a privacy notice that identifies what information they collect from children and how it will be used;

- Obtain express parental consent to the planned collection and use of children's personal information;

- Provide a reasonable method for parents to access and review the personal information collected about their child and provide an opportunity to refuse to permit its further use;

- Not condition a child's participation in any activity or game upon the child disclosing more personal information than is reasonably necessary;

- Establish and maintain reasonable procedures to protect the confidentiality, security and integrity of children's personal information; and

- Hold data only as long as reasonably necessary and delete it when no longer needed.

As is the case with adult online privacy, the FTC has brought numerous enforcement actions against alleged violators of the children's privacy rules, all of which have been settled. The websites involved in FTC enforcement cases have included social networking sites aimed at children, such as Xanga.com, Skid-e-kids, Emily apps and Pony Stars.

SEC. D CHILDREN'S ONLINE PRIVACY

Artist Arena, a music celebrity fan website, also settled charges by the FTC under COPPA. In 2019, the FTC settled charges against the popular mobile app known as TikTok, which agreed to pay a record $5.7 million penalty for violating the FTC's COPPA rules. *United States v. Musical.ly Corp.,* Case No. 2:19-cv-199, Stipulated Order (C.D. Cal. 2019), available at ftc.gov.

The FTC's COPPA regulation also provides for the possibility of industry self-regulatory programs approved by the FTC under a "safe harbor" provision. 16 C.F.R. § 312.11.

The FTC's 2013 revision of the COPPA rules left the basic structure of notice and consent by parents prior to the use of their children's personal information the same, but modernized the implementation of the regulation. The definition of "children's personal information" now includes the tracking of a child's online activities via "cookies," as well as geo-location, photos, videos and audio recordings pertaining to children. The parental approval process was streamlined and updated to include alternative means of providing consent in addition to emails, including use of mail, fax or scan, as well as the use of a credit card for payment. Specific data security protections and deletion methods for children's personal information collected online are also now required.

COPPA has been criticized for not protecting teenagers, who may be just as vulnerable as children under thirteen. It has also been pointed out that the Act places a burden on parents but doesn't do much to actually protect children's privacy or safety since the parental consent can become automatic or can be easily evaded by tech-savvy children.

The FTC has brought related children's online information cases for violations of the FTC Act that are not covered by COPPA. For instance, the FTC charged Apple, Inc. with an FTC Act violation for not informing adult account holders that upon entering their password on an Apple-sponsored mobile app aimed at children, a 15-minute window would open during which a child could make unlimited charges to the account without requiring any further action by the account holder. *In re Apple, Inc.*, C-4444 (March 25, 2014), available at www.ftc.gov. Similar cases were settled with Amazon.com and Google.

E. DATA SECURITY

While there is no specific federal statute or regulation governing the data security procedures for companies that handle consumers' personal information, a series of FTC enforcement actions dating back to the early 2000s have delineated what amounts to a set of specific requirements in this area. The FTC has charged that exposing customers to an unreasonable risk of having their information stolen can amount to an unfair trade practice. Also, if a company has assured its customers that it is employing reasonable security procedures and it does not in fact do that, then the company may have committed a deceptive trade practice.

As defined by FTC policy, an unfair trade practice is one that results in a substantial consumer injury, that consumers cannot reasonably avoid, and the harms of which outweigh the benefits. 15 U.S.C. § 45(n). Failing to provide adequate security for consumer information harms consumers because it can expose them to identity theft, which in turn can result in a ruined credit record and the burden of cleansing that record. Also, consumers who are told of such a breach then experience the burden of taking appropriate steps, such as changing account numbers or monitoring their credit reports, to protect themselves. This type of injury is completely out of the consumer's control so the individual cannot reasonably avoid the injury. Such sloppy security practices also do not benefit competition (although they may save money for the company). Such considerations make companies who use unreasonable security procedures prime candidates for FTC unfair trade practices charges.

FTC cases involving unreasonable data security measures have included charges against DSW, a discount shoe retailer, as well as BJ's Wholesale Club. *In re DSW, Inc.,* C-4157 (FTC 2006); *In re BJ's Wholesale Club, Inc.,* C-4148 (FTC 2005), available at www.ftc.gov. The FTC also took the social media site Twitter to task for having lax security that allowed hackers to gain administrative control of the system, sending phony "tweets" from then-President-elect Barack Obama, among others. *In re Twitter, Inc.,* C-4316 (FTC 2011), available at www.ftc.gov. Ironically, the "LifeLock" company, which touts its identity theft prevention service, allegedly placed consumers' personal information on an insecure, unencrypted system, and allowed the information to be shared indiscriminately. *FTC v. LifeLock, Inc.*, Stipulated Final Judgment (D. Ariz. 2010), available at www.ftc.gov. Snapchat was also sued by the FTC for promising consumers that the photos and messages they sent to their friends would be available for only a short time and would then disappear. Unfortunately, the mobile app was vulnerable to hackers and other misuse. *In re Snapchat, Inc.*, C-4501 (FTC 2014). Many other companies have also been pursued by the FTC, resulting in many detailed consent orders concerning proper data security measures.

The series of FTC enforcement cases in the data security area have resulted in a litany of specific measures needed to reasonably protect consumer data. Guidance can be found in the FTC's publication *Start with Security: A Guide for Business*, which contains "lessons learned from FTC cases," and is available on their website. Companies handling personal information of consumers should be aware of these duties and seek to implement them to avoid being challenged by the FTC. The FTC orders have required the establishment of sound internal controls on and procedures to protect sensitive personal information. Encryption, as well as controls on third parties dealing with consumer information, may be required. Companies should also engage in risk assessment and use available/reasonable technical solutions to prevent security breaches. Training employees on proper handling of data security issues, as well as testing their systems to check for potential or actual security breaches may be necessary. Also, a company that makes promises regarding the

SEC. E DATA SECURITY 111

reasonableness of their data security measures should hold to those promises or risk being charged by the FTC with a deceptive trade practice. For example, Venmo, a peer-to-peer payment system owned by PayPal, allegedly misled consumers about data security measures; it settled the charges with the FTC in 2017. *In re PayPal, Inc.*, FTC Docket No. C-4651, Consent Order (2017), available at ftc.gov.

One company, Wyndham Worldwide Corporation, challenged the FTC's authority to sue them for unfair and deceptive trade practices, despite the fact that Wyndham experienced at least three security breaches affecting consumers' personal information stored on Wyndham-branded hotel computer systems. Wyndham's motion to dismiss was denied, and the Third Circuit Court of Appeals upheld the FTC's authority to find that unreasonable cybersecurity practices could constitute an unfair trade practice. *FTC v. Wyndham Worldwide Corp.*, 799 F.3d 236 (3d Cir. 2015).

The Consumer Financial Protection Bureau (CFPB) has concurrent jurisdiction with the FTC with regard to financial services. Online payment systems provided by financial service providers may put consumers' personal information at risk in the absence of adequate data security practices. In 2016, the CFPB filed its first data security action, alleging that an online payment system provider had committed a deceptive practice by falsely claiming that its data security practices exceeded industry standards, when in fact they did not. The case was settled and the company agreed to fix its security practices and pay a significant civil penalty. *In re Dwolla, Inc.*, Consent Order, File 201603 (March 2, 2016).

In 2017, Equifax, one of the three large consumer reporting agencies (credit bureaus) in the U.S. experienced a massive data breach that exposed sensitive personal financial information of about 147 million consumers. The FTC, the CFPB and the state attorneys general joined forces to sue Equifax for its alleged negligence and other violations involved in allowing this breach to occur. A global settlement resulted, in which Equifax agreed to pay from $575–700 million to consumers who suffered losses, to provide free credit monitoring services to affected consumers and to provide up to six free credit reports each year for seven years. The company also agreed to pay $175 million to 48 states, as well as $100 million to the CFPB in civil penalties. A final stipulated judgment filed in 2019 also requires the company to establish and implement a comprehensive information security program. https://www.ftc.gov/enforcement/cases-proceedings/172-3203/equifax-inc.

Most states now have so-called "security breach notification" laws. Thus, when a company discovers that it has suffered a security breach, under the relevant state law it must notify all consumers who have been affected, and often the company must also notify the news media and regulators. Consumers who receive such notices sometimes seek to sue the company that suffered a data breach for various federal and state causes of actions, such as FCRA violations, or common law breach of contract, ι negligence. In the state of California, as of 2020, consumers have a private right of action for damages stemming from data breaches, under that state's comprehensive California Consumer Privacy Act. Cal. Civ. Code § 1798.150. New York's Department of Financial Services promulgated a comprehensive cybersecurity regulation in 2017. N.Y. Comp. Codes R. & Regs. Tit. 23, § 500.

The biggest obstacle to these consumer suits, which often take the form of class actions challenging data breaches, has been standing to sue and "injury in fact," which is an Article III constitutional requirement for suit in federal court. The cases have produced mixed results thus far. Some consumers whose information was hacked but whose credit or debit cards were cancelled by the issuer and who were not held responsible for the attempted charges, were found not to have suffered sufficient injury to have standing to sue. *See, e.g., Whalen v. Michaels Stores, Inc.,* 689 F. Appx 89 (2nd Cir. 2018); *Beck v. McDonald,* 848 F.3d 262 (4th Cir. 2017); *Engl v. National Grocers by Vitamin Cottage, Inc.,* 2016 WL 8578252 (D. Colo. 2016). In other cases, courts have held that consumers who experienced an increased risk of identity theft and spent time and effort monitoring their credit did suffer sufficient injury to have standing to sue, even if they were not held responsible for *any fraudulent charges. See, e.g., Attias v. Carefirst, Inc.,* 865 F.3d 620 (D.C. Cir. 2017); *Lewert v. P.F. Chang's China Bistro, Inc.,* 819 F.3d 963 (7th Cir. 2016); *Galaria v. Nationwide Mutual Insurance Co.,* 663 F. Appx 384 (6th Cir. 2016). In

...ners have been able to proceed on ...ntract or state consumer protection ...ons in situations where the ... policy made specific promises to ...or consumers' personal information that were broken, resulting in the hacking of consumer information. *See, e.g., In re Premera Blue Cross Customers Data Security Breach Litigation*, 2017 WL 539578 (D. Or. 2017); *Fero v. Excellus Health Plan, Inc.*, 236 F. Supp. 3d 735 (W.D. N.Y. 2017).

F. FINANCIAL PRIVACY & THE GRAMM-LEACH-BLILEY ACT

Many of the aspects of consumer privacy discussed in the previous sections encompassed the consumer's interest in financial privacy, but there is also a specific statute and regulation creating a duty of certain financial institutions to protect the privacy of the personal information they collect regarding their customers. This statute is the Gramm-Leach-Bliley Act (GLBA) passed by Congress in 1999. 15 U.S.C. §§ 6801 to 6809. Regulations were initially issued by the FTC, but since 2011, they have been under the jurisdiction of the CFPB. 12 C.F.R. Part 1016 (Regulation P). The basic thrust of this privacy statute is to require covered financial institutions to provide notice of their information sharing practices to consumers, and to allow consumers to opt out of such sharing under certain circumstances. The GLBA is enforced by the CFPB, the FTC and other relevant regulatory agencies. There is no private right of action.

The scope of the financial institutions covered by the law has been broadly defined and applied in the courts to include not only banks and other depositary institutions, but also credit card issuers, retail stores, credit reporting agencies and credit counseling services. The law does not apply to attorneys engaged in the practice of law, however. *See American Bar Assoc. v. FTC*, 430 F.3d 457 (D.C. Cir. 2005) (although it could apply to attorneys who advise financial institutions without litigating).

The statute requires all covered financial institutions to provide an initial notice to consumers describing their information collection and sharing practices, including the circumstances under which they may disclose nonpublic personal information about a consumer to nonaffiliated third parties. 15 U.S.C. § 6803(a); 12 C.F.R. § 1016.4. If the financial institution plans to share nonpublic personal information outside of its own affiliates, it must also provide disclosure of that fact and notify the consumer of opt-out procedures to prevent such sharing. 15 U.S.C. § 6803(b); 12 C.F.R. §§ 1016.7 & .10.

Once the initial disclosure has been provided, if the consumer continues to be in a customer relationship with the financial institution, then that institution must also provide an annual disclosure. These annual disclosures were criticized for creating an undue paperwork burden on the financial institutions. This criticism resulted in a significant streamlining of the requirements for annual disclosures as of 2016. Under a statutory amendment, if the financial institution does not disclose nonpublic personal information of consumers to non-affiliate third parties, other than as permitted by certain exemptions, *i.e.,* if it is not required to provide an opt out notice, and the institution has not changed its privacy policies and practices since its most recent disclosure, then the financial institution is completely excused from sending an annual report. 15 U.S.C. § 6803(f); 12 C.F.R. § 1016.5(e).

An FTC regulation issued pursuant to the GLBA requires all financial institutions under its jurisdiction to develop their own written information security plans. These plans must include: designating an employee or employees to coordinate the security program; identifying reasonably foreseeable risks to customer information; designing and implementing the safeguards; overseeing service providers; and evaluating and adjusting the information security program as changes occur over time. 16 C.F.R. Part 314. As a designated enforcer of the GLBA, the FTC has enforced this regulation as part of its efforts to promote consumer data security, as discussed in the prior section. For instance, in 2017, the FTC settled charges with TaxSlayer, LLC, an online tax preparation service, for failing to provide adequate safeguards for consumers' private financial data, and for failing to have a strong privacy policy, in violation of the GLBA regulation. *In re TaxSlayer,* LLC, FTC Docket No. C-4526, Consent Order (2017), available at ftc.gov.

The GLBA also prohibits "pretexting," which means the use of false pretenses, including fraudulent statements and impersonations, to obtain consumers' personal information, such as bank balances. 15 U.S.C. §§ 6821 & 6822. The FTC has relied on this authority to pursue several pretexting cases. For instance, the FTC challenged a Canadian company that telephoned elderly consumers posing as Social Security representatives, in order to obtain the consumers' bank account and routing information, which was then used to charge them for phony Medicare insurance or drug discount cards. *FTC v. Xtel Marketing, Inc.*, Stipulated Permanent Injunction, 2005 WL 2248709 (N.D. Ill. 2005), available at www.ftc.gov. The FTC has also used its authority under the GLBA to address the practice of "phishing," which involves the use of deceptive emails and web sites that give consumers the impression they are dealing with legitimate companies. Consumers are then fooled into providing personal information to the fraudsters.

CHAPTER FIVE
CREDIT REPORTS, IDENTITY THEFT, AND EQUAL ACCESS TO CREDIT

A. CREDIT REPORTS

1. USE

Before a creditor will extend credit to a consumer, the creditor will often obtain the consumer's credit report. Some creditors may undertake to conduct their own credit investigation of the consumer. Most creditors, however, simply rely on credit reports generated by local or national credit reporting agencies, also known as credit bureaus or consumer reporting agencies (CRAs).

Credit bureaus generate the reports used by creditors who want to know whether a consumer is credit worthy. The credit bureau reports are mostly confined to financial information about a consumer, although some CRAs also generate information for insurance or employment purposes, which may have more personal information. For example, these reports will provide creditors with the amounts and locations of an individual's bank accounts, credit card accounts and other debts, along with information concerning the individual's marital status, income, occupation and any pending or prior lawsuits. Information such as maximum credit limits and the current balance on each account are included in the reports, along with a payment history to reflect the timeliness of payments made.

Nationally, there are three major consumer reporting agencies: Equifax, Experian and TransUnion. These entities compile credit information for subscribers (e.g., creditors). The subscribers not only use the CRAs to obtain credit reports about consumers, but they also furnish the CRAs with information about their own dealings with consumers which may be used by other merchants. In addition to credit reports, the CRAs and other entities such as FICO also provide credit scores on individual consumers. A credit score is a numerical summary based on various algorithms of a consumer's creditworthiness as contained in the credit report.

An individual's credit report and credit score may be obtained anytime by the individual himself for a fee. Generally, if a consumer has been turned down for credit by a merchant, he may obtain a copy of his credit report via one of the three major credit bureaus without paying a fee. Consumers are also entitled to receive one free credit report (but not a free credit score) each year from each of the nationwide CRAs, by accessing the website annualcreditreport.com. Credit scores are also provided free to consumers voluntarily by some creditors, such as credit card issuers. Consumers are entitled to a free credit score under limited circumstances, such as when a creditor turns them down for credit or offers credit on less favorable terms due to the credit score or when they apply for a loan from a mortgage lender. There are a variety of entities that formulate credit scores, however, and the score received by a consumer for "educational" purposes may differ from the one used by the actual creditor.

Credit reports and credit scores can have significant effects on the consumer's access to credit. In many instances, a bad credit report or credit score may cause a consumer to be unable to purchase a car or a house on credit or to obtain a credit card, or may result in the consumer only being able to obtain credit on less favorable terms. Credit reports may contain negligent errors on the part of the credit bureaus, such as "mixed files" of persons with similar names, or may also reflect the use of the consumer's identity by an unauthorized person. Thus, many consumers have a keen interest in assuring that the information in their credit report is both secure (i.e., not subject to theft or other unauthorized use) and accurate. In addition to the availability of free annual credit reports, all of the CRAs offer to sell consumers credit reports on a more frequent basis to help consumers keep track of what is in their credit report.

2. COMMON LAW PROTECTION

The common law is not a very useful source of legal protection for consumers injured by inaccurate credit reports. Prior to federal legislation in 1970, lenders did not even have to disclose the fact that a credit report had been obtained or which agency provided the report, making it difficult for consumers to even know that there were harmful mistakes in such reports. Even if a consumer had knowledge of an inaccurate report, her common law remedies were still hindered by other legal obstacles.

Defamation claims based on false information in a credit report were seldom successful because most jurisdictions regarded credit bureaus as having a "qualified or conditional privilege to fairly publish to its own legitimately interested business customers the information it received in the course of its investigations without being liable for defamatory matter therein, provided it did not exceed or abuse the privilege . . . " *Wetherby v. Retail Credit Co.,* 235 Md. 237, 201 A.2d 344, 345 (1964). In jurisdictions which recognize a qualified privilege, a plaintiff can succeed on a defamation claim only if he shows that the credit bureau acted with malice or in bad faith.

Like defamation, an invasion of privacy claim is also difficult to maintain. First, the plaintiff must be able to show that the bureau made a public disclosure of private facts. Second, the plaintiff must show that the private facts disclosed would be highly offensive and objectionable to a reasonable person of ordinary sensibilities. One problem is that credit reports are not exactly public information but are circulated only to subscribers and to others who have a legitimate business purpose, thus undermining the argument of public disclosure of private facts. Another problem is that much of the information disclosed by a credit bureau, such as financial information and marital status, would not be considered highly offensive to a reasonable person.

The Fair Credit Reporting Act, discussed below, helped consumers in many ways, but it also granted immunity from these common law actions to credit bureaus, users or furnishers of information in a consumer report unless false information was furnished with malice or intent to injure the consumer. 15 U.S.C. § 1681h(e). This provision makes it even more difficult for consumers to succeed in challenging information in their credit report under common law.

3. FAIR CREDIT REPORTING ACT

In 1970, Congress passed the Fair Credit Reporting Act (FCRA), Title III of the Consumer Credit Protection Act. This Act was significantly revised in 1996 and again in 2003 to provide further protection for consumers.[1] The FCRA is aimed at protecting both the accuracy and the privacy of consumer credit reports, as well as helping consumers prevent and correct the special problems associated with identity theft.

a. Scope

The Fair Credit Reporting Act, codified at 15 U.S.C. §§ 1681, et seq., applies to "consumer reports" generated by "consumer reporting agencies."

---

[1] For a thorough background on the history, scope and remedies available under the FCRA, *see* DEE PRIDGEN, RICHARD M. ALDERMAN & JOLINA CUARESMA CONSUMER CREDIT AND THE LAW, Chapters 2 & 2A (2019–2020 ed.); NATIONAL CONSUMER LAW CENTER, FAIR CREDIT REPORTING (9th ed. 2018).

A "consumer report" is defined as:

(1) any written, oral or other communication of any information by a consumer reporting agency

(2) bearing on a consumer's credit worthiness, credit standing, credit capacity, character, general reputation, personal characteristics or mode of living

(3) which is used or expected to be used or collected in whole or in part for the purpose of serving as a factor in establishing the consumer's eligibility for

(a) credit or insurance to be used primarily for personal, family or household purposes;

(b) employment purposes; or

(c) any other purpose authorized under section 604 [15 U.S.C. § 1681b]."

15 U.S.C. § 1681a(d) (paragraphing and brackets added for clarity and ease of reading).

The Act is focused on consumer-related credit reports. Credit reports prepared to determine the creditworthiness of business entities are clearly not covered. What the definition doesn't tell us is whether reports on individuals compiled for use in commercial transactions are covered by the act. For example, are credit reports regarding individuals seeking to purchase commercial property included under the Act? 15 U.S.C. § 1681a(c) defines a "consumer" as an "individual," thereby covering such a transaction. However, the Act, as quoted above, defines "consumer report" as a communication of information for credit to be used "primarily for personal, family or household purposes," which indicates it would not be covered. The case law is divided on this question.

Consumers who do not have any credit cards or conventional loans, but who may pay rent or utilities, or patronize fringe lenders who do not report information to credit bureaus, are not likely to have a "consumer report." This group, common among low-income consumers, has become known as the "credit invisibles." CFPB, Data Point: Credit Invisibles (2015). Not having a conventional "credit report" on file is a handicap for obtaining credit, but the law does not require that consumer reporting agencies prepare reports on anyone.

So-called "prescreened lists," are considered consumer reports under the Act but their issuance by consumer reporting agencies is subject to certain conditions. Prescreened lists are typically generated by consumer reporting agencies and consist of a list of potential credit customers who satisfy the criteria specified by the requesting creditor. These lists are then used by marketers to solicit customers for credit cards or other credit offerings. While these lists are very useful for creditors and for some consumers, and are a lucrative business for the credit bureaus, consumers may have concerns about the privacy of their financial information or may not want to be flooded with solicitations. Thus, the FCRA specifies that prescreened lists can only be supplied if there is a "firm offer of credit or insurance." 15 U.S.C. § 1681b(c)(1)(B)(i). Even an offer of credit subject to a low credit limit and excessive fees can be considered a "firm offer" for FCRA purposes as long as the offer has some value to the consumer and is actually offered by the creditor to all qualified consumers. *Perry v. First Nat'l Bank*, 459 F.3d 816 (7th Cir. 2006).[2] Consumers receiving a solicitation based on a prescreened list must also be offered the chance to opt out of participating in similar marketing efforts in the future. 15 U.S.C. § 1681b(c)(1)(B)(iii) & 1681b(e); 12 C.F.R. § 1022.54. Consumers under the age of 21 cannot be on a prescreened list without their prior consent, an "opt-in" approach. 15 U.S.C. § 1681b(c)(1)(B)(iv).

According to the Act, a "consumer reporting agency" includes "any person which, for monetary fees, dues, or on a cooperative nonprofit basis, regularly engages in whole or in part in the practice of assembling or evaluating consumer credit information or other information on consumers for the purpose of furnishing consumer reports to third parties, and which uses any means or facility of interstate commerce for the purpose of preparing or furnishing consumer reports." 15 U.S.C. § 1681a(f).

Based on this definition as well as the definition of consumer reports, the major credit bureaus, such as Equifax, clearly are consumer reporting agencies under the Act because they disseminate consumer

---

[2] As of 2010, however, under amendments to TILA, credit cards cannot have fees totaling more than 25% of the credit limit in the first year. 15 U.S.C. § 1637(n), 12 C.F.R. § 1026.52.

reports regularly to third parties. Businesses which assemble or evaluate information for their own purposes are not consumer reporting agencies as long as the information is not provided to third parties. Nor are businesses that pass on information regarding consumers solely as to transactions between the consumer and that business. Businesses that provide background checks on individuals for various purposes, but that do not collect the information with the intent of furnishing "consumer reports" as defined, may not be considered within the scope of the FCRA. *See Kidd v. Thomson Reuters Corp.*, 925 F.3d 99 (2d Cir. 2019). Check verification services or providers of "bad check" lists may be considered consumer reporting agencies. "Resellers," who assemble and merge information from consumer reporting agencies but do not themselves maintain a database producing new consumer reports, are not considered consumer reporting agencies, but have some limited duties under the Act, such as a duty to reinvestigate. 15 U.S.C. § 1681a(u).

Within the scope of the FCRA, as defined, there are four main players under the Act: (1) the consumer reporting agency; (2) the user of the credit report (3) the furnisher of information to the agency; and (4) the consumer. Each of the players have separate rights and duties under the Act, as will be discussed in the next few sections.

b. Requirements for Consumer Reporting Agencies

The requirements for consumer reporting agencies can be divided into two parts: (1) provisions relating to the distribution of consumer reports and (2) provisions relating to the accuracy of consumer reports.

One way that Congress chose to achieve the Act's purpose of protecting privacy was by regulating how the consumer reports are to be distributed and used. 15 U.S.C. § 1681b limits the distribution of consumer reports by consumer reporting agencies to third parties who have certain "permissible purposes," which include:

(1) for use in credit transactions with the consumer,

(2) employment,

(3) insurance,

(4) eligibility for government license or benefit,

(5) investment transactions, and

(6) any other legitimate business transaction.

A consumer, of course, can request to have her report disclosed to her or as specified by her written instructions. Government agencies dealing with child support obligations may request a consumer's report. Consumer reports may also be released in response to a court order.

The Act requires that consumer reporting agencies obtain the identity of the party requesting a consumer report and insure that such recipient uses the report only for the permissible purposes listed in the Act. The consumer reporting agency is required to "maintain reasonable procedures" designed to avoid violations of the permissible purposes restriction. 15 U.S.C. § 1681e(a).

As to the accuracy of the information in the consumer report, the FCRA requires that "whenever a consumer reporting agency prepares a consumer report it shall follow reasonable procedures to assure maximum possible accuracy of the information concerning the individual about whom the report relates." 15 U.S.C. § 1681e(b). This means that the consumer reporting agency must do more than just pass on information from furnishers to its subscribers without any type of screening procedure to ferret out inaccurate information. Now that identity theft has become more prevalent, CRAs must have some reasonable procedures to verify that the information being given by a furnisher is on the same individual they are investigating. One way to avoid such mix-ups is for CRAs to require a minimum number of "points of correspondence" beyond a matching social security number before accepting the information as belonging to the consumer in question. *See, e.g., Andrews v. TRW, Inc.,* 225 F.3d 1063 (9th Cir. 2000), *rev'd and remanded on other grounds,* 534 U.S. 19 (2001). On the other hand, since the Act requires only "reasonable" procedures, some courts have determined that a consumer reporting agency would not have to examine millions of account entries to determine if any of them contain anomalous information, such as a mention of bankruptcy for one account, when no other accounts were so labeled for that consumer. *Sarver v. Experian Information Solutions*, 390 F.3d 969 (7th Cir. 2004).

The FCRA does not prohibit the reporting of what might be deemed irrelevant information, as long as it meets the statutory standards for accuracy. Sometimes even accurate information can be misleading, however. Although some early cases had held that such technically accurate information could not form the basis for CRA liability, later cases say that "reports containing factually correct information that nonetheless mislead their readers are neither maximally accurate nor fair to the consumer who is the subject of the reports." *Koropoulos v. Credit Bureau, Inc.*, 734 F.2d 37, 40 (D.C. Cir. 1984). Examples include noting a tax lien, without also noting that the lien had been satisfied, or a notation of "litigation pending" when the suit had been brought by the debtor, not the creditor. To determine how complete the reporting must be to avoid CRA liability for failing to maintain reasonable procedures for accuracy, most courts balance the burden on the CRA of obtaining more complete information, against the harm to the consumer from the potentially misleading entry. *See Richardson v. Fleet Bank*, 190 F. Supp. 2d 81 (D. Mass. 2001).

Another statutory provision promoting accuracy is the requirement that the CRAs delete from consumer reports certain defined types of obsolete information. Adverse information such as arrests, suits and judgments, defaults and accounts placed for collection may not be reported more than seven years after the occurrence. Bankruptcies may not be reported after ten years. 15 U.S.C. § 1681(c). Veterans' medical debts receive special treatment under the Act, which requires CRAs to suppress reporting about such debts until one year has passed from the rendering of medical services, and also requires deletion of such debt information if the veteran provides documentation showing that the Department of Veterans' Affairs is in the process of making a payment on that debt. 15 U.S.C. § 1681c(a)(7) & (8), and § 1681i(g).

Consumer reporting agencies have extensive duties with regard to investigating the accuracy of their consumer reports in the case of a dispute by a consumer. 15 U.S.C. § 1681i. They also have duties to disclose the information in the report to consumers under certain circumstances. 15 U.S.C. § 1681g. These duties will be discussed in more detail in the section on the rights of consumers *infra*.

The other provisions regulating consumer reporting agencies deal with investigative reports. As defined by 15 U.S.C. § 1681a(e) of the Act, an "investigative consumer report" is one which contains information on a consumer's character, general reputation, personal characteristics or mode of living obtained from personal interviews with friends, neighbors or other associates of the consumer. These types of reports are most commonly used in connection with insurance or employment.

Before a consumer reporting agency may conduct an investigative consumer report, certain disclosures must be made to the consumer. The party requesting such a report must have informed the consumer in writing three days after the report was requested that an investigative report may be made on the consumer. The CRA also cannot report adverse information based on personal interviews unless it has followed reasonable procedures to obtain confirmation of the information from an independent source with direct knowledge. 15 U.S.C. § 1681d. Adverse information developed in an investigative consumer report cannot be used again in a subsequent consumer report unless it is less than three months old or is verified again. 15 U.S.C. § 1681(*l*). The purpose here is to purge the reports of dated and inaccurate information that relates to matters beyond the creditworthiness of the consumer.

c. Requirements for Users of Consumer Reports

A user of a consumer report has two primary duties. First, the user must make certain required disclosures to the consumer. Second, the user must make sure that the report is used for a permissible purpose. Note that a "user" of a consumer report, *e.g.*, a creditor using a consumer report to determine whether and on what terms to offer credit to a particular consumer, may also later be a "furnisher" of information to the CRA on the same consumer. Thus, creditors who use consumer reports and subscribe to a consumer reporting agency, may have different duties depending on which role in the process they happen to be playing. The duties of "furnishers" are discussed *infra*.

The Act requires that users of consumer reports who have taken an adverse action against a consumer based on a consumer report must provide notice to the consumer. "Adverse action" includes not only rejection of the credit application but also the offering of less favorable credit terms based on risk-based pricing. For instance, a lender may be willing to make the loan in the requested amount, but at a higher interest rate than charged to other consumers because the lender deems the applicant to pose a greater risk of defaulting. Special "risk-based pricing" notices must be provided by creditors who offer credit on materially less favorable terms than the terms available to a substantial proportion of consumers. 12 C.F.R. §§ 1022.70 to .75.

The notice to the consumer must state that the action was taken due to information in a credit report and give the relevant contact information for the consumer reporting agency which furnished the report. As of 2011, the creditor in this situation must also give the numerical credit score used in taking the adverse action, as well as related information such as the range of possible credit scores, key factors that adversely affected the consumer's credit score, the date the score was created, and the name of the entity that provided the credit score. The user must also give the affected consumer a notice of the right to a obtain a free copy of the consumer report from the consumer reporting agency, and the right of the consumer to dispute the accuracy or completeness of the information in the report with the consumer reporting agency. 15 U.S.C. § 1681m(a).

Employers and insurance companies that use credit reports as a basis for taking an adverse action also have similar duties for notifying the subject of the report (consumer or job applicant). In a 2007 case, the U.S. Supreme Court held that an offering of insurance at a higher rate on the basis of a consumer credit report could be an adverse action triggering these duties. *Safeco Ins. Co. of America v. Burr*, 551 U.S. 47 (2007).

The user must also provide the consumer with the reason the adverse action was taken, but that requirement is found in a separate provision of the Equal Credit Opportunity Act, discussed *infra*. The credit report user can combine these notifications in one letter to the consumer.

The second major obligation of users is to use the reports only for permissible purposes. As stated above, it is the consumer reporting agency's duty to identify the user and the user's purpose. However, what if those steps have been taken but the user does not use the report for permissible purposes?

Persons who obtain a consumer report for non-permissible purposes may be liable either criminally or civilly. The FCRA provides "Any person who knowingly and willfully obtains information on a consumer from a consumer reporting agency under false pretenses shall be fined . . . imprisoned . . . or both." 15 U.S.C. § 1681q. The Act also directly prohibits obtaining a report for an unauthorized purpose, and provides for civil liability for such activity. 15 U.S.C. §§ 1681b(f), and 1681n(a)(1)(B) & (b). Examples of non-permissible purposes for obtaining a consumer report are quite varied, but commonly center on domestic disputes and non-debt related litigation. Businesses can be held vicariously liable under a theory of apparent authority for their employees' misuse of a consumer report. *Jones v. Federated Financial Reserve Corp.,* 144 F.3d 961 (6th Cir. 1998).

d. Requirements for Furnishers of Information

In 1996, Congress made some amendments to the FCRA which included, for the first time, rules concerning businesses which furnish information to the credit reporting agencies. Thus, not only do credit reporting agencies have the task of ensuring that information is accurate but businesses have the task of ensuring that the information they provide is correct.

Basically, the FCRA prohibits furnishers of information to consumer reporting agencies from providing incorrect information. Furnishers are prohibited from reporting information with actual knowledge or reasonable cause to believe the information is inaccurate. 15 U.S.C. § 1681s–2(a)(1)(A) & (D). This rule, however, does not apply to furnishers who provide consumers with an address to notify them of any inaccuracies. If a consumer uses the notification address and claims that information is inaccurate, the furnisher must refrain from providing that information to a reporting agency if it is in fact inaccurate. 15 U.S.C. § 1681s–2(a)(1)(B), (C). Yet, if the furnisher is unable to determine that the information is inaccurate, the furnisher may only report the information by noting that it is disputed. The dispute then must also be noted by the credit reporting agency. Additionally, the amendment requires that furnishers who regularly supply information to reporting agencies, inform the agency of any necessary corrections.

Any financial institution that furnishes negative information to a consumer reporting agency must provide a written notice to the consumer no later than 30 days after such furnishing, which includes information concerning a customer's delinquencies, late payments, insolvency or default. 15 U.S.C. § 1681s–2(a)(7). Furnishers also have a duty to investigate claims of inaccuracy based on consumers' direct complaints. 15 U.S.C. § 1681s–2(a)(8).

These duties of furnishers are not subject to a private right of action, however, and can only be enforced by the relevant government agency, such as the FTC or the CFPB. The furnisher's duty to investigate as triggered by a notice of dispute from a consumer reporting agency, set forth in 15 U.S.C. § 1681s–2(b), however, is subject to a private right of action. *See Peart v. Shippie*, 345 Fed. Appx. 384 (11th Cir. 2009). This topic will be discussed more fully in the section on remedies, *infra*.

"Regulation V" requires each furnisher of information to CRAs to "establish and implement reasonable written policies and procedures regarding the accuracy and integrity of the information relating to consumers that it furnishes to a consumer reporting agency." 12 C.F.R. § 1022.42. Both the CFPB and the FTC have been active in enforcing this aspect of Regulation V, as well as challenging other violations of the FCRA itself. The CFPB also provides supervisory guidance to furnishers, to help ensure compliance.

e. Rights of Consumers

Many rights of the consumer have been discussed in the previous pages, i.e., the right to be notified of a user's reliance on adverse information in a credit report, right to privacy, and the right to accurate information. The consumer also has a right to see the contents of his report and dispute any inaccurate information, thus triggering a reasonable investigation by either the CRA or the furnisher or both. The consumer has a right to a free annual credit report from each of the three nationwide consumer reporting agencies, and can also receive a free report in the case of certain triggering events, such as receipt of an adverse action notice. 15 U.S.C. § 1681j. Although many websites advertise "free" credit reports, the only website providing the free copy as required by federal law is AnnualCreditReport.com.

The FCRA, at 15 U.S.C. § 1681g, allows consumers access to all information in a consumer's file, including the sources of the information, the identification of each person that procured a consumer report, the dates, original payees and amounts of any checks upon which is based any adverse characterization of the consumer and a record of all inquiries received by the agency during the one-year period preceding the request. Additionally, the CRA must also include a summary of the consumer's rights with the disclosure, including disclosures to identity theft victims. On request by the consumer, credit reporting agencies must also disclose information concerning credit scores, but they can charge a reasonable fee if the score is not covered by a specific requirement. Sources of information acquired solely for use in preparing an investigative report do not have to be disclosed.

An individual has greater access to his consumer report now more than ever because of the scope of the Internet. There are many websites dedicated to furnishing an individual his report in a matter of seconds. The cost of these reports is limited to $8.00 per report. Due to consumer complaints about misleading advertising for "free" credit report websites that were actually advertising free trial offers that lapsed into a paid monthly subscription unless the consumer took some action, regulations now require prominent disclosures directing consumers to the official free annual credit report site. 12 C.F.R. §§ 1026.136–138.

If a consumer receives a credit report, he or she should check the report for accuracy. Over the years, several studies have found that a significant percentage of reports contain some errors. If a consumer finds an inaccurate statement, and duly notifies the consumer reporting agency, the CRA must follow strict procedures to reinvestigate disputed information. 15 U.S.C. § 1681i.

The agency must conduct a reasonable reinvestigation of the disputed matters free of charge and record the current status of the disputed information or delete the information within 30 days of receiving notice of a dispute by a consumer. The 30-day time limit may be extended fifteen days if the agency receives additional information from the consumer requiring additional consideration. However, the 15-day extension is inapplicable if the agency has already determined that the disputed information is inaccurate.

Aside from the time limits, the question of what actions constitute a "reasonable" reinvestigation is not specified in the statute. Depending on the circumstances, the CRA may have to go beyond simply conveying the dispute information back to the furnisher and relying on their response. *Jones v. Experian Information Solutions, Inc.*, 982 F. Supp. 2d 268 (S.D.N.Y. 2013).

As part of its reinvestigation, the agency must consider all relevant information provided by the consumer. Additionally, the agency will within five days of receiving notice of a dispute, provide notification of the dispute to the person who provided any item of information in dispute.

Upon notification of a dispute by the CRA, the furnisher of the information must investigate the accuracy of the disputed information. 15 U.S.C. § 1681s–2(b). Similar to the duties of the agency, the furnisher (1) must conduct an investigation of the disputed information within a reasonable time; (2) review all relevant information furnished to it by the agency and (3) report the results of its investigation to the agency. If the investigation results in the finding of inaccurate information, the furnisher must also report the results to all other reporting agencies to which it had reported the original information. This provides a method of checks and balances between the credit reporting agency and the furnisher. This also provides greater protection for the consumer against inaccurate information.

If the furnisher does not conduct a "reasonable" investigation upon receipt of a dispute notice from the CRA, it is liable under the Act, including by private suit. *Johnson v. MBNA America Bank*, 357 F.3d 426 (4th Cir. 2004). This is in contrast to the furnisher's duty under 15 U.S.C. § 1681s–2(a)(8), which is by statute not subject to private suit. 15 U.S.C. § 1681s–2(c). Unfortunately, most consumers who become aware that a creditor is reporting a delinquency or other adverse information based on identity theft, for instance, would likely complain directly to the creditor rather than complaining to a consumer reporting agency that would in turn send a notice of dispute to the creditor. If the consumer never sends a notice of dispute directly to the CRA, however, the consumer may lose his right to sue the furnisher who performs an unreasonable investigation. *See Burrell v. DFS Services, LLC*, 753 F. Supp. 2d 438 (D.N.J. 2010).

The CRA can refuse to reinvestigate a dispute raised by a consumer if the agency determines that the dispute is frivolous or irrelevant. If, however, a reinvestigation was conducted, the agency must provide the consumer with the results within five days of its completion, regardless of the outcome. All inaccurate or incomplete information must be promptly deleted or corrected. If a reinvestigation is conducted, but the dispute is left unresolved, the consumer may file a brief statement setting forth the nature of the dispute. The consumer's statement, or the agency's clear and accurate summary of the statement, must then be presented in any subsequent consumer report containing the information in dispute.

Furthermore, at the consumer's request, the reporting agency is required to give "notification" that an item has been deleted or that the disputing statement or summary has been added "to any person designated by the consumer" who has received a consumer report within the past two years for employment purposes or within the past six months for any other purpose. The agency must "clearly and conspicuously" disclose to the consumer his right to make such a request.

Once disputed information has been deleted after a reinvestigation, consumers should watch out for its sudden reappearance on the credit report. The disputed information can only be reinserted into a consumers report after certain steps have been taken by the agency. First, the agency must get certification from the furnisher of the information that the information is accurate and complete. Second, the agency must notify the consumer, in writing, within five business days after reinsertion that the information was reinserted; the name and address of the furnisher; and that the consumer has a right to add a statement to his file about the disputed information.

f. Identity Theft Protections

As stated earlier in this chapter, consumers should check their credit reports periodically for mistakes. Some of the mistakes found may be inadvertent, while others may be the result of fraud. When a credit card, a social security number or other item of identification is lost or stolen, consumers may become victims of identity theft, a growing problem in the 21st century. Identity theft has topped the list of consumer complaints to the FTC for years.

Identity theft is a crime. In 1998, Congress passed the Identity Theft and Assumption Deterrence Act. This law makes it a crime to "knowingly transfer or use, without lawful authority, a means of identification of another person with the intent to commit, or to aid or abet, any unlawful activity that constitutes a violation of Federal law, or that constitutes a felony under any applicable State or local law." 18 U.S.C. § 1028(a)(7). Prior to the enactment of this criminal law, identity theft usually was considered a fraud on the creditors or financial institutions with whom the imposter was dealing, because they were the ones who usually ended up with the direct loss for the fraud. There was little recognition of the victimization of the person whose identity was stolen, however, resulting in many indirect adverse financial consequences and the burden of correcting her credit record.

The 2003 FACTA amendments to the FCRA added several provisions specifically aimed at protecting victims of identity theft. Consumers who have a good faith suspicion that they have been or are in danger of becoming a victim of identity theft can require the consumer reporting agencies to place a one-year (formerly 90-day) initial fraud alert on the consumer's file. This status requires the CRA to take certain steps to verify the identity of the consumer before opening a new account, increasing the credit limit or issuing additional cards on an existing account. 15 U.S.C. § 1681c–1(a)(1). A consumer who is on active military duty may also file a similar alert that lasts at least one year. 15 U.S.C. § 1681c–1(c)(1). Active duty military personnel must be excluded from "pre-screened" credit offers for two years following a fraud alert request. They are also entitled to take advantage of free electronic credit monitoring services offered by credit reporting agencies for as long as they are on active duty. 15 U.S.C. § 1681c–1(k), 16 C.F.R. § 609. An "extended" alert lasting up to seven years is available to any consumer but must be based on the consumer's submission of an "identity theft report," which must include a copy of a police report filed by the consumer. 15 U.S.C. § 1681c–1(b).

Effective in 2018, the FCRA also requires that all consumers have the option of placing a "security freeze" on their credit records, free of charge. 15

U.S.C. § 1681c–1(i). A security freeze, once placed by the consumer, is very strong protection against identity theft as it prohibits the CRA from releasing a credit report to anyone unless the consumer "unfreezes" their credit record. This prevents would-be imposters from obtaining credit in the consumer's name because any creditor being used by the imposter would not be able to obtain a credit report in the victim's name. There are exceptions to the impenetrability of the security freeze for existing creditors who are monitoring an account, law enforcement investigations and for the fulfillment of a credit monitoring subscription, among other things. The 2018 amendments also establish the availability of a security freeze for persons under the age of 16, and incapacitated persons, or persons for whom a guardian or conservator has been appointed. 15 U.S.C. § 1681c–1(j). Such persons could be vulnerable to identity thieves because they are not likely to be actively monitoring or using their credit records. The FTC is tasked with issuing regulations to implement the national security freeze legislation. Both the CRAs and the FTC are required to have webpages that will help consumers request security freezes. Information about the security freeze, as well as the fraud alerts, will be added to the required FCRA "notice of rights" consumer disclosures.

Prior to the 2018 federal law, many states had required the major CRAs to allow consumers to place a security freeze on their credit records, often for a fee. These state laws are now preempted by the federal law, and the standards for security freezes are uniform nationwide.

Other identity theft protections include the requirement that credit card receipts print only the last five digits of the credit card account on the receipt, and that creditors send a change of address verification. 15 U.S.C. § 1681c(g) & (h). A victim of identity theft can force the CRA or a furnisher to block fraudulent information in the victim's consumer report upon the provision of proper documentation by the consumer. 15 U.S.C. § 1681c–2(a), (b). Such a victim can also require the business who accepted a credit application from an unauthorized person to supply copies of the application and transactions. 15 U.S.C. § 1681g(e).

As to users of credit reports, they must establish an Identity Theft Program and respond appropriately to certain "red flags" that indicate possible identity theft. 12 C.F.R. § 41.90. Finally, all users of individually identifiable consumer information must use proper disposal measures to protect against unauthorized use. 12 C.F.R. § 41.83.

g. Administrative Remedies

The Federal Trade Commission is invested with the principal responsibility for administrative enforcement of the FCRA. Violations of any requirement of the FCRA are declared to be unfair or deceptive practices under Section 5(a) of the FTC Act. The FTC is also authorized to enforce provisions of the Act through cease and desist orders with respect to consumer reporting agencies, users of reports and others not regulated by federal agencies. The Consumer Financial Protection Bureau and several other agencies also have enforcement powers under the Act but the CFPB is the main rulemaking authority for the FCRA. 15 U.S.C. § 1681s.

h. Civil Liability

The Act imposes civil liability against any person who willfully or negligently fails to comply with any requirement under the Act with respect to any consumer. If there is willful noncompliance, a consumer may recover actual damages of not more than $1,000 or less than $100, punitive damages and attorney's fees. 15 U.S.C. § 1681n. "Willful" violations under the FCRA include both knowing and reckless violations. *Safeco Ins. Co. of America v. Burr*, 551 U.S. 47 (2007). A "willful" violation includes a violation of an unambiguous statutory requirement, even in the absence of any prior court or agency interpretation. *Syed v. M-1, LLC*, 853 F.3d 492 (9th Cir. 2017). Any person who was negligent in failing to comply with the FCRA's requirements is liable to the consumer for actual damages and attorney's fees, but not punitive damages. 15 U.S.C. § 1681o. Obtaining a consumer report under false pretenses or knowingly without a permissible purpose is also subject to civil liability of actual damages or $1,000, whichever is greater. 15 U.S.C. § 1681n(a)(1)(B).

Class actions are not specifically provided for under the FCRA, but there have been some successful class actions under the Act. One of the biggest impediments to class actions is the inclusion of arbitration clauses with class action waivers in consumer contracts. *See, e.g., Anglin v. Tower Loan* of *Mississippi, Inc.*, 635 F. Supp. 2d 523 (S.D. Miss. 2009).

Another major hurdle for private actions brought in federal court is the requirement of Article III standing, as articulated in the U.S. Supreme Court case of *Spokeo, Inc. v. Robins*, 136 S. Ct. 1540 (2016). In that case, the named plaintiff in a class action alleged statutory violations of the FCRA by the consumer reporting agency Spokeo, including an allegation that the defendant failed to "follow reasonable procedures to assure maximum accuracy," as required by the statute. In this case, the Supreme Court held that in order to have standing to sue in federal court, the plaintiff would have to show "injury in fact," which in turn must be both "particularized" (individualized) and "concrete" (real, not hypothetical).

Since *Spokeo* was decided, lower courts have struggled to determine the issue of standing, not only for FCRA cases, but for other cases involving federal consumer statutes as well. In the FCRA context, the cases have been mixed. For example, potential harm from failure to truncate credit card information on receipts was not considered sufficient injury in fact where there was no allegation of actual harm. *See, e.g., Basset v. ABM Parking Servs., Inc.*, 883 F.3d 776 (9th Cir. 2018). On the other hand, in the *Spokeo* case itself, the plaintiff had alleged that the information disseminated about him was inaccurate, in that it portrayed him as older, more educated and more financially well off than he actually was. The Supreme Court remanded for a finding that there was "concrete" as well as "particularized" injury. On remand, the Ninth Circuit held that there was standing because the plaintiff was actually harmed by the presence of misrepresentations about him that might be relevant to potential employers. 867 F.3d 1108 (9th Cir. 2017).

A final observation relating to obtaining civil remedies is that the FCRA preempted most common law actions. The Act provides that "no consumer may bring an action or proceeding in the nature of defamation, invasion of privacy or negligence with respect to the reporting of information ... against any consumer reporting agency, any user of information, or any person who furnishes information to a consumer reporting agency, based on information disclosed pursuant to [various provisions of the FCRA] except as to false information furnished with malice or willful intent to injure such consumer." 15 U.S.C. § 1681h(e). Basically, due to the difficulty of proving malice or willful intent to injure, that provision means that a consumer may sue under common law, but not if the information on which the suit is based was obtained through the Act. The practical problem of obtaining information outside the Act makes any common law claim unlikely.

4. STATE LAWS

Almost all states have enacted legislation attempting to regulate credit bureaus and protect consumers, most of which mirror the federal law but with some additional or differing aspects. *See, e.g.,*

Cal. Civ. Code §§ 1785.1–.36.[3] Some states have promulgated regulations to protect consumers against security breaches on data bases held by CRAs. *See* N.Y. Comp. Codes Rules & Regs. Tit. 23, § 201.00 (2018).

The federal Fair Credit Reporting Act (FCRA), however, has preempted at least some provisions of most of these statutes. The preemption provisions of the federal statute, many of which affect enforcement options, are both specific and complex, resulting in much conflicting case law.

B. CREDIT REPAIR ORGANIZATIONS ACT

Aside from the problem of identity theft, consumers should also be aware of credit repair scams. Consumers who are mired in debt often are desperate for a way out. Those are the people towards whom these scams are aimed. So-called "credit repair" businesses often promised (falsely) that consumers could erase any and all adverse information in their credit reports even if the information was accurate. In most cases, these companies tried to inundate the consumer reporting agencies with disputes and requests for investigation of accurate information, in the hopes that the CRAs would delete the information because they couldn't verify it within the statutory time limits. In the most egregious cases, some companies would offer consumers a chance to hide unfavorable credit

---

[3] *See* DEE PRIDGEN, RICHARD M. ALDERMAN & JOLINA CUARESMA, CONSUMER CREDIT AND THE LAW, Appendix 2A (2019–2020 ed.), for a list of these state statutes.

information by establishing a new credit identity, which actually involved the consumer in a type of fraud.

Although not all credit repair agencies were engaging in misleading or fraudulent practices, because of the potential for abuse, Congress passed the Credit Repair Organizations Act (CROA) in 1996 to regulate this industry. 15 U.S.C. §§ 1679–1679j. The Act requires these companies to give consumers three days to rescind a contract for credit repair. This right to cancel must be disclosed to consumers on the contract. Additionally, the Act mandates that the companies make certain required disclosures to the consumer such as "a full and detailed description of the services to be performed." Furthermore, the company must inform the consumer of her right to self-help through the FCRA, allowing the consumer to police and correct inaccuracies themselves, without the need for a credit repair organization.

The Act also prohibits certain types of conduct. Credit repair organizations cannot make any false or misleading statements or statements which in the exercise of reasonable care would be known to be false or misleading, provide misleading advice, engage in any kind of deception or make any statement encouraging consumers to alter their identification. The credit repair organizations are also barred from receiving advance payments before the promised services are fully performed.

To be subject to these duties, a person or entity must fit the definition of "credit repair organization." The statute says it includes "any person who uses any instrumentality of interstate commerce or the mails to sell, provide, or perform (or represent that such person can or will sell, provide, or perform) any service, in return for the payment of money or other valuable consideration, for the express or implied purpose of—(i) improving any consumer's credit record, credit history, or credit rating; . . ." 15 U.S.C. § 1679a(3). This language has been applied in court to cover certain online credit monitoring service providers, because they marketed themselves as being able to help consumers improve their credit records or credit scores. *See, e.g., Stout v. FreeScore*, 743 F.3d 684 (9th Cir. 2014).

The Act provides civil liability as well as government enforcement, mainly by the FTC. Consumers who have been victims of credit repair scams can recover the greater of actual damages or the amount paid to the organization. Punitive damages may also be allowed, as well as attorney's fees. There is a five year statute of limitations for actions under the Act.

CROA has a "non-waiver" provision that invalidates contractual waiver of the Act's protections. 15 U.S.C. § 1679f. This "non-waiver" provision does not apply, however, to a mandatory arbitration agreement contained in the underlying credit repair contract. As the U.S. Supreme Court held, the non-waiver provision of the statute applies only to rights created by the statute and does not cover the right to sue in court. *CompuCredit Corp. v. Greenwood*, 565 U.S. 95 (2012). Class action suits may also be waived despite the statutory "non-waiver" clause. *King v. Capital One Bank*, 2012 WL 5570624 (W.D. Va. 2012).

The FTC has been relatively aggressive in enforcing CROA, mainly using joint enforcement sweeps with state attorneys general. The FTC won a major judgment in 2001 against a credit repair organization in California that was co-managed by an attorney. This company had made false promises of guaranteed credit repair through widespread advertising, including on a radio talk show that was actually an infomercial. The FTC won a permanent injunction banning the defendants from engaging in the credit repair business in the future, and also obtained a judgment for over $1,000,000. *FTC v. Gill*, 265 F.3d 944 (9th Cir. 2001). The CFPB has also pursued companies offering credit repair services if they engage in deceptive practices, such as representing, without any reasonable basis, that they can remove negative entries on a consumer's credit history, whether the entry is accurate or not, and can substantially increase a consumer's credit score. *See, e.g., CFPB v. Commercial Credit Consultants*, Stipulated Final Judgment & Order, No. 2:17-cv-04720 (C.D. Cal. 2017); and *CFPB v. Park View Law, Inc.*, Stipulated Final Judgment & Order, No. 2:17-cv-04721 (C.D. Cal. 2017).

C. DISCRIMINATION IN ACCESS TO CREDIT

1. SCOPE OF EQUAL CREDIT OPPORTUNITY ACT

The Equal Credit Opportunity Act, enacted in 1974 and amended in 1976, prohibits discrimination against any credit applicant with respect to any aspect of a credit transaction on the basis of race, color, religion, national origin, sex, marital status, age, the fact that all or part of the applicant's income is derived from public assistance, or the fact that the applicant has in good faith exercised any right under the Consumer Credit Protection Act. 15 U.S.C. § 1691(a).

The Equal Opportunity Act is one title of the Consumer Credit Protection Act. Regulations under the Act were originally promulgated by the Federal Reserve Board, and are now under the jurisdiction of the Consumer Financial Protection Bureau (CFPB). The ECOA regulations are known as Regulation B and are codified at 12 C.F.R. Part 1002. Banks, finance companies, retail stores, credit card issuers, and generally, anyone who regularly extends credit is subject to the regulations. In addition, the law may apply to those who arrange financing, such as real estate brokers or automobile dealers. Also, unlike the Fair Credit Reporting Act, there is no question that the Equal Credit Opportunity Act does apply to business credit. Other federal anti-discrimination statutes that apply to consumer credit in the housing area include the Fair Housing Act, the Community

Reinvestment Act and the Home Mortgage Disclosure Act, but these laws are beyond the scope of this volume.

2. DISCRIMINATION IN OBTAINING INFORMATION AND SIGNATURES IN CREDIT APPLICATIONS

Although the Equal Credit Opportunity Act does not regulate the contents of credit applications, Regulation B does. 12 C.F.R. § 1002.5 prohibits creditors from requesting information concerning an applicant's spouse or former spouse, unless the spouse will be liable for the account, will have access to the account, or the applicant is relying on the spouse's income. Information concerning an applicant's sex, marital status, child-bearing, race, color, religion and national origin are also prohibited. This prohibited information, however, may be gathered for monitoring or self-testing purposes.

Creditors are also prohibited from requiring the signature of an applicant's spouse (other than a joint applicant) on any credit application or credit instrument if the applicant on his or her own can meet the creditor's standards of creditworthiness. 12 C.F.R. § 1002.7(d). This rule was authorized as a way of implementing the Act's ban on marital status discrimination. *Anderson v. United Finance Co.*, 666 F.2d 1274 (9th Cir. 1982).

There are model application forms available from the CFPB. Although creditors are not required to use the model forms, if a creditor chooses to use the model forms, the creditor is deemed to be acting in compliance with Regulation B's credit application requirements.

3. PROVING ILLEGAL DISCRIMINATION IN CREDIT TRANSACTIONS

The Act prohibits discrimination on a prohibited basis with regard to "any aspect" of a credit transaction, but the main area in which this may arise is in the evaluation of the credit application. In an early case, treating an unmarried couple jointly applying for a mortgage loan less favorably than a similarly situated married couple was held to be prohibited discrimination of the basis of marital status. *Markham v. Colonial Mortg. Service Co., Associates, Inc.,* 605 F.2d 566 (D.C. Cir. 1979). Similarly, a credit card issuer's policy of terminating a credit card based on a change in marital status, i.e., the death of a spouse, was also considered illegal credit discrimination, without the need to prove specific intent to discriminate. *Miller v. American Exp. Co.,* 688 F.2d 1235 (9th Cir. 1982). Yet from the outset, it has been clear that most credit discrimination will not manifest itself in overtly discriminatory policies of the creditor. This has led to the use of indirect methods of attempting to prove discrimination, such as "disparate impact" or "disparate effects" tests, borrowed from the law of employment discrimination.

Most creditors today generally use a statistical analysis of the applicant's past credit experience, *i.e.*, "credit scoring," for evaluating credit applications. There may also be some use of subjective evaluation of the individual applicant, *i.e.*, a "judgmental system," but these systems have not been widely used in recent years. Credit scoring is a statistical method of assessing credit risk which rates the likelihood that an individual will pay back the loan by considering the information contained in the consumer's credit report, including past delinquencies, type of credit, how often credit is applied for and number of inquiries.

Creditors use credit scores produced by different scoring models, with the most widely used being the Fair, Isaac Company or FICO score. Generally, credit bureaus (also known as Consumer Reporting Agencies or CRAs) provide the risk scores to their subscribers who then use the score to objectively evaluate an applicant's credit worthiness. Each lender uses the scores differently. The scores only become meaningful and useful within the context of a particular lender's own cutoff points and risk guidelines.

Credit scoring is arguably more reliable than the judgmental method because it is based on real data and statistics. Credit scoring systems consider many factors, but what they cannot consider are any of the prohibited characteristics such as race, sex, marital status, national origin or religion. 15 U.S.C. § 1691. The use of certain characteristics such as zip code or occupation, however, can be proxies for one or more of the prohibited categories, and as such can be challenged as violating the ECOA under the so-called "effects test," to be discussed in more detail below.

The newest iteration of credit evaluation was pioneered by online lenders in the "fin tech" sector, who use algorithms and machine learning to scour and analyze a much wider range of data about consumers. These lenders may start with a credit score, but also consider such factors as education, shopping patterns, and social media posts to make judgments about creditworthiness. The fintech lenders are totally online, with no paper applications or in person interviews, thus cutting costs and streamlining the credit application process. Proponents of this method say it can include more consumers because more factors are considered than the old model based on credit scores and personal evaluation. Critics say that the lack of transparency involved in these proprietary systems can mask the presence of factors that are proxies for prohibited criteria and that the complexity of the systems may make it well nigh impossible for plaintiffs to make a case of discriminatory impact.

The consideration of a person's age, however, is a different story. Credit scoring systems can use age as a consideration. The system must not assign a negative factor or value to elderly applicants, however. What may be considered is the fact that the applicant's income may be reduced because of retirement. Creditors are allowed to consider the age of an elderly applicant if such age is used to favor the applicant in extending credit. If the creditor is using a judgmental method, then age can only be considered for the purpose of determining a pertinent element of creditworthiness. 12 C.F.R. § 1002.6(b)(2).

The effects test permits an ECOA plaintiff to show that some criterion used by a creditor, often as part of the credit scoring system, has the effect of discriminating against a protected class, thus eliminating the need to prove an intent to discriminate on an unlawful basis. This approach, while promising, has historically been difficult for plaintiffs to use successfully due to the steep burden of proof. *See, e.g., Cherry v. Amoco*, 490 F. Supp. 1026 (N.D. Ga. 1980).

Illegal credit discrimination can also be shown using the so-called "disparate treatment" test, by which a plaintiff who is a member of a protected class must show that he or she was qualified for the loan or credit in question but was nonetheless turned down. This approach has proved to be more difficult for plaintiffs and has not been universally accepted by all courts as being applicable in ECOA cases.

A related theory of ECOA liability is the "disparate impact" test, a concept borrowed from employment law. The CFPB began using this theory to challenge "indirect" automobile lenders based on lending policies that facilitated discriminatory finance charge markups imposed on African Americans by automobile dealers. Typically, the dealers arrange financing for prospective buyers by sending the information to several lenders. In turn, the lenders will send back a "buy rate" which they would be willing to charge, and the dealer is often allowed to add a discretionary "dealer markup." The CFPB alleged that this dealer discretion resulted in disproportionately higher rates being paid by African

American and other buyers in one or more of the ECOA protected classes. The CFPB was successful in obtaining several settlements against auto lenders in the mid-2010s, and also released a Compliance Bulletin in 2013 cautioning auto lenders that allowing dealers to mark up the rates at their discretion might result in a disparate impact on minorities in violation of the ECOA. Congress responded in 2018 to the CFPB's perceived overstepping by exercising a Congressional veto of the CFPB's 2013 Bulletin, so that the use of disparate impact theory in indirect auto lending cases became moot. It remains to be seen whether courts will recognize disparate impact as a viable ECOA theory in private cases. *See* Winnie F. Taylor, *The ECOA and Disparate Impact Theory: A Historical Perspective*, 26 J. of Law & Policy 575 (2018).

4. NOTIFICATION

The Equal Credit Opportunity Act requires the creditor to provide applicants with notification of any action it takes regarding an application for credit, and furthermore, the creditor must provide a statement of reasons for any adverse action taken. 15 U.S.C. § 1691(d). Regulation B, 12 C.F.R. § 1002.9, specifies what must be included in the notification and when notice is required. Basically, the section requires creditors to provide notice (1) within 30 days after receiving a completed application, (2) within 30 days after taking adverse action on an incomplete application; (3) within 30 days after taking adverse action on an existing account or (4) within 90 days after notifying the applicant about a counter offer, if the applicant does not expressly accept or use the credit offered.

If adverse action has been taken, the creditor must give, in addition to other transaction details, a statement of the specific reason(s) for the action taken or a disclosure of the applicant's right to a statement of specific reasons within 30 days if a request for such a statement is made within 60 days. 12 C.F.R. § 1002.9(a). The rationale for this requirement is to force the creditor to articulate legitimate reasons for adverse actions, thus possibly preventing some discriminatory actions from taking place. Also, this requirement gives consumers the opportunity to learn about possible mistakes in their credit application or credit record and permits them to take steps to correct such mistakes or deficiencies. Adverse action under the ECOA is defined as a refusal to grant credit in substantially the amount or on substantially the terms requested in an application, a termination or unfavorable change in the terms of an account, or a refusal to grant a requested increase in credit. 12 C.F.R. § 1002.2(c)(1). Note that the Fair Credit Reporting Act also requires creditors to provide a notice to the consumer if adverse action was taken based on information in a credit report. 15 U.S.C. § 1681m(a). The notices required by these two statutes can be combined.

The reasons for adverse action must be both specific and accurate. *See, e.g., Fischl v. General Motors Acceptance Corp.*, 708 F.2d 143 (5th Cir. 1983). A statement that the applicant "failed to achieve a qualifying score on the creditor's credit scoring system" would be considered insufficient. 12 C.F.R. § 1002.9(b)(2). If using a credit scoring system, the creditor should list the factors actually used that most significantly affected the adverse decision.

5. EFFECT OF EQUAL CREDIT OPPORTUNITY ACT ON STATE LAW

The Equal Credit Opportunity Act preempts state credit discrimination statutes which are "inconsistent" with the Act. A state which has laws that are more protective of credit applicants than the Act are not inconsistent with the Act. 15 U.S.C. § 1691d(f).

The CFPB, along with its other duties, is invested with the power to determine whether a State's law is inconsistent with the Act. This grant of authority, however, does not seem to be exclusive. Courts may make this determination and so may creditors, at their own risk.

The Act also provides an exemption by CFPB regulation for transactions subject to "substantially similar" state requirements or more protective state requirements. 15 U.S.C. § 1691d(g).

6. REMEDIES

Any creditor that fails to comply with a requirement imposed by the Act or Regulation B is subject to civil liability for actual and punitive damages in an individual or class action. 15 U.S.C. § 1691e(a) & (b). Damages, however, are limited to actual damages plus punitive damages of not more than $10,000 in individual actions and the lesser of $500,000 or one percent of the creditor's net worth in class actions. 15 U.S.C. § 1691e(b). Equitable and declaratory relief may also be granted, as well as, costs and reasonable attorney's fees. 15 U.S.C. § 1691e(c) & (d).

The administrative enforcement for the act is delegated to several agencies, depending on the type of credit involved, with the overall enforcement authority given to the Federal Trade Commission and the Consumer Financial Protection Bureau. The CFPB has the sole authority to issue regulations under the Act, a function that belonged to the Federal Reserve Board prior to 2011. The CFPB has taken the position that discrimination in debt servicing, as well as in the initial credit application process, can violate the ECOA. The agency settled a case against American Express that alleged the company had discriminated against minority populations in Puerto Rico and other U.S. territories by requiring those residents to pay more to settle debts than customers in mainland U.S. *In re American Express Centurion Bank*, Consent Order, available at www.consumerfinance.gov.

Although state law remedies may still be available to credit applicants, an applicant cannot recover under both the federal and the state statutes.

CHAPTER SIX

CREDIT DISCLOSURES: TRUTH IN LENDING OVERVIEW AND CLOSED-END TRANSACTIONS

A. NEED FOR DISCLOSURE LEGISLATION AND HISTORY OF TILA

Congress enacted what is commonly known as the Truth in Lending Act, or TILA, to require uniform disclosure of the cost of credit in consumer transactions. The volume of consumer credit exploded in the years after World War II. Yet consumers were unable to comparison shop for credit because of the chaotic state of credit cost information. State usury laws were not helpful because creditors used loopholes to conceal the true cost of credit.

Prior to the enactment of TILA in 1968, the disclosures creditors provided to consumers varied widely. It was often impossible for consumers to determine the true cost of the credit, and some creditors did not disclose the rate of interest; they only disclosed the number and amount of monthly payments.

Before TILA, those creditors that did disclose the interest rate did so in a variety of ways. Creditors offering a revolving charge plan commonly quoted a monthly rate, generally one and one half percent a month. Other creditors quoted the rate of interest in terms of a dollar add-on. For example, a creditor might explain the finance charge on a new car as $7 per $100 per year for 3 years. Another method of stating the rate of interest was the discount method, where the finance charge was deducted from the face amount of the note at the time the credit was extended. During this early period, the Federal Trade Commission successfully used the FTC Act to challenge the advertising of "add-on" rates by the major automobile manufacturers in a manner that was likely to confuse consumers into assuming that the add-on rate was the same as simple interest. Because simple interest is a percentage rate applied to a declining balance, whereas an add-on rate is a rate applied to the amount financed as a whole, an add-on rate of 6% would be the equivalent of a simple interest rate of 11.5%. *See Ford Motor Company v. FTC*, 120 F.2d 175 (6th Cir. 1941); *General Motors Corp. v. FTC*, 114 F.2d 33 (2d Cir. 1940). Yet case-by-case policing of deceptive advertising of consumer credit rates was not sufficient to provide consumers with the needed information about the comparative cost of credit offerings.

After nearly a decade of debates and hearings, Congress adopted the Truth in Lending legislation, effective July 1, 1969, which basically required creditors to disclose the cost of credit in a uniform manner. 15 U.S.C. §§ 1601–1667. The stated purpose of TILA is "to assure a meaningful disclosure of credit terms so that the consumer will be able to compare more readily the various credit terms available to him and avoid the uninformed use of credit, and to protect the consumer against inaccurate and unfair credit billing and credit card practices." 15 U.S.C. § 1601(a). TILA authorized the Federal Reserve Board to issue regulations (Regulation Z) and official staff commentary to help practitioners and courts interpret and apply the statute. As of 2011, responsibility for rulemaking and staff commentary was transferred to the Consumer Financial Protection Bureau (CFPB). At that time the numbering of the regulations changed from 12 C.F.R. Part 226 to 12 C.F.R. Part 1026. This volume will use the current numbering, but older cases refer to the original numbering.

The Truth in Lending Act has undergone a series of revisions since its enactment. During the first ten years after its passage, it became evident that the disclosures were overly burdensome to creditors and caused consumers to suffer from "information overload." The federal courts were swamped with TILA cases alleging technical violations that resulted in excessive damages. Thus, in 1980, Congress simplified TILA through a complete revision of the statute. The major purposes of the so-called Simplification Act were to provide consumers with simpler, more understandable information, to make compliance easier for creditors, and to limit creditor liability for statutory penalties to significant rather than technical violations. One major format innovation of this legislation was to require that all the federal disclosures be segregated from the rest of the contract into what has come to be known as "the federal box." At this juncture, the Federal Reserve Board was also empowered to produce model disclosure forms that could provide a safe haven for creditors seeking to comply with the law.

In 1988, TILA was amended to add the Fair Credit and Charge Card Disclosure Act, which requires cost disclosures at the time of solicitation and application for a credit card. Prior to that change, credit card issuers did not need to provide the TILA comparative cost disclosures until just prior to the consumer's first transaction using the credit card, a time which would obviously be too late to be useful for comparison shopping. These solicitation disclosures must be given in readable tabular form, and have come to be known as the "Schumer Box," referring to Senator Charles Schumer, one of the sponsors of the legislation. TILA's 1988 amendment also included the Home Equity Loan Consumer Protection Act, which is concerned with open-end lines of credit secured by the consumer's principal dwelling. This part of the law is aimed at educating consumers on the costs and details of so-called "Home Equity Lines of Credit," or HELOCs, and requires specific disclosures on applications and advertisements for these types of loans.

In 1994, sparked by abuses in subprime home-secured loans made to low income home owners, often in connection with shoddy home repair services, Congress amended TILA to include the Home Ownership and Equity Protection Act (HOEPA). These loans were high cost compared to the traditional lending market and carried a high risk of foreclosure. For this category of loans, consumers were given additional disclosures, a cooling-off period, and some substantive protections against particularly oppressive terms, such as balloon payments, negative amortization and prepayment penalties. The scope and protections of HOEPA were later broadened by the 2010 Dodd-Frank Act.

In 1995, TILA was again revamped, to refine the definition of finance charge, and to increase the error tolerance, in response to concerns raised by lenders who made closed-end, non-purchase money mortgage loans.

Further changes in TILA were brought about in response to the subprime mortgage foreclosure crisis, the stock market plunge and the "great recession" of 2007–2008. The Credit CARD Act of 2009 contained significant reforms in credit card disclosures, and also contained substantive limits on certain unfair and deceptive credit card practices. In 2010, Congress passed the historic Dodd-Frank Wall Street Reform and Consumer Protection Act. This Act resulted in the creation of the Consumer Financial Protection Bureau, which took over the administration and enforcement of TILA from the Federal Reserve Board and other bank regulatory agencies. The FTC remained as an enforcing agency for non-bank creditors within their jurisdiction, however. Dodd-Frank also contained within it the Mortgage Reform and Anti-Predatory Lending Act, which amended TILA in significant ways with regard to residential mortgage loans. This law requires a unified mortgage loan disclosure that combines the previously separate RESPA and TILA disclosures, requires creditors to verify the consumer's ability to repay the loan, and contains many other substantive provisions to protect consumers.

B. TRUTH IN LENDING ACT—OVERVIEW

1. INTRODUCTION

The "Truth in Lending Act," or "TILA," is the popular name for Title I of the Consumer Credit Protection Act, codified at 15 U.S.C. §§ 1601, et seq. The Consumer Credit Protection Act is an umbrella statute that contains not only TILA, but also the Fair Credit Billing Act, the Fair Credit Reporting Act, the Equal Credit Opportunity Act, the Fair Debt Collection Practices Act and the Electronic Fund Transfer Act. These other federal consumer credit laws are discussed elsewhere in this volume.

TILA originated as essentially a disclosure statute. A creditor is free to impose any charges for credit permitted by state or other federal law. The legislation does not generally restrict or confine the price of credit, or the terms and conditions of the extension of credit, although more substantive limits on credit terms in some types of transactions were included in the 2010 amendments under the Dodd-Frank Act. Generally speaking, however, TILA requires that creditors apprise consumers of the terms, conditions and costs of credit in a uniform manner that can be used to compare the cost of credit before consumers enter into a consumer credit contract.

2. REGULATION Z AND OFFICIAL STAFF COMMENTARY

Congress originally empowered the Federal Reserve Board to prescribe regulations to carry out the purposes of TILA. This function is now vested in the Consumer Financial Protection Bureau, which was created to consolidate consumer financial regulation and eliminate the prior situation of multiple federal bank regulatory agencies regulating consumer credit based solely on the type of entity involved. In 1969, the Federal Reserve Board published a comprehensive set of regulations in 12 CFR Part 226, commonly known as "Reg. Z." These regulations are now contained in 12 CFR Part 1026. Regulation Z restates many of the TILA sections, but is generally a more thorough statement of the law. There is also an Official Staff Commentary, which is to Regulation Z, what Regulation Z is to TILA. The Official Staff Commentary makes TILA more user-friendly, with comments and examples that clarify the law. In analyzing any TILA section, both the Regulation Z provision and the corollary Official Staff Commentary should be reviewed.[1] Regulation Z and the Staff Commentary can be readily accessed via the "Interactive Bureau Regulations" platform available on the CFPB website, http://www.consumerfinance.gov/eregulations/. Also, the official up-to-date site for all federal regulations, including Regulation Z, is www.ecfr.gov.

---

[1] Many good reference works providing more detail on TILA and Regulation Z are available, including DEE PRIDGEN, RICHARD M. ALDERMAN & JOLINA CUARESMA, CONSUMER CREDIT AND THE LAW, Chapters 4–9A and 14–15 (Thomson Reuters 2019–2020); and NATIONAL CONSUMER LAW CENTER, TRUTH IN LENDING (10th ed. 2019).

3. SCOPE OF APPLICATION OF TILA

The Truth in Lending Act has no single, comprehensive scope provision. Congress intended it to apply broadly and to apply to most consumer credit transactions.

To determine the scope of application of TILA, it is necessary to consider a number of the Act's sections in conjunction with sections from Regulation Z and the Official Staff Commentary. The following discussion considers these sections according to four principal factors that determine the applicability of TILA:

(a) amount of credit,

(b) purpose of credit,

(c) status of debtor,

(d) status of creditor.

a. Amount of Credit

Large transactions are exempt from TILA requirements, through the operation of 15 U.S.C. § 1603(3). If more than $50,000 (subject to annual adjustments for inflation) is being financed, TILA generally does not apply. One major exception to this maximum is any extension of credit secured either by real property or personal property that is used or expected to be used as the consumer's principal dwelling. 12 C.F.R. § 1026.3(b). The purpose of the property exception to the large transaction exemption is to make the purchase on credit of a home, trailer, condominium, and so on, also subject to TILA.

b. Purpose of Credit

For TILA to cover the consumer credit transaction, the transaction must be "primarily for personal, family, or household purposes." 15 U.S.C. § 1602(i); 12 C.F.R. § 1026.2(a)(12). The phrase "personal, family, or household" should be taken at face value.

The extension of credit for business, commercial, or agricultural purposes is exempt from TILA. 15 U.S.C. § 1603; 12 C.F.R. § 1026.3(a). Loans issued pursuant to student loan programs under the Higher Education Act are also exempt from TILA, but have their own required disclosures under the HEA. Private education loans are covered by TILA, however, and are subject to extensive disclosure rules. 15 U.S.C. § 1650; 12 C.F.R. § 1026.46.

In applying the coverage of TILA to credit transactions for "personal, family, or household" purposes, as opposed to business purposes, the courts will look at the "overall purpose" for which the loan was taken out or for which the account was opened. Thus, if a consumer buys a personal automobile and occasionally uses it for business purposes, the Act still applies. *Gallegos v. Stokes*, 593 F.2d 372 (10th Cir. 1979). Even if some of the proceeds of the loan or some of the charges on a credit card are used for a business purpose, TILA may apply if the overall purpose was personal. *See Citibank (South Dakota) v. Mincks*, 135 S.W.3d 545 (Mo. Ct. App. 2004) (credit card was opened primarily for consumer purposes, and thus TILA applied to an extension of credit on that account even though that particular transaction was for business purposes); *Semar v. Platte Valley Fed. Sav. & Loan Ass'n,* 791 F.2d 699 (9th Cir.1986) (loan "primarily" for personal purpose even though 10 percent of proceeds used for a business purpose).

"Credit" is "the right granted by a creditor to a debtor to defer payment of debt or to incur debt and defer its payment." 15 U.S.C. § 1602(f); 12 C.F.R. § 1026.2(a)(14). This term includes so-called "check cashing" services which are actually short-term high-interest "payday" loans in which the consumer writes a post-dated check several weeks in advance of the check date for an amount higher than the cash advanced. Thus, this type of loan is subject to all of the disclosure requirements of TILA, including the disclosure of Annual Percentage Rates (APRs) in the range of 300–800%.[2] Rent-to-own or rental purchase agreements, on the other hand, are generally not covered by TILA because they are typically terminable at will by the consumer, and thus no credit for a set amount has actually been extended. Regulation Z's definition of "credit sale" specifically excludes leases that are "terminable without penalty

---

[2] The CFPB issued a rule in 2017 to regulate on a federal level some fringe, nonbank lenders, such as payday lenders, car title lenders and pawn shops. This regulation would have required lenders of these types of loans to make an initial determination of the borrower's ability to repay the loan in full when it is due. 82 Fed. Reg. 54472 (Nov. 17, 2017).

In 2020, however, the CFPB amended the regulation so as to eliminate most of the substantive aspects of the rule but retained the limit on repeated attempts to collect payments from consumer accounts. 85 Fed. Reg. 44382 (July 22, 2020).

at any time by the consumer." 12 CF.R. § 1026.2(a)(16).

c. Status of Debtor

The Truth in Lending disclosure requirements apply only to transactions involving a debtor who is a "natural person." "Natural person" is not defined in either the statute or the regulations, but the concept is incorporated in the definition of "consumer." 15 U.S.C. § 1602(i); 12 C.F.R. § 1026.2(a)(11). Presumably this eliminates from coverage credit extended to business entities or other types of organizations.

d. Status of Creditor

The scope of TILA's disclosure requirements are not only limited by the type of debtor—an individual obtaining credit for consumer purposes—but they are also limited by the type of creditor. The creditor must be a person who, in the ordinary course of business regularly extends credit that is subject to a finance charge or is payable in more than four installments, and to whom the obligation is initially payable. 15 U.S.C. § 1602(g); Reg. Z § 1026.2(a)(17)(i). A natural person or an organization can be a "person" who is a creditor.

Thus, a TILA creditor must, essentially, be a "professional creditor." This does not mean that the creditor's regular business must be extending credit; it means that whatever the creditor's business, he or she must regularly extend credit in the ordinary course of business.

Regulation Z includes a mathematical test to determine if a person "regularly" extends credit and is, therefore, a creditor. To meet this test, the person must have extended consumer credit more than 25 times in the preceding calendar year. This numerical standard is lower for real estate secured loans. If a person extends credit more than five times in the preceding calendar year and each of those transactions was secured by a dwelling, then that person also "regularly" extends credit within the meaning of Regulation Z. If a person extends consumer credit for more than one HOEPA loan, or one or more credit extensions through a mortgage broker, that will also satisfy the "regular" extension of consumer credit requirement. 12 C.F.R. § 1026.2(17)(v).

To be a creditor under TILA, not only must a person regularly extend credit, but the credit extended also must meet one of two alternative tests. The credit must either (1) be subject to a finance charge, or (2) be payable by written agreement in more than four installments.

Under the first alternative test, if the consumer credit is subject to a finance charge, then the person extending the credit is a creditor. The definition of a finance charge will be discussed at some length *infra*.

Under the second alternative test, if a person extends consumer credit payable by a written agreement in more than four installments, not including the down payment, then that person is a creditor regardless of whether or not a finance charge is imposed. An oral agreement to pay consumer credit in more than four installments does not qualify a person as a creditor. The four-installment rule was meant to bring within the TILA disclosure regime those creditors who allow consumers to pay for goods in installments, but do not separately charge a finance charge, instead absorbing the cost of credit into their overhead costs.

Finally, to be a creditor subject to TILA, the person must be the one to whom the obligation is initially payable. This generally excludes contract assignees, i.e., entities that purchase these consumer credit contracts from automobile dealers, mobile home dealers or other retail dealers who sell financing to consumers in conjunction with the sale. Assignees may be liable for TILA violations that are apparent on the face of the contract, however. 15 U.S.C. § 1641(a). Assignees of high-cost mortgages regulated by HOEPA are subject to liability for both apparent and non-apparent TILA violations. 15 U.S.C. § 1641(d).

4. ORGANIZATION OF TILA AND REGULATION Z

Truth in Lending divides consumer credit transactions into two broad categories: open-end credit transactions and closed-end credit transactions. TILA provides different disclosure requirements for each category. So while TILA's disclosure requirements apply to all credit transactions which meet the relevant requirements, the actual requirements will not be the same for all such transactions. After determining that TILA covers a specific transaction, it is then necessary to classify that transaction as open-end or closed-end.

An "open end credit plan" is defined at 15 U.S.C. § 1602(j) and 12 C.F.R. § 1026.2(a)(2). It is a plan under which the creditor reasonably contemplates repeated transactions, which prescribes the terms of such transactions, and which provides for a finance charge which may be computed from time to time on the outstanding unpaid balance. If the finance charge is precomputed at the inception of the transaction, it is not an open-end transaction. The most common type of open-end plan is a credit card account. This category also includes Home Equity Lines of Credit (HELOCs), which is a type of open-end credit secured by the consumer's home.

The other major category of consumer credit in TILA is closed-end credit, which Regulation Z defines as "other than open-end credit." 12 C.F.R. § 1026.2(a)(10). Closed-end credit usually involves one transaction and is extended for a specific period of time. The total finance charge and amount financed, payment amounts, number of payments, and due dates are generally agreed upon by the creditor and the customer at the time of the transaction. Common examples of closed-end credit include a mortgage loan to buy a home and installment contract sales of relatively expensive items such as cars, furniture, and major appliances.

The open-end credit disclosures are in some ways less onerous than the closed-end disclosures, because they do not require the disclosure of a total finance charge, total costs of the transaction, monthly payments and how long it will take to repay. On the other hand, open-end disclosures must be made repeatedly over the course of the open end account, whereas closed-end disclosures are made only once at the outset. There has been a gradual shift to open-end credit plans since TILA was originally passed, with old-style retail installment contracts being replaced in many sectors by credit card sales. In some cases involving open end credit for big-ticket items, however, the question has come up whether this is tantamount to "spurious" open end credit which should in fact be regulated as a closed-end transaction. Cases have been mixed on this issue, which will be discussed in more detail, *infra*.

5. GENERAL DISCLOSURE REQUIREMENTS

As stated above, precisely what must be disclosed under TILA depends on whether the consumer credit transaction is open-end or closed-end and whether it is a loan or credit sale. However, there are some general requirements that apply to all TILA disclosures. Regulation Z, 12 C.F.R. §§ 1026.5(a)(1) and .17(a)(1), requires creditors to make disclosures "clearly and conspicuously," "in writing," and "in a form that the consumer may keep."

The clear and conspicuous standard requires that disclosures be in a "reasonably understandable form." Such disclosures must be meaningful to the average consumer. Thus, in a case involving disclosure of cash-advance rates applicable to the purchase of virtual currency, the creditor argued that it was obvious that such purchases were "cash-like transactions" (as disclosed) and thus subject to the cash advance rate. The court agreed with the plaintiffs, however, that this wording did not clearly disclose that the acquisition of cryptocurrency would be subject to cash advance rates. *Tucker v. Chase Bank USA, N.A.*, 399 F. Supp. 3d 105 (S.D.N.Y. 2019).

Closed-end disclosures must be grouped together but do not have to be located in any particular place. Official Staff Commentary ¶ 17(a)(1). The format for open-end disclosures varies depending on whether they are in the solicitation, the account-opening disclosure or the periodic statement.

Regulation Z, 12 C.F.R. § 1026.17(a)(2), requires that in closed-end credit disclosures, the terms "finance charge" and "annual percentage rate," when required to be disclosed with a number, must be disclosed more conspicuously than other required disclosures, except in a few limited circumstances. A creditor may also choose to disclose these items more conspicuously even when the regulations do not so require.

According to the Official Staff Commentary, "more conspicuous" requires that the actual words "finance charge" and "annual percentage rate" should be accentuated. They can be highlighted by capitalizing the relevant words, when other disclosures are printed in lower case. They can be printed in bold print or contrasting color. They can be underlined, set off with asterisks or printed in larger type. Official Staff Commentary, ¶ 17(b)–2. It is fitting that these two terms receive special attention, because they are at the heart of the notion that TILA should provide critical information to consumers who are shopping for credit. The finance charge and APR are the clearest expressions of the true cost of credit.

Another disclosure requirement is that the disclosures must be in writing. Reg. Z § 1026.17(a)(1) and .5(a)(1). And the consumer must be given a copy of the written disclosures. The consumer's written copy is relevant for determining whether required disclosures are "clear and conspicuous," and whether they comply with TILA in other respects, as well as for comparison shopping purposes.

Electronic disclosure is permitted if the creditor complies with the consumer consent and other requirements of the E-Sign Act, which basically seeks to promote e-commerce by declaring that electronic transactions, contracts and signatures may not be denied validity simply because they are electronic and not paper-based. The Act provides that consumer disclosures (including those in TILA) can be made electronically if certain conditions, such as consumer consent, are met. 15 U.S.C. § 7001(c). Regulation Z incorporates this approach but also allows certain disclosures, such as those contained in electronically delivered solicitations and advertisements, to be made electronically without consumer consent. 12 C.F.R. §§ 1026.5(a)(iii) and .17(a)(1). The burgeoning "fintech" sector, which offers online platforms for consumer lending, promises to make electronic disclosures even more prevalent.

TILA's disclosure requirements are detailed and complex. One must first determine the nature of the credit (open-end or closed-end), then examine the statute, Regulation Z and the Official Staff Commentary for guidance. In order to assist creditors who face the daunting task of compliance with TILA, there are published model disclosure forms and clauses upon which creditors can rely. 15 U.S.C. § 1604(b). Use of the forms is not required, but a creditor who uses one of the forms (and not just the language on the forms) is deemed to be in compliance with the disclosure provisions of TILA, other than the numerical disclosures (where the creditor might make an error). *Id.* However, if a creditor starts to use homemade forms loosely patterned after the model forms, the protection may be lost. And if the creditor uses the wrong form, the protections of 15 U.S.C. § 1604(b) are lost. *In re Melvin*, 75 B.R. 952 (Bankr.E.D.Pa.1987).

C. CLOSED-END CREDIT DISCLOSURES

1. TIME FOR DISCLOSURE

TILA requires that closed-end credit disclosures be made "before the credit is extended." 15 U.S.C. § 1638(b)(1). Regulation Z uses the phrase "before consummation." 12 C.F.R. § 1026.17(b). Requiring that credit disclosures be made available to consumers before they enter into credit transactions theoretically encourages comparison-shopping. It is meant to help consumers make careful, rational economic choices and to further competition in the consumer credit market. 15 U.S.C. § 1601(a). Determining a time frame when disclosures will actually help consumers comparison shop for credit, however, has been an issue plaguing TILA disclosures since the law was passed.

The timing and content of TILA disclosures for closed-end real estate transactions has become more complex over time, particularly so as a result of the Dodd-Frank Act of 2010. Thus, the TILA requirements for these types of consumer credit transactions are treated in a separate section on real estate transactions, *infra*.

Regulation Z, 12 C.F.R. § 1026.17(b), uses the phrase "before consummation" to describe the time within which creditors or lenders must make closed-end disclosures. "Consummation" is "the time that a consumer becomes contractually obligated on a credit transaction." 12 C.F.R. § 1026.2(a)(13). Whether a consumer becomes contractually obligated is a matter of state law. Consummation does not occur when the consumer merely becomes contractually committed to buy the goods, unless the consumer also becomes legally obligated to accept a particular credit arrangement. For example, paying a nonrefundable deposit to purchase a car does not constitute "consummation" unless the consumer also contracts for financing at that time. Official Staff Commentary ¶ 2(a)(13).

For most closed-end credit transactions, other than those secured by the consumer's dwelling, the requirement of providing TILA disclosures before consummation of the credit transaction can be fulfilled by providing the disclosures "moments before the consumer signs the contract." *Spearman v. Tom Wood Pontiac-GMC, Inc.*, 312 F.3d 848 (7th Cir.

2002). This includes a situation in which the disclosures are part of a retail installment contract handed to the consumer for her signature, and which in theory she is free to keep without signing should she choose to use the disclosures for comparison shopping. *Id.* Other cases have held that the TILA disclosures in closed-end credit transactions do not have to be on a separate document from the Retail Installment Sales Contract itself, that the consumer's copy does not have to be physically separated from the other copies prior to the consumer signing, and that there is no generally applicable waiting period for consummation after the disclosures are given. Obviously, this type of scenario raises some questions as to how useful these disclosures will be for comparison shopping, since the consumer at that point in time is usually already committed to the credit transaction.

Timing issues for TILA disclosures also arise in a type of automobile financing known as "yo-yo financing" or "spot delivery." In this scenario, the automobile dealer may offer the consumer a relatively favorable financing deal contingent on the dealer successfully identifying a finance company willing to buy the contract on the disclosed terms. At the same time, the consumer is allowed to take home the vehicle subject to a bailment agreement with the dealer. If the initially disclosed financing does not come through, however, the consumer is called back to the dealership (like a yo-yo on a string) and given a second financing contract with a second set of TILA disclosures at a higher rate. In this situation, there may well be two consummations and two disclosures for TILA purposes but there is no violation of the TILA disclosure timing requirements provided the dealership would have honored the first contract had the contingency been fulfilled. The objection to this type of arrangement is that the consumer may be locked in to the purchase and financing under the first (albeit conditional) offer once they have taken possession of the car, and thus can be pressured into agreeing to less favorable credit terms that are not revealed until later. Consumer plaintiffs have been unsuccessful thus far in challenging such arrangements under TILA.

2. DISCLOSURE OF THE FINANCE CHARGE

a. In General

Many disclosures are required by TILA but the disclosure of the cost of credit in dollars and cents is probably the most important concept in TILA. The finance charge is the cost of credit as a dollar amount, whereas the APR reflects that cost on an annual percentage rate basis. The finance charge in effect tells the consumer the total cost of credit, which can be used to compare the transaction to cash, whereas the APR tells the comparative cost of different credit deals.

The basic definition of a "finance charge" is broad and is contained within its own separate regulatory section. The finance charge, as a ratio to the amount financed, and stated on an annual basis, determines the APR, which determines which credit offering appears most competitive compared to other credit deals. As generally defined by TILA and Regulation Z, a finance charge is: (1) the sum of all charges, (2) payable directly or indirectly by the consumer, (3) imposed directly or indirectly by the creditor, (4) as an incident to or a condition of the extension of credit. 15 U.S.C. § 1605(a); 12 C.F.R. § 1026.4(a). It does not include any charge of a type payable in a comparable cash transaction.

An accurate disclosure of the finance charge (within a slight "tolerance" for error allowed by TILA) is viewed as so critical that a failure to properly disclose the finance charge gives rise to statutory damages as well as actual damages. 15 U.S.C. § 1640(a)(4); 15 U.S.C. § 1602(v). Statutory damages and the right of rescission are available only for material disclosure violations.

For both the creditor and the consumer, determining the accurate cost of credit for TILA purposes involves breaking down the components of the total obligation into two basic classifications: (1) the amount financed, and (2) the finance charge. The amount financed is comprised of those legitimate components of the obligation which are advanced by the lender directly to the borrower or paid to others on the borrower's behalf. The finance charge is the cost of the credit. These two categories are mutually exclusive.

TILA has an all-inclusive definition of the cost of credit. The term "finance charge" is intended to reflect the true cost of the credit to the borrower and it is often broader than what may be described as the "interest rate." TILA generally reflects an approach

SEC. C CLOSED-END CREDIT DISCLOSURES

that focuses on what the borrower pays. TIL approach, is distinct from the principle underlying most usury laws, which focus on what the creditor receives as interest.

The finance charge can include fees and amounts charged by someone other than the creditor if (1) the creditor requires the use of a third party as a condition of the extension of credit, even if the consumer can choose the third party, or (2) if the creditor retains a portion of the third-party charge, to the extent of the portion retained. 12 C.F.R. § 1026.4(a)(1). Thus, if a creditor requires the borrower to hire an attorney to prepare a security interest in the financed property, the attorney's fee will be counted as part of the finance charge, even if the consumer selects and pays the attorney directly. There is a special rule for mortgage broker fees, which are considered part of the finance charge even if the creditor does not require the consumer to use a mortgage broker and even if the creditor does not retain any portion of the charge. 12 C.F.R. § 1026.4(a)(2).

The regulation lists examples of finance charges in § 1026.4(b), and examples of charges excluded from the finance charge in § 1026.4(c). Note that some of the examples in (b) describe a general category, such as "appraisal, investigation, and credit report fees," but then a subset of that general category may be excluded in part (c), e.g., appraisals and credit report fees are excluded in § 1026.4(c)(7) if they are associated with a transaction secured by real property. Credit insurance and property insurance ded in the finance charge under 8), but are excluded under meet certain prerequisites, such and properly disclosed for credit being properly disclosed and son of the consumer's choice for property insurance. Certain security interest charges, which theoretically should be considered finance charges under the general definition as a charge that would not be payable in a comparable cash transaction, nonetheless are excluded from the finance charge under § 1026.4(e), if itemized and disclosed and if certain conditions are met.

Charges that are included in the finance charge are described in 15 U.S.C. § 1605(a) and Regulation Z, 12 C.F.R. § 1026.4(b). The following charges are included in the finance charge:

(1) interest;

(2) time price differential;

(3) any amount payable under an add-on or discount system of additional charges;

(4) service, transaction, activity and carrying charges;

(5) points;

(6) loan fees;

(7) assumption fees, finder's fees and similar charges;

(8) appraisal, investigation and credit report fees;

SEC. C CLOSED-END CREDIT DISCLOSURES

(9) premiums or other charges for any guarantee or insurance protecting the creditor against the consumer's default or other credit loss;

(10) charges imposed on a creditor by another person for purchasing or accepting a consumer's obligation, if the consumer is required to pay the charges in cash, as an addition to the obligation, or as a deduction from the proceeds of the obligation;

(11) premiums or other charges for credit life, accident, health, or loss-of-income insurance, written in connection with a credit transaction, except where otherwise treated as part of the finance charge;

(12) premiums or other charges for insurance against loss of or damage to property, or against liability arising out of the ownership or use of property, written in connection with a credit transaction;

(13) discounts for the purpose of inducing payment by a means other than the use of credit; and

(14) charges or premiums paid for debt cancellation or debt suspension coverage written in connection with a credit transaction, whether or not the coverage is insurance under applicable law.

On the other hand, the following charges are *not* part of the finance charge:

(1) application fees charged to all applicants for credit, whether or not credit is actually extended;

(2) actual unanticipated late payment charges for exceeding a credit limit, or for delinquency, default or a similar occurrence;

(3) overdrawn account charges, unless previously agreed upon;

(4) charges imposed by a financial institution for paying items that overdraw an account, unless the payment of such items and the imposition of the charge were previously agreed upon in writing;

(5) fees charged for participation in a credit plan, whether assessed on an annual or other periodic basis;

(6) seller's points;

(7) discounts offered to induce payment for a purchase by cash, check or other means, as provided in Section 167(b) of the Act;

(8) other taxes and fees prescribed by law which actually are or will be paid to public officials for determining the existence of or for perfecting or releasing or satisfying any security related to the credit transaction; and

(9) in transactions secured by real property, fees for, title examination, abstract of title,

title insurance, property survey, preparing deeds and mortgages, reconveyance, settlement and similar documents, notary, appraisal, credit reports, and amounts required to be paid into escrow or trustee accounts, if the amounts would not otherwise be included in the finance charge.

b. Credit Insurance

Credit insurance products receive special treatment under TILA and Regulation Z with regard to their inclusion or exclusion in the finance charge. Their inclusion in consumer credit contracts has always been a point of controversy. Credit life insurance pays off the loan in the event of the death of the borrower. Credit disability insurance, sometimes described as "accident and health" (A & H), typically picks up the monthly payments while a debtor is disabled. Credit property insurance covers the collateral where the loan is secured. Involuntary unemployment insurance covers the monthly payments in the event the debtor loses his or her job through such things as a lay-off or plant closing. And non-filing insurance covers the interest of the secured creditor in the event the creditor is unable to retrieve the collateral (after default) due to the creditor's failure to file a financing statement. Debt cancellation or debt suspension is a type of provision whereby, for a fee, the creditor agrees to cancel the debt for amounts exceeding the value of the collateral, or to cancel or suspend the debt in the event of the loss of life, health, or income or in the case of an accident.

The controversy in consumer credit insurance comes from allegations that lenders and credit-sellers use credit insurance and related products as a way to squeeze additional revenue from the borrower, and that the credit insurance premiums should be treated as part of the finance charge, because they represent part of the "cost of credit." Consumer groups also argue that creditors tie the purchase of insurance to the extension of credit as a means of avoiding the limitations on interest under the usury laws.

Industry groups counter that credit insurance serves to protect legitimate interests of consumers and should not be included as a finance charge because the premium is for a product that has value to the consumer and is not like the stated interest on a loan. Creditors hold the view that the charge for insurance has nothing to do with the cost of credit.

TILA's approach is a compromise between these positions. Credit life or health insurance premiums are a part of the finance charge if the creditor requires the consumer to buy it. Property or liability insurance is a part of the finance charge if the creditor requires the consumer to buy it from or through the creditor. In most instances, however, the creditor will comply with the requirements specified in the law to allow them to exclude these items from the finance charge.

If the creditor complies with all of the following three requirements, credit life, accident and health insurance, and loss-of-income insurance premiums, as well as debt cancellation or debt suspension fees, do not need to be included in the finance charge. First, the creditor must not require the insurance or other related product. Second, the fact that insurance is not required by the creditor must be clearly and conspicuously disclosed in writing to the consumer. Finally, after receiving the "voluntariness" disclosure, the consumer must sign or initial the affirmative written request for insurance. 12 C.F.R. § 1026.4(d)(1) & (3).

TILA's treatment of property insurance is somewhat different. Premiums for required insurance protection against loss or damage to property do not need to be included in the finance charge. However, they can only be excluded if the creditor discloses in a clear, conspicuous, specific written statement: (1) the cost of insurance if obtained through the creditor, and (2) the freedom of the customer to choose the person from whom the insurance is to be obtained. 12 C.F.R. § 1026.4(d)(2).

The premium for non-filing insurance may be excluded from the finance charge to the extent that the premium does not exceed the filing cost that would be paid if the creditor chose to record its security interest in the public record. Taxes and fees prescribed by law that actually are or will be paid to public officials for perfecting, releasing or satisfying a security interest are also excluded from the TILA finance charge. The exclusion of these items is permitted if properly itemized and disclosed. 12 C.F.R. § 1026.4(e).

c. Hidden Finance Charges

Another controversial credit practice occurs when the cost of credit is hidden or buried in the cash price, or when credit buyers pay a higher price than cash customers, without the price difference being disclosed as a finance charge.

If a seller offers its wares for a truly unitary price, *i.e.,* the same price whether paid upfront or in installments, then it has not charged a hidden finance charge under TILA, but instead would simply be absorbing the cost of credit as part of its overhead. Official Staff Commentary, ¶ 4(a)–2. If the installments number more than four, however, that seller is still a TILA creditor and must give the relevant disclosures, 12 C.F.R. § 1026.2(a)(17), albeit they may disclose the finance charge as $0.

In many cases, dealers do not hold their installment sales contracts, but sell their paper to a finance company at a discount. For example, a car dealer may sell a car to Smith for $10,000 plus a $3,000 finance charge. This contract may be sold to Acme Finance for $9,500, a $500 discount below the $10,000 sales price. The auto dealer will make money if he bought the car at an auto auction for some amount less than $9,500. And Acme finance will make money because it paid $9,500 for an asset that will return $13,000 over the life of the loan; that is, the $10,000 amount financed and the $3,000 in interest. This so-called "discount financing," is common in used car auto finance, and most particularly in the subprime credit market.

The question that has been raised in litigation is whether the $500 discount amount should be disclosed to the borrower as a finance charge. Consumer advocates argue that the assignee's total return above the amount it paid for the contract, should be characterized and disclosed as interest because the "true" cash price being realized by the auto dealer is only $9,500. The argument is that the interest rate reflects (in part) the risk on the contract represented by the borrower, and if the assignee has insisted on the discount because the $3,000 finance charge is viewed by the finance company as being inadequate to compensate for the risk, the additional $500 should be lumped together with the $3,000 and disclosed to the borrower as the "true cost of credit."

Whether the amount of the discount which is built into the cash sales price is a finance charge under TILA has not been easy for the courts to resolve. The particular facts of the case must be analyzed, in light of the following passage from ¶ 4(a)–2 of the Official Staff Commentary:

Costs of doing business. Charges absorbed by the creditor as a cost of doing business are not finance charges, even though the creditor may take such costs into consideration in determining the interest rate to be charged or the cash price of the property or services sold. However, if the creditor separately imposes a charge on the consumer to cover certain costs, the charge is a finance charge if it otherwise meets the definition. For example, a discount imposed on a credit obligation when it is assigned by a seller-creditor to another party is not a finance charge as long as the discount is not separately imposed on the consumer.

It is important to note that under TILA, the "creditor" in an installment sales contract is the person to whom the debt is initially made payable. 15 U.S.C. § 1602(g). Thus, since the installment sales contract is initially made payable to the car dealer, although later assigned (bought) by the bank or finance company, the car dealer is the creditor who may be absorbing the discount as a cost of doing business. That is, in the auto example above, the creditor had to give up the $500 in order to get $9,500 cash for the contract, where the car was sold for $10,000.

If the dealer absorbs the loss (discount) as a cost of doing business, the discount may not be viewed as a finance charge. For example, in *Perino v. Mercury Finance*, 912 F. Supp. 313 (N.D.Ill.1995), the judge held that although the buyer of the automobile did not receive a disclosure that the paper would be sold at a discount, the alleged failure to disclose is specifically authorized by TILA and that the discount was not a finance charge but a "cost of doing business" absorbed by the creditor. On the other hand, if a dealer negotiates "inflated" cash prices with credit customers high enough to cover the discounts, but negotiates lower prices with cash customers, the dealer may have to disclose the discount as a finance charge. *Walker v. Wallace Auto Sales*, 155 F.3d 927 (7th Cir.1998). The *Walker* Court noted that a dealer need not disclose the cost of a

SEC. C   CLOSED-END CREDIT DISCLOSURES

discount as a finance charge if he recoups the discounts at which he sells the retail installment contracts by negotiating for comparable vehicles the same, relatively high price for all customers.

Automobile manufacturers commonly offer promotional APRs and/or cash rebates on their cars in order to entice customers. When both a rebate and a low APR are offered, typically the customer must forego the cash rebate in order to take advantage of the low APR. This practice has been argued to be a hidden finance charge because the end result of this type of promotion is that the customer who opts for the low APR is going to pay a higher cash price for the car because they will not qualify for the rebate. This argument has not been successful, however, because the higher cash price is not imposed solely because the consumer is buying on credit, but only because they are buying pursuant to a special credit offer. Other credit customers not taking the promotional APR can still get the rebate. *Virachack v. University Ford*, 410 F.3d 579 (9th Cir. 2005).

Discounts for cash are excluded under § 1026.4(c)(8) in specific situations covered by TILA. The Act states in pertinent part that in open-end credit (credit cards), where the seller is not the card issuer, the card issuer may not prohibit the seller from offering a discount to a cardholder to induce the cardholder to pay by cash, check, or a similar means other than a credit card. 15 U.S.C. § 1666f(a). And any discount from the regular price offered by the seller for the purpose of inducing payment by cash or check or other means not involving a credit card shall not constitute a finance charge if such discount is offered to all prospective buyers and its availability is disclosed clearly and conspicuously. 15 U.S.C. § 1666f(b). Sellers are not required to provide a discount to cash buyers, but they have the option to do so.

Thus, there is an incentive to characterize this type of deal as a "discount" for cash since such a discount can be excluded from the finance charge even though a "surcharge" for credit might be considered a finance charge. Also, many contracts between merchants and credit card issuers prohibit the use of "surcharges" for credit card use (but not discounts for cash) because it is widely believed that consumers are less likely to use their credit cards if they have to pay a surcharge, whereas they may not be so swayed by the fact that they could get a discount for cash.

Aside from the TILA treatment of discounts v. surcharges for credit cards, some states have prohibited merchants from imposing a "surcharge" for credit card sales, even though the same merchants are freely allowed to offer a discount for cash. The net economic effect on the customer of a discount for cash is the same as a surcharge for credit cards. The issue of whether such laws are an unconstitutional restriction on commercial speech was considered by the U.S. Supreme Court in *Expressions Hair Design v. Schneiderman*, 137 S. Ct. 1144 (2017). The Court held that the New York law regulating the surcharge wording was in fact a regulation of commercial speech (as opposed to conduct), but declined to rule on whether or not the law was barred by the First Amendment.

Relatively minor charges, such as a courier fee charged by a settlement agent in a real-estate transaction, are not considered hidden finance charges and may be excluded from the disclosed finance charge if it is not required by the creditor or retained by the creditor. 12 C.F.R. § 1026.4(a)(2). Also, in real-estate secured closed end transactions, errors of up to $100 in the finance charge are tolerated. 15 U.S.C. § 1606(f).

Other examples of hidden fees that are not well-handled by TILA disclosures appear to be prevalent in the subprime automobile loan sector. When low income consumers finance the purchase of inexpensive used cars, dealers (who are exempt from CFPB jurisdiction) often add "dealer reserves" to the interest rate, employ "spot delivery" as a means to get customers to accept higher interest rates, and may insist that financing is not available unless the customer agrees to unwanted "add-ons" such as rust proofing or service contracts. Dealer reserves represents the higher rate offered to the customer above what a third party creditor is willing to accept, with the dealer retaining the difference as a type of finder's fees, the auto loan equivalent to the old mortgage loan "yield spread premium." While the actual interest rate is disclosed, it is not clear to the consumer that part of this is actually a fee retained by the dealer. These practices not only make auto financing more expensive to the consumer but are often not made evident in TILA disclosures.

3. ANNUAL PERCENTAGE RATE

In addition to the finance charge discussed above, the other item that is required to be disclosed more conspicuously than other terminology is the APR, or "annual percentage rate." 12 C.F.R. § 1026.17(a)(2). The APR reflects the effective cost of credit expressed as a percentage, when declining balances are taken into account, unlike an add-on rate.

Most consumer credit transactions are multiple installment transactions. For example, suppose X and Y both borrow $1,000 for one year. Both agree to pay $100 finance charge. X is to repay the loan in one lump sum at the end of the year. Y is to repay the loan in 12 equal monthly installments. Using R = I / PT to compute the annual percentage rate, the rate in the two transactions would be identical.

The comparison would be misleading in Y's transaction, however. The formula fails to take into account the fact that Y is paying installments over the 12 months of the loan and that each installment payment reduces the amount of credit. Y, unlike X, does not have the use of the entire $1,000 for the entire year. After the first month, Y only has the use of less than the full $1,000. After the second month, Y only has the use of even less. Accordingly, the annual percentage rate disclosed to Y should be higher than the annual percentage rate disclosed to X. Therefore, something more "sophisticated" than R = I / PT must be used to compute the true cost of the credit in transactions in which the debtor pays in installments.

SEC. C   CLOSED-END CREDIT DISCLOSURES

The calculation of APR under TILA recognizes the real cost of the credit, both because of the reduction of principal over time, but also because TILA has a more inclusive definition of "finance charge" than merely the interest on a loan. For example, a state may exclude a certain fee imposed by a lender from the calculation of whether the loan is usurious, but TILA would include the fee in the calculation of the finance charge and APR if the charge is one "imposed by the creditor as a condition to the extension of credit." 15 U.S.C. § 1605(a). Thus, the APR, which is based on the more expansive definition of "finance charge," often exceeds the "interest rate" shown on the contract.

The mathematical equation and technical instructions for determining the APR in accordance with the actuarial method are set forth in 12 C.F.R. § 1026.22 & Appendix J. The Consumer Financial Protection Bureau also provides "Regulation Z Annual Percentage Rate Tables" to supplement Regulation Z. In general, the annual percentage rate disclosed in closed-end credit transactions is considered accurate if it is not more than 1/8 of 1 percentage point above or below the APR determined in accordance with the procedures outlined in the regulation. 12 C.F.R. § 1026.22(a)(2). Other (higher) tolerance levels apply to irregular transactions and mortgage loans.

4. OTHER CLOSED-END CREDIT DISCLOSURE REQUIREMENTS

a. In General

"Finance charge" and "annual percentage rate" are the most critical disclosures available to consumers in comparing the cost of credit, but they are not the only disclosures required by TILA in closed-end consumer credit transactions. Special disclosure requirements required for real estate secured transactions will be covered in the next chapter. The "triggered" disclosures for closed-end credit advertisements are covered in Chapter Three, *supra*.

The following are generally applicable additional disclosure requirements for closed-end loans, as set forth in 12 C.F.R. § 1026.18.

(a) The identity of the creditor making the disclosures must be made. Recall that the creditor is the party to whom the obligation is originally made payable.

(b) The "amount financed" must be disclosed using that term, and a brief description such as "the amount of credit provided to you or on your behalf."

(c) A separate written itemization of the amount financed must be made, including:

(1) the amount of any proceeds distributed directly to the consumer;

(2) the amount credited to the consumer's account with the creditor;

(3) any amounts paid to other persons by the creditor on the consumer's behalf.

The creditor does not need to comply with these requirements if the creditor provides a statement that the consumer has the right to receive a written itemization of the amount financed, together with a space for the consumer to indicate whether it is desired, and the consumer does not request it. 12 C.F.R. § 1026.18(c)(2).

(d) If the APR may increase after consummation in a transaction not secured by the consumer's principal dwelling, or in a transaction secured by the consumer's principal dwelling with a term of one year or less, the consumer must be informed of the circumstances under which the rate may increase, any limitations on the increase, the effect of any increase and be provided with an example of the payment terms that would result in an increase.

If the annual percentage rate may increase after consummation in a transaction secured by the consumer's principal dwelling with a term greater than one year, the consumer must be informed that the transaction has a variable rate feature and must be provided with a statement that variable rate disclosures have been provided earlier.

(e) The number, amount, and due dates or period of payments scheduled to repay the total of payments must be provided.

(f) The "total of payments," and a descriptive explanation of the term such as "the amount you will have paid when you have made all scheduled payments," must be disclosed.

(g) The creditor must disclose the demand feature, if the obligation has one.

(h) In a credit sale, the creditor must disclose the "total sale price," using that term, and a descriptive explanation (including the amount of any down payment), such as "the total price of your purchase on credit, including your down payment of $_____."

(i) Descriptive explanations of the terms "amount financed," "finance charge," "annual percentage rate," "total of payments," and "total sale price" as specified by the regulation, must be provided.

(j) The creditor must disclose whether or not a penalty will be imposed in the event of prepayment, when an obligation includes a finance charge computed from time to time by application of a rate to the unpaid principal balance.

(k) The creditor must disclose any dollar or percentage charge that may be imposed before maturity due to a late payment, other than a deferral or extension charge.

(*l*) The information required in order to exclude credit insurance from the finance charge must be provided.

(m) There must be a contract reference that the consumer should refer to the appropriate contract document for information about nonpayment, default, the right to accelerate the maturity of the obligation, and prepayment rebates and penalties.

(n) In a residential mortgage transaction the creditor must disclose whether a subsequent purchaser of the dwelling from the consumer may be permitted to assume the remaining obligation on its original terms.

(*o*) The creditor must provide a statement that the APR does not reflect the effect of the required deposit, if the creditor requires the consumer to maintain a deposit as a condition of the specific transaction.

b. Security Interests

Among other disclosures that creditors must make, they must disclose whether they have or will acquire a security interest in the property being purchased as part of the transaction or in property not purchased as part of the credit transaction. 15 U.S.C. § 1638(a)(9). The TILA disclosure is quite general. A creditor who wishes to preserve its security interest(s) may need to include a separate more detailed security interest agreement or mortgage outside of the TILA disclosures.

The regulation has a relatively narrow definition of "security interest." The term is defined as "an interest in property that secures performance of a consumer credit obligation and that is recognized by state or federal law." 12 C.F.R. § 1026.2(a)(25). It does not include "incidental interests such as interest in proceeds, accessions, additions, fixtures, insurance proceeds (whether or not the creditor is a loss payee or beneficiary), premium rebates, or interests in after-acquired property." *Id.*

If creditors err in their disclosures, they should err on the side of inclusion of disclosed security interests. Courts strictly enforce creditors' duty to disclose whether they have or will acquire a security interest in the property being purchased. For instance, in payday loan situations, the consumer must provide a post-dated check as security for the loan, and this type of security interest must be disclosed under TILA. *See, e.g., Van Jackson v. Check 'N Go of Illinois, Inc.*, 123 F. Supp. 2d 1079 (N.D. Ill. 2000).

c. Private Education Loans

In 2008, TILA was amended to add new disclosure requirements and some substantive limitations with regard to private education loans. 15 U.S.C. § 1638(e). These loans are distinct from the federal student loans that remain exempt from TILA, but which require their own set of disclosures under the Higher Education Act. The TILA amendment regarding private education loans was passed in response to reports that the private student loan industry was creating conflicts of interest with school financial aid staff by cooperating too closely with them and providing benefits to staffers or schools in return for recommending their loan programs to students.

Under TILA as amended, creditors providing private education loans are required to provide three sets of special disclosures in addition to the normal TILA disclosures. These special disclosures must be made to the prospective student borrowers at the following junctures: first, with the application or solicitation; second, when the loan is approved; and third, when the loan proceeds are disbursed. 12 C.F.R. § 1026.46. The purpose of these special disclosures is to ensure that students will be able to freely compare alternative methods of financing their education, armed with complete information about both federal and private offerings.

With the application or solicitation, the private loan creditor must disclose detailed information about the applicable interest rate or rates being offered, fees, consequences of default or late payment, repayment terms, the fact that student loans may not be later discharged in bankruptcy, a cost estimate example, eligibility requirements, alternatives to private education loans, such as federal student loan programs, and the rights and duties of the consumer with regard to the loan. 12 C.F.R. § 1026.47. These disclosures must be made within three business days after the consumer has applied. 12 C.F.R. § 1026.46(d).

Further disclosures must be made upon approval of the loan, which would include the definite terms being offered. Final disclosures must be provided after the consumer accepts the loan, and should include interest rate information, fees and default or late payment costs, repayment terms and notice of the three day right to cancel the loan without penalty. 12 C.F.R. § 1026.48.

"Co-branding" of private educational loans is prohibited. There are also limits on financial aid officials being paid by private lenders for service on advisory boards of the lender, and the lenders are prohibited from offering gifts to an educational institution in exchange for any advantage or special consideration in relation to the lender's private loan activities. 15 U.S.C. § 1650.

Private education loans make up a relatively small portion of the student loan market, as the federally issued student loans are usually more beneficial to borrowers. Nonetheless, the federal loans have caps and many students need to supplement them with private education loans. In the 2010s, so-called "fintech" companies began to act as loan brokers for student loans, setting up internet-based platforms that connect student loan applicants to private lenders, either for their initial loans or to consolidate existing loans. These lenders (or lending platforms) function completely online and use "big data" factors that go beyond traditional credit scores to determine eligibility and terms of credit. This can be helpful to students who are often "credit invisible" due to their youth and lack of credit experience. But some have criticized the use of education detail... and even social media posts to... eligibility, because these factors ma... embedded racial biases.[3] The law... reports, credit scoring and discrimin... covered in more detail in Chapter Five, *supra*.

d. Location of Disclosures

TILA, and Regulation Z at 12 C.F.R. § 1026.17(a)(1), require that the disclosures must be "segregated from everything else, and shall not contain any information not directly related" to the disclosures required by Regulation Z, 12 C.F.R. § 1026.18. This requirement was added in the 1980 Simplification Act, and is aimed at not loading consumers with so much information that it is difficult for them to understand a lot of it. It was also meant to address the issue of having the TILA disclosures mixed in with general contract terms in a way that they did not stand out sufficiently to be noticed or that was confusing to consumers.

There are some exceptions to the segregation rule. First, the itemization of the amount financed may not be included with the segregated disclosures. It must be disclosed separately. Second, the creditor may exclude any or all of the following disclosures from the segregated disclosures: (1) the creditor's identity, (2) variable-rate example, (3) insurance disclosures, and (4) security interest charges. Finally, the segregated disclosures may include any or all of the

---

[3] Christopher K. Odinet, *The New Data of Student Debt*, 92 SO. CAL. L. REV. 1617 (2019).

following: (1) acknowledgment of receipt, (2) date of the transaction, and (3) the consumer's name, address, and account number. 12 C.F.R. § 1026.17(a)(1).

The disclosures may be grouped together and segregated in a variety of ways. The segregated disclosures may appear by themselves, with other information, on the back of documents, or may be continued from one page to another. Official Staff Commentary ¶ 17(a)(1)–(3). The segregation is often accomplished by surrounding the federal disclosures with a black box to separate them from the contract terms, a format that is referred to as "the federal box."

CHAPTER SEVEN

CREDIT DISCLOSURES: OPEN-END CREDIT AND REAL ESTATE SECURED TRANSACTIONS

A. INTRODUCTION

In Chapter Six, the Truth in Lending Act was introduced, with its goal of informing consumers about the cost of credit transactions and encouraging comparison shopping. The disclosures required under TILA are organized according to the type of transaction involved. Closed-end credit, one-time extension with terms set at the outset, is the type of credit that was most basic and very prevalent at the time TILA was passed in the late 1960s. Closed-end credit disclosures form a foundation for the remaining aspects of TILA, *i.e.,* open end credit and real-estate related credit, which tend to be more complex. Also, more substantive limitations were added to the traditional disclosure approach under TILA for both open-end credit card accounts, as well as for real-estate secured credit, by federal legislation passed during 2009–2010.

This chapter will treat the federal regulation of open-end credit, mainly credit cards and home equity lines of credit, as well as real estate secured closed-end loans, and related topics.

B. OPEN-END CREDIT

1. OVERVIEW

An open-end credit plan is one under which the creditor reasonably contemplates repeated transactions, which prescribes the terms of such transactions, and which provides for a finance charge that may be computed from time to time on the outstanding unpaid balance. 15 U.S.C. § 1602(j) and 12 C.F.R. § 1026.2(a)(25). The most common form of open-end credit in the lives of most consumers is a credit card. Home equity lines of credit is also a type of open-end credit. In open-end credit, rather than disclosing a total finance charge at the execution of the contract, the creditor applies an interest rate against the unpaid balance to arrive at a monthly finance charge.

Open-end credit has increased in popularity with consumers since TILA was passed in 1968. Credit cards in particular are becoming more important than installment credit even for relatively high-priced items such as furniture and electronics. At the other end of the spectrum, consumers use credit cards for small purchases due to the convenience of swiping a card versus paying cash or writing a check. Credit cards are also useful for online or telephone purchases. By the 21st century, debit cards had also become increasingly popular for use by consumers for small purchases and for online transactions. Prepaid general-purpose debit cards fill this need particularly for the unbanked population. The regulation of debit cards is covered in Chapter Twelve.

Open end disclosures in some ways are less onerous than closed end ones, due to the lack of an overall total finance charge, but open end disclosures are more frequent than closed end, and have also become more complex due to the complexity of credit card offerings. Credit card consumers may be subject to a variety of fees, such as late fees, over-the-limit-fees, balance transfer fees and annual fees. There are also now multiple APRs applied in open-end credit, including an APR for purchases, another for cash advances, initial teaser rates, penalty rates for late payers, etc.

Open-end credit has undergone two major legislative revisions. First, the Fair Credit and Charge Card Disclosure Act was enacted into law in 1988. 15 U.S.C. § 1637(c). This law required detailed disclosures of the cost of credit to be made with credit card solicitations. Prior to 1988, consumers did not get the TILA disclosures for credit card accounts until they received the actual card in the mail. The solicitation-disclosure approach was aimed at helping consumers get information about various credit card offerings at a time when they could still shop around for the best deal.

The 2009 Credit CARD Act also contained major consumer protection reforms. This law focused on rate increases, credit card fees, payment and billing practices, and the use of credit cards by young consumers. These substantive limits on credit cards are covered in Chapter Twelve, *infra*. At about the same time, the Federal Reserve Board launched an overhaul of the formatting of open-end credit card disclosures, to improve their readability and utility to consumers.

2. SCOPE OF OPEN-END CREDIT

One of the requirements for the establishment of open-end credit is that the creditor "reasonably contemplates" repeat transactions. Consumer advocates have argued that certain creditors were trying to avoid closed-end disclosures, by setting up sales under open-end credit, even though no subsequent transactions were contemplated. The use of private label credit cards to finance door-to-door sales of satellite dishes and other "big ticket" items was a common example of alleged "spurious" open-end credit.

Despite these arguments, an influential Seventh Circuit case validated the use of open-end credit in most of these sales. In *Benion v. Bank One*, 144 F.3d 1056 (7th Cir.1998), the federal appeals court upheld the view that Bank One's expectations for repeat transactions were "reasonable." As long as the creditor could point to some objective evidence of contemplated repeat transactions, such as data for another lender's similar program, showing that repeat sales constituted more than 10 percent of total sales, the plan would satisfy the open-end credit definition. Judge Posner noted that courts should be reluctant to plug a loophole, where a regulatory agency such as the Federal Reserve Board had the regulatory expertise and the power to do so and had not done so. On the other hand, in an Alabama case in which the door-to-door seller of satellite dishes had no retail outlets and neither the seller nor the private label credit card provider did any advertising of additional services available for purchase on the card, the court declined to grant summary judgment to the seller on the open-end credit issue. *Myers v. First Tennessee Bank*, 136 F. Supp. 2d 1225 (M.D. Ala. 2001).

3. DISCLOSURES WITH SOLICITATIONS AND APPLICATIONS

For open-end credit transactions, the creditor is bound to make certain specified disclosures at three distinct times: first, with any solicitation or applications; second, at account opening; and third, periodically, in the form of periodic statements, usually issued every month. Each of these disclosures have their own specific format and content rules, which will be discussed in turn below. The "triggered" disclosures required for open-end credit advertisements are discussed in Chapter Three, *supra*.

Since 1988, TILA and Regulation Z have mandated detailed early disclosures of cost information for credit cards in an easy to read tabular format. These special disclosures are required for direct mail or email applications and solicitations, telephone solicitations and other applications and solicitations made available to the general public.

Under the law, any solicitation or application to open a credit card account under an open-end consumer credit plan that is mailed or sent electronically to consumers shall disclose the following information, in tabular format:

(1) the APR, variable rate information, discounted initial rate, premium initial rate, penalty rates, risk-based rates, and any other applicable rate;

(2) annual and other fees, such as a minimum finance charge or transaction charge;

(3) any grace period under which charges must be paid to avoid a finance charge, using the phrase "How to Avoid Paying Interest on Purchases," or the fact that one is not offered;

(4) the name of the balance calculation method if it is one defined in the regulation, or a detailed explanation of the balance calculation method used;

(5) information on cash advance fees, late fees and over-the-limit fees; and

(6) a reference to the CFPB website and a statement that consumers may obtain information about shopping for and using credit cards on that site.

See 15 U.S.C. § 1637(c); 12 C.F.R. § 1026.60(b).

The solicitation disclosures, like the disclosures in closed-end credit transactions, must be segregated from other items such as a cover letter touting the benefits of the credit card offering. The disclosures are divided into two parts, one for "interest rates and interest charges" and another for "fees." This disclosure in its tabular format is often referred to as the "Schumer" box after Senator Charles Schumer who sponsored the bill that added this requirement to TILA. Model forms are available from the CFPB to assist creditors in complying with the detailed format and substantive requirements.

The balance computation method, either by name or using an explanation, may be disclosed outside the Schumer box. Balance computation methods determine the actual balance to which the various disclosed periodic rates will be applied. The method used can make a substantial difference in the amount of the finance charge, especially for larger balances. In the aggregate, the choice of a particular balance computation method can add up to big dollars for the credit card issuers. Unfortunately, most consumers do not fully comprehend the significance of this item. Credit card issuers are allowed to use only the name of the balance computation method on the solicitation disclosure, if they use one of the methods listed in the regulation. These designated methods, which are defined within the regulation, are as follows:

- **Average daily balance (including new purchases)**—balance figured by adding the outstanding balance (including new purchases and deducting payments and credits) for each day in the billing cycle, and then dividing by the number of days in the billing cycle;

- **Average daily balance (excluding new purchases)**—balance determined by adding the outstanding balance (excluding new purchases and deducting payments and credits) for each day in the billing cycle, and then dividing by the number of days in the billing cycle;

- **Adjusted balance**—balance figured by deducting payments and credits made during the billing cycle from the outstanding balance at the beginning of the billing cycle;

- **Previous balance**—the outstanding balance at the beginning of the billing cycle; and

- **Daily balance**—for each day in the billing cycle, taking the beginning balance each day, adding any new purchases, and subtracting any payment and credits.

12 C.F.R. § 1026.60(g).

The adjusted balance method is the most favorable to consumers, whereas the previous balance method has been criticized for not giving consumers credit for payments made during the billing cycle. Average daily balance methods are widespread and are popular with creditors. If the credit card issuer wishes to use a balance calculation method that is not one of those listed in the regulation, that is permitted, but in that situation the issuer must give a detailed explanation in lieu of just using the name. The use of "two-cycle" billing, in which the periodic interest rate is applied to balances incurred in the previous billing cycle when the balance is not paid in full in the current cycle, however, has been prohibited since 2010. 15 U.S.C. § 1637j.

Solicitation disclosures must be accurate and cannot be used in a type of "bait and switch" scheme. For instance, a Third Circuit case held that a credit card solicitation that advertised "no annual fee" in a situation where it was alleged that the issuer actually intended to impose such a fee within a year of card issuance, violated the principle that solicitation disclosures must not be misleading. *Rossman v. Fleet Bank*, 280 F.3d 384 (3d Cir. 2002). The court stated that "[s]olicitation disclosures are intended to alert the consumer to the basic costs of the credit card he is considering—a purpose unserved where the issuer conceals the temporary nature of a favorable fee or rate." *Id.* at 399.

For telephone solicitations, the disclosures may be given orally, or they may be mailed within 30 days of the consumer request or the date of delivery of the card, whichever is earlier. To qualify for this later disclosure, the creditor must disclose that the consumer is not obligated to accept the card and will not be obligated to pay any fee unless he accepts the card by using it after receiving the disclosures. 12 C.F.R. § 1026.60(d). So-called "take-one" applications or solicitations made available to the general public may use an abbreviated disclosure, providing general information without any specific terms if the application or solicitation states there are costs associated with the credit card and that the applicant may contact the creditor to request the disclosure at a specified toll free telephone number or by writing to a given mailing address. The creditor may also give the detailed disclosures associated with direct mail, but must also say that the information is correct as of a specified date, is subject to change and state how the consumer can obtain current information. 12 C.F.R. § 1026.60(e).

4. ACCOUNT-OPENING DISCLOSURES

The account-opening disclosures must be provided before the first transaction by which the customer becomes obligated in the plan. In a case where a consumer simultaneously opens a plan and makes a purchase, disclosure must be made before that purchase.

Regulation Z, 12 C.F.R. § 1026.6(b)(2) lists the required disclosures to be included in the account-opening disclosures, formerly known as the "initial statement." As of 2010, the account-opening disclosures were made more accessible for consumers by requiring a tabular disclosure whose format and content are substantially similar to the solicitation disclosures discussed above, including a listing of the various APRs, the grace period ("how to avoid paying interest"), all applicable fees, and a CFPB web site reference. For both the solicitation disclosures and the account-opening disclosures, the prominence of a single APR is diminished, replaced by a more straightforward disclosure of all the rates applicable in various transactions, such as for purchases, balance transfers, cash advances, and penalty APRs. Specific disclosures must be made for variable rates and introductory, short-term rates. The use of an "historical" or "nominal" APR has been eliminated.

All charges that may be imposed as part of the open-end plan must be disclosed as follows:

(1) the conditions under which a finance charge may be imposed and an explanation of how it will be determined;

(2) the time period (if any) within which any credit extended may be repaid without incurring a finance charge;

(3) the method of determining the balance upon which a finance charge will be imposed;

(4) the method of determining the amount of the finance charge; including any minimum or fixed amount imposed as a finance charge; any service charges, such as those commonly imposed by bank check credit plans, or minimum charges, such as those imposed on some revolving charge accounts, must be disclosed;

(5) identification of other charges which may be imposed such as voluntary credit insurance, debt cancellation or debt suspension;

(6) if the indebtedness is or will be secured, a statement to that effect with an appropriate identification of the collateral; and

(7) a statement as to billing error rights and the right to assert claims and defenses.

5. PERIODIC STATEMENTS

Creditors must send periodic statements at the end of each "billing cycle" in which there is (1) a closing debit or credit balance in the account of more than $1.00, or (2) any finance charge has been imposed. Reg. Z, 12 C.F.R. § 1026.5(b)(2)(i). Neither the Act nor the regulations require the use of any particular billing cycle. The most commonly used billing cycle, though, is the calendar month. The periodic statement is quite different from either the solicitation or the account-opening disclosures, because the periodic statement is focused on the transactional activity since the prior monthly statement, and not so much on the comparison shopping function.

Extensive formatting changes for the periodic statement became effective in 2010. First, the payment due date (date by which the new balance must be paid to avoid finance charges) must be disclosed on the first page, as well as the amount of the late payment fee and any applicable penalty APR, in the form of a late payment warning. This disclosure is aimed at helping consumers avoid paying a late fee or triggering a penalty APR by giving better notice of the payment deadline and the consequences of paying late. The ending balance and the minimum payment must also be disclosed in close proximity. 12 C.F.R. § 1026.7(b)(13). A minimum payment warning, telling how long it would take to repay the balance and how much interest would accrue if only the minimum payments are made, is also required. 12 C.F.R. § 1026.7(b)(12). This warning is meant to educate consumers on the drawbacks of making only the minimum payment each month. Any changes in terms, including any increased rates, must be disclosed prominently on the front of the periodic statement. 12 C.F.R. § 1026.7(b)(7). Model forms available from the CFPB provide the best way for card issuers to comply with these disclosure and formatting requirements.

Neither TILA nor the regulations specify how soon after the end of the billing cycle the periodic statement must be sent. Yet under Regulation Z, 12 C.F.R. § 1026.5(b)(2)(ii), periodic statements must be mailed at least 21 days prior to the payment due date and the card issuer must not treat as late for any purpose a required minimum periodic payment received by the card issuer within 21 days after the mailing or delivery of the periodic statement disclosing the due date for that payment. Payments received by 5:00 PM on the due date must be posted promptly to avoid the imposition of a finance charge. If payments are not accepted on a due date, i.e., if the due date falls on a weekend or holiday, the creditor must consider as timely a payment received on the next business day. 12 C.F.R. § 1026.10(d). The payment due date for credit card accounts must be the same day each month. 15 U.S.C. § 1637(*o*)(1).

In addition to the disclosures noted above, under 15 U.S.C. § 1637(b) and 12 C.F.R. § 1026.7(b), creditors are required to make the following disclosures in each periodic statement.

(1) the beginning balance;

(2) the amount and date of each credit extension with an identification of each;

(3) the amount credited during the billing period;

(4) the amount of any minimum finance charges;

(5) each periodic rate, and the range of balances to which it applies;

(6) the finance charges attributable to each periodic rate using the term "interest charge" and the range of balances to which it applies as well as the total interest charged for the statement period and the year to date;

(7) the balance on which the finance charge is computed and how the balance was determined;

(8) the closing date of the billing cycle and the outstanding balance at the end of the period;

(9) the creditor's address for billing error purposes.

The periodic statement must also include the amount of any other non-interest charges debited to the account. These charges must be itemized and identified by type and disclosed under the heading "Fees." These "fees" include:

(1) membership fees;

(2) late charges;

(3) default or delinquency charges;

(4) charges for exceeding the credit limit on an account;

(5) fees for providing copies of documents in connection with billing error procedures;

(6) taxes imposed on the credit transaction as such;

(7) charges in connection with a real estate transaction which have been excluded from the finance charge;

(8) other charges imposed on credit transactions; and

(9) charges imposed on both cash and credit customers, to the extent that the charge to credit customers exceeds the charge to cash customers.

6. HOME EQUITY LINES OF CREDIT (HELOC)

Home equity lines of credit, or HELOCs, constitute a distinct category of open end credit. Basically a HELOC is an open-end real estate-secured credit transaction. They are subject to open-end disclosures, similar to credit cards, but also provide a three day right of rescission, similar to closed-end real estate mortgages. HELOCs allow consumers to have a credit plan that is open-end, accessed through checks or credit cards, and usually subject to variable interest rates. These plans provide consumers access to relatively large credit lines because they are secured by the existing equity in the consumer's home (i.e., the difference between the current market value and the current indebtedness). They are regulated by TILA and Regulation Z as open-end credit plans, including specific requirements for account-opening disclosures, 12 C.F.R. § 1026.6(a), and periodic statements, 12 C.F.R. § 1026.7(a). There are also special disclosure requirements applicable only to home equity plans. 12 C.F.R. § 1026.40. Since these home equity plans are often secured by the consumer's principal dwelling, they are also subject to a three-day right of rescission. 15 U.S.C. § 1635; 12 C.F.R. § 1026.15.

Home equity lines of credit emerged as a popular alternative in the consumer credit market in the late 1980s, possibly due to changes in the tax laws that favored real-estate secured interest payments as tax deductions. Yet there were some pitfalls for consumers who took on this type of credit obligation. First, open end creditors, such as credit card issuers, are allowed to change the terms over the course of the relationship, which when occurring in the context of a HELOC, could result in unexpected hardship to consumers with large balances secured by their homes. Many HELOCs also featured a "draw" period during which only interest is paid, followed by a balloon payment of the balance, which could be quite large. If the consumer could not pay or refinance a large balloon payment, the result could be the loss of the home. Also, the common use of variable interest rates in HELOCs posed some uncertainty about future payments. Congress felt that HELOC consumers should get special disclosures that would help them make informed choices about these types of transactions, and thus it amended TILA in 1988 to add these home equity credit provisions. 15 U.S.C. § 1637a.

HELOC disclosures must be given within three days of receiving an application. No nonrefundable fee may be charged in connection with such an application until three business days after the consumer receives the required disclosures. 12 C.F.R. § 1026.40(h). Since many consumers are not familiar with HELOCs and may not fully appreciate the risks involved with home-secured credit, all home equity creditors and third parties who provide applications for such plans must provide consumers with a brochure of general information about this type of credit. 12 C.F.R. § 1026.40(e). The CFPB website contains a suitable brochure than can be used by creditors to fulfill this requirement, and that can be downloaded by any interested consumer as well.

The home equity disclosures furnished with the application must be grouped together and segregated from all other unrelated information, in a manner reminiscent of the "federal box" requirement for closed end credit. There must be a highlighted disclosure that the creditor will acquire a security interest in the consumer's dwelling and that the consumer could lose his or her home in the event of default. 12 C.F.R. § 1026.40(d)(3). Other disclosures specific to the risks of home equity credit plans, such as possible balloon payments and term modifications, must also be given. Additionally, the HELOC disclosures must include information about payment terms, annual percentage rate, fees imposed by the creditor and/or third parties, negative amortization, transaction requirements, a disclaimer about tax implications, and any applicable variable rate disclosures.

Creditor termination of the plan, or unilateral changes in terms in home equity plans are not prohibited, but are limited to certain circumstances. 12 C.F.R. § 1026.40(f). Advertisements for home equity plans, like for other types of open-end credit, is also subject to triggered disclosures if the advertisement uses any of the triggering terms, such as the finance charge or payment terms. Additional disclosures are required for discounted initial rates not based on the index that will be used later, if a minimum payment will result in a balloon payment, and if the home-secured credit exceeds the fair market value of the home. 12 C.F.R. § 1026.16(d).

C. REAL ESTATE SECURED TRANSACTIONS

1. OVERVIEW

Generally, an extension of credit in which the amount financed exceeds $50,000 (or a higher figure as adjusted annually for inflation) is exempt from TILA. However, there is one major exception to this general rule. If the amount financed exceeds the normal TILA ceiling and the credit extended is secured by either *real property or by personal property used or expected to be used as the consumer's principal dwelling*, TILA disclosure and other requirements are applicable. 15 U.S.C. § 1603(3).

Consumer credit transactions secured by a consumer's dwelling are considered to be a particularly high-stakes type of transaction for most consumers. These types of loans tend to be longer in duration and larger in amount, and feature complex terms and multiple charges that make comparison shopping difficult for most people. They are also inextricably connected to the "American dream" of owning the family home. Thus under TILA this type of transaction is subject to special protective rules that go beyond those applicable to other closed-end or open-end credit transactions discussed above.

This section will focus on the special TILA and Regulation Z provisions that apply to these types of credit transactions. Note that in addition to the TILA provisions, there is also the Real Estate Settlement Procedures Act (RESPA), that provides for disclosures of settlement costs, and also prohibits kickbacks for real estate related services, and requires disclosures of good faith estimates of closing costs well ahead of the actual settlement. RESPA was formerly enforced by the Department of Housing and Urban Development but is now under the jurisdiction of the CFPB. RESPA will be discussed in more detail in Chapter Eight, *infra*.

First, there are specific timing rules applicable to home-secured loans, providing for both early, more detailed disclosures, and other expanded disclosures required three days prior to the closing. In 2010, with the passage of the Mortgage Reform and Anti-Predatory Lending Act, the previously separate and confusing disclosures required by TILA and its sister statute, the Real Estate Settlement Procedures Act (RESPA), have been combined into an integrated set of mortgage disclosures.

Second, there are specific rules for Adjustable Rate Mortgage (ARMs) disclosures, specific real estate related rules for determining the finance charge, as well as specific disclosures for interest rates and payment schedules.

Third, for certain home mortgages considered "high-cost," there are both additional disclosures required as well as substantive limitations on certain types of provisions considered particularly unfavorable to consumers. These loans, first identified and given special protections by the Home Owners Equity Protection Act (HOEPA) enacted in 1994, were mainly secondary mortgages solicited by unscrupulous lenders in conjunction with home repair contractors. In 2010, with the passage of the Mortgage Reform and Anti-Predatory Lending Act, the scope of the HOEPA provisions was significantly widened, so that it is now applicable to many more loans.

Fourth, also under the 2010 legislation, TILA now contains more substantive limits on home-secured credit transactions. These include a duty for creditors to determine that their potential borrowers have an ability to repay their obligations, combined with a "qualified mortgage" package that contains many pro-consumer provisions and also gives creditors a safe harbor for fulfilling the ability to repay requirements. Loan originators are banned from steering consumers into unfavorable loans, and broker-compensation through "yield-spread premiums" is also limited. Mortgage servicing and appraisals, businesses associated with residential mortgage credit, have also been brought under special consumer protection regulations.

Fifth, reverse mortgages in which the homeowner receives advances from a lender based on the equity in their home, are popular among older homeowners and have unique advantages and drawbacks. They have a separate regulation which attempts to provide consumer safeguards.

Each of these aspects of real estate secured consumer credit transactions will be considered in turn below. Special rules related to the advertising of home mortgage credit products are discussed in Chapter Three, *supra*.

2. SPECIAL TIMING RULES

As noted in the preceding chapter, the default rule for most closed-end credit transactions is that the TILA disclosures can be given any time prior to consummation, i.e., moments before the consumer signs the credit contract. For home mortgages, however, if credit cost disclosures were not given until the parties were about to finalize the credit transaction, this would be too late to do much good for the average consumer. Also, at the point of finalizing a relatively large real estate transaction, if the consumers did not like the disclosed costs, most would have a difficult time to decline the credit offer. For a buyer to back out of a home purchase at closing, they might have to lose their deposit, as well as losing the home in which they have psychologically invested. Thus, TILA requires that mortgage lenders give preliminary or "good faith estimates" of the costs of credit within three days of receiving the consumer's written application. 12 C.F.R. § 1026.19(e)(1)(iii).

Real estate transactions, unlike other consumer credit transactions, also involve significant charges that are due at the loan closing or "settlement," such as appraisal fees, credit checks, title insurance, origination fees, etc. The Real Estate Settlement Procedures Act (RESPA) was enacted by Congress in 1974 to require early estimated disclosures of such fees so that consumers would have advance notice of them. These disclosures were, until 2015, separate from the TILA disclosures.

Early disclosures can be quite useful to consumers contemplating a major home purchase transaction, but since there is typically a large gap in time between the loan application and the final closing, there can be significant changes in the costs. Thus, both TILA and RESPA require "final" disclosures as well as early estimated disclosures. But if there is a significant increase in costs between the estimated disclosures and the final disclosures, consumers can feel they have been duped. For instance, in the case of *Brophy v. Chase Manhattan Mort. Co.*, 947 F. Supp. 879 (E.D. Pa. 1996), there was a nearly $3,000 increase in final closing costs from the estimated disclosures. The early disclosures were upheld as being made in good faith, despite the discrepancies, because the mere change alone was insufficient to prove a lack of good faith.

Under current law, effective in 2015, the combined TILA/RESPA good faith estimates of both credit costs and closing costs must be made within three business days after the creditor receives the consumer's written application, for most closed-end consumer mortgages (and at least seven days prior to consummation). 12 C.F.R. § 1026.19(e)(1)(iii). These integrated early disclosures are called a "Loan Estimate," and must be provided by either the mortgage broker or the creditor. This requirement covers any mortgage loan secured by a consumer's dwelling, including home improvement loans, vacation homes, or refinancing. It does not include home equity lines of credit, reverse mortgages, timeshares, or mortgages secured by a mobile home or dwelling not attached to real property. Consumers cannot be charged any application fee until they receive the early TILA/RESPA combined disclosures. 12 C.F.R. § 1026.19(e)(2)(i).

The integrated TILA/RESPA disclosures, promulgated by the CFPB as required by the Dodd-Frank Act, were designed to enhance consumer understanding of the complex details involved in home financing. They have been dubbed the "Know Before You Owe" program. The CFPB also provides consumers with various resources and reference tools to assist them in using the revised disclosures to comparison shop for mortgage loans.

The content of the Loan Estimate disclosure includes: general information about the loan terms and costs; a description of various clauses as applicable, such as negative amortization, balloon payments, and prepayment penalties; a breakdown of projected payments and potential adjustments that may occur over time; detailed closing costs; adjustable rate and interest tables, contact information, and a cost comparison chart. 12 C.F.R. § 1026.37. For adjustable rate loans, special information about adjustable rate payments and interest rates must also be included.

As of 2015, there is also a required, combined "Closing Disclosure," replacing the HUD-1 form and the final TILA disclosures, that must be provided at least three business days prior to closing. 12 C.F.R. § 1026.19(f). This creates in effect a three-day waiting period between the receipt of the final disclosures and the actual closing, meant to allow the consumer sufficient time to read and understand the disclosures before committing to the loan. The consumer can waive the waiting period if the credit is needed to meet a bona fide personal financial emergency, subject to certain procedural safeguards. 12 C.F.R. § 1016.19(e)(1)(v). If there are significant changes, such as an over 1/8 of a percentage point change in the APR, a change in the loan product (e.g., fixed rate loan to variable rate loan), or the addition of a prepayment penalty, between the "closing disclosure" and the actual closing, the creditor will have to provide a new three-day waiting period. Other less significant changes can be disclosed at the settlement

As discussed above, given the normally lengthy period of time between receipt of a mortgage loan application and the final closing, some of the early disclosures may be subject to change prior to consummation, and thus there are the final or "closing disclosures." However, the early disclosures must be made in good faith and there are limits as to how much of a change there can be in the various categories to ensure that a good faith estimate has been made. For instance, if a third party service fee increases by less than 10%, it is presumed to be in good faith. Other items, such as interest, insurance premiums, escrow amounts, etc., will be considered to have been made in good faith if they were consistent with information reasonably available at the time of disclosure and the revisions are caused by changed circumstances, or revisions requested by the consumer, among other things. 12 C.F.R. § 1026.19(e)(3). While there is still some room for significant changes, these guidelines provide more certainty as to what is or is not a good faith estimate.

The content of the Closing Disclosure is somewhat similar to the Loan Estimate, and includes a comparison of the amounts disclosed in the Loan Estimate to those same items in the Closing Disclosure. The CFPB has published model forms for both the Loan Estimate and Closing Disclosure. The model forms were based on consumer research aimed at helping consumers read and understand the disclosures. Nonetheless, these forms are quite lengthy and contain much complex, albeit quite useful, information.

3. SPECIFIC REAL ESTATE DISCLOSURE RULES

Many home mortgages feature variable rates and are known as ARMs (adjustable rate mortgages).

Such mortgages, including most subprime ones, have a rate set by adding a specific number, the margin, to another number, the index. The index is typically controlled by an entity separate from the lender, such as the LIBOR or the prime rate as published in the Wall Street Journal. With ARMs, it is impossible to know in advance the exact cost of a mortgage loan because the rate is subject to changing over the course of the loan in ways that are not necessarily predictable. Thus, TILA provides special disclosure rules for ARMs, which include a Consumer Handbook and information about each variable rate program in which the consumer has expressed an interest which must be provided with the application. 12 C.F.R. § 1026.19(b). Under the rules that went into effect in 2015, the Loan Estimate and Closing Disclosure must include tables showing a range of projected payments through the loan term, as well as an adjustable payment table and adjustable interest rate table. 12 C.F.R. § 1026.37(i) & (j); & .38(m) & (n). For ARMs, there is no total finance charge nor total of payments, unlike other closed-end credit transactions.

The finance charge, which can be determined for fixed rate mortgages, has some special rules under TILA. Prepaid finance charges, or "points" (one point for each percent) are common in such transactions. Points or other loan fees generally must be disclosed as part of the finance charge, but "seller's points," or points paid by the seller, are excluded from the finance charge, even if they are passed on to the buyer in the form of a higher sale price. 12 C.F.R. § 1026.4(c)(5).

Certain settlement charges are specifically excluded from the finance charge disclosed under TILA, if they occur in a transaction secured by real property or in a residential mortgage transaction, provided the fees are bona fide and reasonable in amount. The charges thus excluded are: fees for title examination, title abstract, title insurance, property survey; fees for document preparation in connection with settlement; notary, appraisal and credit report fees; and amounts paid in escrow or trustee accounts, 12 C.F.R. § 1026.4(c)(7).

Given the great variety of applicable interest rates and payments that may be found in various modern real-estate secured loans, such as adjustable rates, step rates, interest only payments, and balloon payments, the normal TILA payment schedule and APR/finance charge disclosures were deemed inadequate to fully apprise consumers of these aspects of their loans. Thus, for most closed-end consumer credit transactions secured by real-property, creditors must provide both early and final disclosures of an interest rate and payment summary in table form. 12 C.F.R. §§ 1026.37(c) and .38(c). There is also a required warning that there is no guarantee that a consumer can refinance the transaction to lower the interest rate or periodic payment at a later time. 12 C.F.R. § 1026.18(t).

In addition, real-estate specific disclosures must include aggregate settlement charges, the total of fees paid to a mortgage originator, and the total amount of interest over the life of the loan as a percentage of the principal. 15 U.S.C. §§ 1638(a)(17),

(18) and (19). For step-rate mortgages, where the interest rate will change by a set amount after a set period of time, as well as for adjustable rate mortgages, the disclosure must show the interest rate at consummation and the period of time until the first interest rate adjustment may occur, the maximum interest rate applicable during the first five years, the earliest date on which that rate may apply, and the maximum interest rate that may apply over the life of the loan. The disclosures must also show how the payments may change with changes in interest rates.

A negative amortization loan is one in which the payment of minimum periodic payments will result in an increase in the principal balance because the payment covers only a portion of the accrued interest and none of the principal. For such loans, special disclosures showing both the minimum payment and the fully amortizing payment must be made. Note that such negative amortization loans are not allowed for "qualified mortgages" or HOEPA loans, discussed in more detail below.

4. HIGH-COST (HOEPA) LOANS

Congressional concern for abuses in the home mortgage market predated the 2010 Mortgage Reform and Anti-Predatory Lending Act. Indeed, the Home Ownership and Equity Protection Act of 1994 (HOEPA) amended TILA to prevent a number of the predatory lending practices found in mortgage lending, particularly in the subprime credit market where interest rates were very high and transactions often packed with credit insurance products and other add-ons. The lenders targeted by HOEPA basically sought to strip the equity from the home by making loans that the borrower could not afford to pay, thus leading to foreclosure. The original version of HOEPA, while somewhat helpful, proved to be too restricted in scope to have much effect. Thus, the 2010 legislation widened the reach of the protective provisions, added other substantive protections for borrowers in this category and brought this type of lending under the auspices of the CFPB.

Although the original legislation was limited to secondary mortgages, the expanded legislation now also covers purchase-money loans and open-end credit plans secured by the consumer's principal dwelling. 15 U.S.C. § 1602(bb); 12 C.F.R. § 1026.32(a). Coverage by HOEPA is also limited to loans that meet certain APR and points and fees "triggers." These triggers, as discussed below, were originally set too high to result in much coverage, with lenders structuring otherwise troublesome loans in ways that could evade the HOEPA provisions. Thus, HOEPA's relatively aggressive consumer protections were not applicable to many of the loans that led to the foreclosure crisis of the late 2000s. As of the 2010 amendments, most of which became effective in 2014, however, HOEPA coverage is now much more inclusive.

Most consumer credit transactions secured by the consumer's principal dwelling will be subject to HOEPA if the transaction qualifies under either the APR trigger or the points and fees trigger, or the prepayment penalty trigger. Thus, such loans will be covered by HOEPA if the APR at the time of consummation exceeds by more than 6.5 percentage points the applicable Average Prime Offer Rate (APOR) for first lien mortgages, or exceeds the APOR by more than 8.5 percentage points for subordinate mortgages and first-lien mortgages of personal property with a loan amount of less than $50,000. 12 C.F.R. § 1026.32(a)(1)(i). For mortgage loans with adjustable interest rates or step rate provisions, coverage will be determined based on the APR resulting from application of the maximum margin applied to the initial index value, or the maximum interest rate that may be imposed during the term of the loan.

The second HOEPA "trigger" is based on the ratio of the points and fees to the total loan amount. Where the total charge for points and fees exceeds 5 percent of the total loan amount, HOEPA will be triggered for loans over $20,000. The third alternative trigger, which was added in the 2010 legislation, is the prepayment penalty trigger. This trigger applies to transactions that permit the creditor to charge prepayment fees or penalties more than 36 months after the transaction closing or if the prepayment penalties exceed more than 2% of the amount prepaid. 15 U.S.C. § 1602(bb)(1)(A).

Points and fees for purposes of calculating the HOEPA trigger are defined broadly, including more items than the finance charge, and are also applicable to open-end credit secured by a consumer's principal dwelling. The relevant definition of points and fees includes:

(a) all items included in the finance charge for the loan, other than interest and any time-price differential;

(b) all compensation paid directly or indirectly by a consumer or creditor to mortgage brokers (thus including Yield Spread Premiums and other indirect compensation);

(c) all settlement costs, unless the charges are reasonable, the creditor receives no direct or indirect compensation and the charge is paid to a third party unaffiliated with the creditor;

(d) premiums for credit life insurance and similar products if payable at or before closing; and

(e) prepayment penalties.

15 U.S.C. § 1602(bb)(4) & (5); 12 C.F.R. § 1026.32(b)(1) & (2).

If HOEPA is triggered, there are certain disclosures that must be made. These disclosure requirements are in addition to disclosures that are mandated by other provisions of TILA.

The following disclosures must be made in conspicuous type:

(a) "You are not required to complete this agreement merely because you received these disclosures or have signed a loan application."

(b) "If you obtain this loan, the lender will have a mortgage on your home. You could lose your home and any money you have put into it, if you do not meet your obligations under the loan."

15 U.S.C. § 1639(a)(1). Other special HOEPA disclosures are also required, as shown on the CFPB model disclosure form. Creditors are also required to obtain confirmation that the consumer has received approved counseling on the advisability of the mortgage prior to extending credit subject to HOEPA. 15 U.S.C. § 1639(u).

Disclosures required by HOEPA must be given at least three days prior to closing. This constitutes a "cooling-off" period that prevents the prior practice of certain unscrupulous lenders who would try to close a home-secured loan on the same day as they first presented a home owner with the TILA disclosures. HOEPA borrowers are also entitled to a three-day right of rescission in addition to the three-day waiting period.

In transactions covered by HOEPA, several types of onerous provisions are prohibited, although there is no set cap on interest rates or fees.

Prepayment penalties are prohibited for HOEPA loans, and the exceptions allowed prior to 2014 have been eliminated. 15 U.S.C. § 1639(c). A prepayment penalty is a charge to the debtor for paying all or part of the principal of the loan amount before the date on which the principal is due. Such penalties had often made it difficult for borrowers to refinance unfavorable loans. Other prohibited terms or practices for HOEPA loans include: default interest rates, balloon payments (subject to certain narrow exceptions), and negative amortization. 15 U.S.C. § 1639(d), (e) & (f). There are also limits on extending credit without regard to the consumer's ability to repay, as well as limits on refinancing by the same lender within one year.

There are special provisions in HOEPA dealing with payments to home improvement contractors.[1] Under 15 U.S.C. § 1639(i), when a creditor finances a home improvement contract, payments in covered loans may not be made in an instrument payable directly to the contractor alone. The payment must be made either to the consumer only or in a jointly payable instrument.

Violations of HOEPA can lead to enhanced remedies for the consumer. Assignees are subject to a greater liability than they are for other types of TILA violations. 15 U.S.C. § 1641(d). The right of rescission is extended by either disclosure or substantive violations. Statutory damages are somewhat increased. 15 U.S.C. § 1640(a)(4). In addition, provisions are made for state attorneys general to enforce the statute. 15 U.S.C. § 1640(e).

---

[1] For a discussion of problems in home improvement lending, *see* Gene A. Marsh, *Lender Liability for Consumer Fraud Practices of Retail Dealers and Home Improvement Contractors*, 45 Ala. L. Rev. 1 (1993).

5. SUBSTANTIVE LIMITS ON ALL HOME-SECURED CREDIT TRANSACTIONS

While TILA has traditionally been focused on disclosure type regulation, the law took a huge step toward more substantive regulation with the passage of the Mortgage Reform and Anti-Predatory Lending Act of 2010.[2] Prior to this legislation, only high cost HOEPA loans were subject to substantive as well as disclosure requirements. These new provisions, applicable to a wide range of home-secured real estate transactions, became effective in 2014. The major substantive real estate credit related provisions to be discussed in this section include: ability to repay and "qualified" mortgages; loan originator compensation (Yield Spread Premiums); prepayment penalties and other prohibited clauses such as mandatory pre-dispute arbitration clauses; mortgage servicing; and appraisals.

The financial crisis leading up to the 2010 legislation was marked by stories of homeowners who took out mortgages they ultimately could not afford, based in part on relatively low introductory rates, and on the hope or unfounded belief that home prices would rise indefinitely. When payment levels increased and home prices fell off sharply, along with a rise in unemployment, the subprime mortgage market experienced a significant rise in foreclosures. In response to this situation, TILA now provides:

---

[2] *See* Dee Pridgen, *Putting Some Teeth in TILA: From Disclosure to Substantive Regulation in the Mortgage Reform and Anti-Predatory Lending Act of 2010*, 24 LOY. CONSUMER L. REV. 615 (2012).

[N]o creditor may make a residential mortgage loan unless the creditor makes a reasonable and good faith determination based on verified and documented information that, at the time the loan is consummated, the consumer has a reasonable ability to repay.

15 U.S.C. § 1639c(a)(1).

This requirement is also aimed at eliminating so-called "no-doc" or "low-doc" loans in which the borrower's qualifications were either not documented or were exaggerated, often resulting in an unfortunate overextension by the consumer. To determine the borrower's ability to repay, the regulation as amended requires the creditor to take into account the following: current or reasonably expected income or assets; current employment status; monthly payment on the mortgage loan at issue as well as monthly payments on any simultaneous loan and payments for other related obligations; current debt obligations, such as credit cards, alimony or child support; monthly debt-to income ratio; and credit history. 12 C.F.R. § 1026.43(c)(2).

The ability to repay regulation was extended by Congress in 2018 to cover an innovative type of home-secured financing called Property Assessed Clean Energy (PACE) financing, in which homeowners can finance energy saving improvements through a special local tax assessment. Congress directed the

CFPB to issue implementing regulations, which were still in progress as of 2020.[3]

In what appears to be a regulatory "nudge" to incentivize creditors to offer loans that have provisions more favorable to consumers, the statute provides a "safe harbor" from the "ability to repay" requirements for creditors who offer residential mortgage loans that fit the blueprint of a "qualified" mortgage. 15 U.S.C. § 1639c(b). The safe harbor is a conclusive presumption of compliance with the ability-to-repay provisions for most loans, but is only a rebuttable presumption for higher-priced loans that exceed the average prime rate for comparable transactions by more than 1.5% for first-lien transactions, and more than 3.5% for subordinate-lien transactions. 12 C.F.R. § 1026.43(b)(4).

A "qualified mortgage" must have the following characteristics:

- Principal balance does not increase over the term of the loan (no negative amortization);
- No deferment of principal repayment (no interest only loans);
- No balloon payments (with limited exceptions);
- The consumer's income and financial resources are documented;

---

[3] Economic Growth, Regulatory Relief, and Consumer Protection Act, Pub. L. No. 115–174, 132 Stat. 1206, § 307 (2018).

- The creditor uses fully amortizing rates for fixed or variable rate loans;

- The creditor complies with debt-to-income guidelines (consumer's total monthly debt to total monthly income does not exceed 43 percent);

- Total points and fees are not more than 3% of the total loan amount; and

- The term of the loan is not greater than 30 years.

12 C.F.R. § 1026.43(e)(2) & (3).

TILA, as amended, also restricts the method of compensation that mortgage originators may use. As the regulation states: "in connection with a consumer credit transaction secured by a dwelling, no loan originator shall receive and no person shall pay to a loan originator, directly or indirectly, compensation in an amount that is based on a term of a transaction. . . ." 12 C.F.R. § 1026.36(d)(1). Thus, the practice of taking "yield spread premiums," (YSPs) from lenders is prohibited, with some limited exceptions. With YSPs, the broker was paid a bonus by the lender for bringing in a loan that had a higher interest rate than the "par" or otherwise available rate. The objections to this previously prevalent method of compensation for mortgage brokers were twofold. First, by keying the broker's compensation to the interest rate, the broker had an incentive to steer the consumer into higher interest loans, while the consumer may have qualified for a lower rate. Second, the average consumer was under the impression that the broker was working only in the consumer's best interest, and was unaware that the broker was being paid by the lender. The regulation also prohibits so-called "dual compensation" in which the broker is paid both through upfront fees from the consumer, as well as YSP compensation from the lender. 12 C.F.R. § 1026.36(d)(2). These two provisions resolve years of controversy over mortgage broker compensation in the form of YSPs.

As part of the 2010 legislation, TILA was also amended to prohibit or severely limit specific mortgage practices deemed unfair to consumers, including prepayment penalties, financing of single premium credit insurance products and pre-dispute mandatory arbitration clauses.

First, prepayment penalties, which were very common in subprime mortgage loans prior to the foreclosure crisis in the late 2000s, are penalties charged to the borrower for repaying the loan prior to its due date. These penalties, which help lenders recoup fees they may have paid to brokers, also had the effect of locking borrowers into high-cost loans. Such penalties are now prohibited for residential mortgage loans that are not "qualified mortgages," that have adjustable rates, or that have higher than average APRs. For "qualified mortgages," prepayment penalties are limited and are not allowed at all after the third year. 15 U.S.C. § 1639c(c)(1) & (3); 12 C.F.R. § 1026.43(g)(1) & (2).

Second, the financing of "single premium" credit insurance products is banned for all loans secured by a dwelling, both open and closed end. 15 U.S.C.

§ 1639c(d); 12 C.F.R. § 1026.36(i). Such insurance financing imposed large upfront premiums that became part of the overall debt, but typically would not benefit consumers if they paid off their loan early.

Third, TILA now prohibits pre-dispute mandatory arbitration clauses in all dwelling secured closed-end consumer loans, and all open-end consumer loans secured by the consumer's principal dwelling. The statute also prohibits waivers of the right to bring suit for a statutory cause of action. 15 U.S.C. § 1639c(e)(1) & (3); 12 C.F.R. § 1026.36(h)(1) & (2). Such clauses were criticized for leading to the forfeiture of the consumer's right to go to court to adjudicate their TILA claims.

Mortgage servicers are the intermediaries between the lender and the borrower who perform the routine tasks of receiving payments, managing escrow accounts, and communicating with residential mortgage borrowers. They also perform duties with regard to handling defaults and often have the discretion to determine whether to foreclose or work out a loss mitigation arrangement for borrowers in default. In the lead-up to the subprime mortgage foreclosure crisis, consumers complained of many issues involving the previously unregulated mortgage servicing industry, including lack of warning of steep payment increases resulting in "payment shock," lack of responsiveness to requests for information, and lack of information about their payment schedules and loss mitigation options upon default, among other things.

Thus, the 2010 legislation resulted in extensive regulation of the mortgage servicing industry under RESPA and its Regulation X. The regulations became effective in 2014, and attempt to address these issues. 12 C.F.R. §§ 1024.39 to .40. The mortgage servicing regulations are actively enforced by the CFPB. They include requirements for special advance notices of upward payment resets, issuance of periodic statements, special provisions regarding escrow accounts, prompt crediting of payments, and prompt responses to requests for payoff amounts. Mortgage servicers are also required to work with borrowers to provide information and assistance with loss mitigation programs that might help prevent unnecessary foreclosures.

Property appraisals are a critical factor in determining the selling price of a home and the amount of credit that a lender will provide to the home buyer. An inflated appraisal can lead a buyer to pay too much for a home, and to incur more debt than necessary. Such appraisals can also contribute to foreclosures or other types of financial distress when borrowers, who borrowed more than the property was objectively worth, end up owing more on the mortgage than the property can sell for. It was widely reported that some mortgage brokers in the subprime market were coercing appraisers into misrepresenting home values in order to raise their own commissions.

In response to these concerns, TILA now imposes "appraisal independence requirements" in all consumer credit transactions secured by the principal dwelling of the consumer. 15 U.S.C. § 1639e; 12 C.F.R. § 1026.42. Coercion of appraisers and misrepresentations of value are prohibited. Further appraisal requirements are imposed on certain "higher-risk" or "higher priced" mortgages, defined as mortgages secured by a consumer's principal dwelling, that has an APR exceeding the average prime offer rate for comparable transactions by 1.5 to 3.5%. 15 U.S.C. § 1639h(f); 12 C.F.R. § 1026.35(c)(4). For such mortgages the creditor is required to obtain a written appraisal by a certified appraiser who conducts a physical property visit, which the consumer receives without charge at least three days prior to the transaction closing date, among other requirements.

6. REVERSE MORTGAGES

A so-called "reverse mortgage" is a special type of home loan targeted to older (62 or older) homeowners who have built up equity in their homes and wish to draw out the value of the equity and defer repayment of the loan until they either die, sell the home or move out. This type of loan provides an alternative to the Home Equity Line of Credit (HELOC) discussed earlier, in that the reverse mortgage pays out the proceeds of the loan without requiring immediate payments. The recipients of such a loan remain responsible for paying the property taxes and homeowner's insurance. The payout can be in the form of an annuity or can be in a lump sum (up to 60% of the loan in the first year). The goal of these loans is to allow homeowners to "age in place" by keeping their homes and gaining some cash or a stream of income for expenses in retirement based on their home equity.

Reverse mortgages, also called Home Equity Conversion Mortgages (HECMs), are insured by the FHA, and are regulated under both TILA and the FHA (through the Department of Housing and Urban Development or HUD). Regulation Z requires a special set of disclosures specifically for reverse mortgages. 12 C.F.R. § 1026.33. The total costs of the loan must be given in the form of a table at least three days prior to consummation. Because the cost of the loan will vary with the appreciation of the property and the life expectancy of the borrower, the projected cost must be given in matrix form with various alternatives shown.

The HUD regulation contains provisions on the qualifications needed to take out a reverse mortgage, such as being at least 62, having no outstanding debts on the home, having the financial resources to pay ongoing property taxes and insurance, and continuing to live in the home. Consumers must also receive free or low cost counseling prior to receiving this type of loan. If the borrower/homeowner dies, moves out or sells, the loan becomes due immediately. In the past, this could displace spouses who were not actually borrowers, often because the spouse was not 62 when the loan was taken out by an older homeowner spouse. Under revisions to the HUD regulation effective in 2015, such spouses are allowed to remain in the home as long as it is their primary residence and taxes and insurance are paid. 24 C.F.R. Part 206. Rule changes announced in 2017 reduced the amount of the loan proceeds that can be accessed by the borrower in a reverse mortgage. The rule changes also require borrowers in many cases to set aside funds up front to pay property tax and insurance premiums, since failure to pay such charges had resulted in widespread foreclosures in the years leading up to the rule change.

In 2012, the Consumer Financial Protection Bureau (CFPB) issued a report on reverse mortgages that found the terms of reverse mortgages are too complex for most borrowers to understand, despite the disclosures required under TILA and Regulation Z and despite the availability of counseling. They also found that most borrowers were opting for a lump sum payout, rather than an annuity, and that the barrage of television and other types of advertisements for these credit products were often misleading. For example, claims that the loans required "no payments" led many homeowners to overlook the fact that they still had to pay their property taxes and property insurance themselves, items that previously had been included in their mortgage payments. The CFPB has settled cases against several mortgage brokers and lenders who have falsely claimed that their reverse mortgage products were affiliated with the federal government. *See, e.g., CFPB v. All Financial Services, LLC*, Case 15:-CV-420-BPG, Stipulated Final Judgment (D. Md. 10/15/15), available at http://consumerfinance.gov.

CHAPTER EIGHT
TRUTH IN LENDING ENFORCEMENT AND RELATED STATUTES

A. INTRODUCTION

Chapter Seven summarized the requirements of the Truth in Lending Act with regard to open end credit (credit cards and HELOCs) and real estate secured consumer credit transactions. In this chapter, the enforcement of TILA will be discussed, both government enforcement and consumer remedies. Consumer remedies include a private right of action for TILA violations, with actual and statutory damages, attorney's fees and class actions. Creditor defenses will also be covered. The right to rescind certain real estate secured transactions, a different type of consumer remedy, will also be discussed. Finally, several statutes that are related to TILA and consumer credit transactions will be summarized. These statutes include the Truth in Savings Act, the Consumer Leasing Act, the Interstate Land Sales Full Disclosure Act, and the Real Estate Settlement Procedures Act.

B. FEDERAL ENFORCEMENT OF TILA

The Consumer Financial Protection Bureau (CFPB), the agency established by the 2010 Dodd-Frank Act, is charged with both rulemaking and enforcement of the Truth in Lending Act, as well as related consumer credit laws. 12 U.S.C. §§ 5561 to 5566. The Federal Trade Commission (FTC) retains its authority, concurrent with the CFPB, to enforce the federal consumer credit laws as to entities within the FTC's jurisdiction, which excludes banks but includes retailers who sell on credit and commercial lenders other than banks. The FTC also retains sole jurisdiction over motor vehicle dealers, which are exempt from CFPB oversight. 12 U.S.C. § 5519.

Prior to 2010, federal enforcement of TILA was shared by various bank regulatory agencies, the Federal Reserve Board and the FTC. The Federal Reserve Board had the sole rulemaking authority. The consolidation of both rulemaking and enforcement power under the CFPB was meant to strengthen the protection of consumers by not splitting the authority among multiple agencies, most of which did not have a focus on consumer protection.

Under 15 U.S.C. § 1607(b), a violation of any requirement of Truth in Lending (including Regulation Z) is also a violation of the Act under which the agency exercises power over creditors regulated by it. Thus, for example, any powers which the FTC can exercise against a violator of the Federal Trade Commission Act can also be exercised against a violator of Truth in Lending. 15 U.S.C. § 1607(e). The enforcing agencies are also allowed to order creditors in serious violation of the Act to adjust accounts of consumers so that they do not have to pay a higher finance charge (or APR) than was disclosed to them. 15 U.S.C. § 1607(e). The CFPB has supervisory powers with regard to very large banks, savings associations and credit unions, as well as

SEC. B FEDERAL ENFORCEMENT OF TILA

certain non-depository entities. 12 U.S.C. §§ 5514 & 5515. This authority means that the CFPB staff can periodically examine records, request information, and conduct onsite visits to determine if a financial institution is in compliance with applicable federal consumer financial laws. This type of activity can often result in compliance without the need to litigate.

Both the FTC and more recently the CFPB have also been very active in bringing administrative cases to enforce the TILA, most of which have resulted in settlements. Many TILA enforcement cases also involve allegations of unfair, deceptive, or abusive practices, as well as other statutory violations. The CFPB has challenged major credit card companies with deceptive marketing of credit card "add-on" products, has joined with state prosecutors to challenge pawnbrokers that understated the APR for small loans secured by personal property, and also sued student loan servicers for deceiving student borrowers regarding repayment options, among other far-reaching cases. While the FTC can obtain restitution only if it goes to court for an injunction, the CFPB in its administrative enforcement of TILA as well as other statutes, has the specific statutory authority to extract civil penalties for violations. The CFPB was very assertive in enforcing TILA in the early years of its existence, but its enforcement levels have significantly decreased with the change in administration resulting from the 2016 election, and the resignation of the CFPB's first Director, Richard Cordray.[1]

The most potent type of TILA enforcement, criminal prosecution, is also the least used. The Act makes it a crime for a creditor to "willfully and knowingly" give false or inaccurate information or to fail to make disclosures required by the Act. Violators are subject to a fine of not more than $5,000 or imprisonment for not more than one year, or both, for each violation of the Act. 15 U.S.C. § 1611. The Department of Justice is responsible for enforcement of these criminal sanctions.

As a practical matter, 15 U.S.C. § 1611 is unlikely to lead to many criminal convictions of creditors in violation of the Act. Federal district attorneys are generally faced with a heavy enough caseload that ferreting out Truth in Lending violators does not rank high on their list of priorities.

C. CONSUMER REMEDIES

1. PRIVATE ACTIONS—OVERVIEW

Private consumer actions under 15 U.S.C. § 1640 historically have been the most effective method of enforcing the disclosure requirements of Truth in Lending. To recover, a consumer must establish: (1) the transaction comes within the Truth in Lending regime; and (2) the creditor failed to comply with the

---

[1] Christopher L. Peterson, *Dormant: The Consumer Financial Protection Bureau's Law Enforcement Program in Decline*, Consumer Federation of America, Washington, D.C., published 03/12/2019.

Act or Regulation Z. The consumer need not show that the creditor's violation resulted in any injury or that it led to the consumer's decision to enter into the credit transaction. Nor must the consumer show that the creditor intended or knew about the violation or that the consumer was deceived. Furthermore, even the slightest, technical violation may be actionable. Note that in recent years, the number of private consumer actions enforcing TILA have been somewhat reduced by the prevalence of mandatory arbitration clauses and class action waivers contained in consumer credit contracts, as well as federal standing requirements and the doctrine of detrimental reliance. TILA violations give rise to several remedies: actual damages, individual statutory damages, class action statutory damages, and attorney fees, each of which are discussed below.

2. STANDING TO BRING CLAIMS FOR DAMAGES

Creditor liability arises when a creditor fails to comply with disclosure requirements "with respect to any person." 15 U.S.C. § 1640(a). Usually, the person seeking remedies is a "consumer" who is the primary obligor in the credit transaction.[2] However, the definition of "person" includes a natural individual or an organization. 15 U.S.C. § 1602(d). Courts have held that the phrase "with respect to any person"

---

[2] A "consumer" is a cardholder or a natural person to who consumer credit is offered or extended. (For purposes of the right to rescind, the definition is expanded.) 15 U.S.C. § 1602(e); 12 C.F.R. § 1026.2(a)(11).

need not be limited to consumers or primary obligors.[3]

Statutory and actual damages are generally available for any violation of TILA Part B (credit transactions), with some exceptions for certain disclosure items.[4] In addition, they are available for violations of Part D (credit billing) and Part E (consumer leases). Statutory damages are available for violations of the general requirements that disclosures must be clear and conspicuous and timely given, as well as for violations of the rescission requirements. On the other hand, there is no liability for either actual or statutory damages for violations of Part C (credit advertising).

Standing to sue in federal court is required by Article III of the U.S. Constitution, and lack of such standing has proved to be an obstacle to consumer plaintiffs seeking recovery of statutory damages under TILA as well as other statutes. The rise of the standing issue in consumer credit cases can be traced to the landmark case of *Spokeo, Inc. v. Robins*, 136 S. Ct. 1540 (2016) which dealt with a Fair Credit Reporting Act claim, as discussed in more detail in Chapter Five, *supra*. *Spokeo* held that to satisfy federal standing requirements, there must be an

---

[3] *See, e.g., Barash v. Gale Employees Credit Union*, 659 F.2d 765 (7th Cir.1981); *Maddox v. St. Joe Papermakers Federal Credit Union*, 572 So.2d 961 (Fla.Dist.Ct.App.1990).

[4] 15 U.S.C. §§ 1631–1651. The exceptions are for some specific open-end disclosures (§ 1637) and some of the closed-end disclosure requirements (§ 1638).

"injury-in-fact" stemming from the law violation, and that injury must be both concrete and particularized.

This ruling was applied by the Second Circuit to a TILA class action, *Strubel v. Comenity Bank*, 842 F.3d 181 (2d Cir. 2016) in which the consumer plaintiffs were seeking statutory damages for several disclosure violations involving a credit card account. The reviewing court applied a painstaking analysis of whether there was a "risk of real harm" from each of the four alleged violations and found only two were satisfactorily "concrete" to provide standing to sue. Other TILA cases filed in federal court and alleging statutory damages have been dismissed for lack standing.[5] Note that Article III standing applies only to cases filed in federal court, and not to those in state court, but federal court is where most TILA consumer class actions are litigated.

3. STATUTORY DAMAGES

The measure of damages in an individual action under TILA is actual damages plus a statutory penalty. 15 U.S.C. § 1640(a). The statutory damage provision is meant to provide an economic spur for creditor compliance with the Act's requirements, and to encourage consumers to act as "private attorneys general" to promote enforcement. *See, e.g., Rodash v. AIB Mortgage Co.*, 16 F.3d 1142 (11th Cir.1994). Once liability is established, damages are mandatory.

---

[5] *See, e.g., Schwartz v. HSBC Bank USA, N.A.*, 2017 WL 95118 (S.D.N.Y. 2017), *aff'd* 750 Fed. Appx. 34 (2d Cir. 2018).

The default statutory penalty for an individual case is twice the amount of the finance charge so long as the amount is not less than $200 or more than $2,000. For a case involving open end consumer credit not secured by real property or a dwelling, the minimum is $500 and the maximum is $5,000. If the transaction giving rise to the claim is closed end and real property or a dwelling is secured, these amounts are $400 and $4,000. For violations of specific duties imposed on high cost (HOEPA) mortgage creditors, violations of the ban on steering incentives by mortgage originators, and violation of the duty to ensure mortgage customers' ability to repay, there is no cap on the statutory damages, which are "the sum of all finance charges and fees paid by the consumer, unless the creditor demonstrates that the failure to comply is not material." 15 U.S.C. § 1640(a)(4).

The statute provides for only a single statutory recovery in a single transaction or open-end account, even for multiple disclosure violations. However, a creditor's "continued failure to disclose after a recovery has been granted shall give rise to rights to additional recoveries." 15 U.S.C. § 1640(g).

In refinancing situations, an apparently single transaction may in fact be a series of separate transactions with statutory damages available for each. For example, in *Dennis v. Handley*, 453 F. Supp. 833 (N.D.Ala.1978), a consumer pawned a ring for $200, renewable each month upon payment of $20 accrued interest. A missed payment would allow the pawnbroker to hold the property free and clear. The court found this arrangement to be a series of separate transactions rather than an account payable in installments. Since each renewal was a new transaction, the consumer was allowed five recoveries, one for the original loan and one for each of four renewals.

Refinancing, or "flipping," of consumer credit transactions, generally gives rise to multiple statutory damages to the extent there are TILA violations in both the original transaction and the refinancing, even if the violations in the separate transactions are identical.[6] A consumer may recover more than two times the statutory damages if there are more than two refinancings with a TILA violation. This is so because a refinancing is by definition a new and separate transaction under Regulation Z. 12 C.F.R. § 1026.20(a).

If there are multiple obligors, such as may occur if a husband and wife both sign a note in a consumer credit transaction, both are considered debtors or obligors. If the creditor violates TILA, these obligors are limited to one recovery of statutory damages. 15 U.S.C. § 1640(d). This limitation does not extend to actual damage claims or class actions, however. In such a case, each obligor may recover separate actual damages.

Statutory damages are not available for all TILA violations, because the statute limits the award of such damages to certain specific violations. 15 U.S.C.

---

[6] *See, e.g., Abele v. Mid-Penn Consumer Discount,* 77 B.R. 460 (E.D.Pa.1987); *Simpson v. Termplan of Georgia, Inc.,* 535 F. Supp. 36 (N.D.Ga.1981).

§ 1640(a). This limitation was meant to "curtail damages awards for picky and inconsequential formal errors." *Brown v. Payday Check Advance, Inc.*, 202 F.3d 987, 991 (7th Cir. 2000). Courts do not have any discretion to award statutory damages for violations not specifically listed in the statute as subject to statutory damages.

4. ACTUAL DAMAGES

In addition to the "statutory damages," a claimant may recover actual damages, costs, and "reasonable attorney's fees as determined by the court." 15 U.S.C. § 1640(a)(2)(A) and (3). Despite this provision, recovery of actual damages for disclosure violations is rare. The reason is that a majority of courts hold that proof of detrimental reliance is required for actual damages under TILA.[7] To establish the prerequisite detrimental reliance for actual damages, consumers must show that: they read the TILA disclosure statement; they understood the charges being disclosed; that had the disclosure been accurate, they would have sought a lower price; and they would have obtained a lower price.[8] This standard has proved nearly impossible to meet in most TILA disclosure cases.

There is a minority view that the consumer is actually damaged in the amount by which the finance

---

[7] *See, e.g., Vallies v. Sky Bank*, 591 F.3d 152 (3d Cir. 2009); *U.S. v. Petroff-Kline*, 557 F.3d 285 (6th Cir. 2009); *In re Smith*, 289 F.3d 1155 (9th Cir. 2002).

[8] *See Peters v. Jim Lupient Oldsmobile Co.*, 220 F.3d 915, 917 (8th Cir. 2000).

charge is understated, without having to prove actual reliance.[9] *In re Russell,* 72 B.R. 855 (Bankr.E.D.Pa.1987). The *Russell* court held that where a disclosure statement contains a substantial TILA violation, as opposed to a simple technical violation, a consumer is entitled to actual damages measured by the difference between the misstated financial charge and the actual amount charged. The court refused to apply a detrimental reliance standard on the ground that TILA is a remedial statute, and that § 1640(b) implies that consumers should be awarded as actual damages a reduction of the debt owed in an amount equal to the undisclosed finance charges or the dollar equivalent of the disclosed APR, whichever is less. The detrimental reliance standard may also not be applicable in situations where the TILA disclosure is obscured or not made in a timely manner since in that situation the consumer could not have read or relied on the substance of the disclosures.[10]

Actual damages may include a claim for consequential damages. Humiliation, harm to one's reputation, and mental or emotional distress have been held to be a proper basis for awarding actual damages under TILA. For instance, in *Iuteri v. Branhaven Motors, Inc.*, No. N-81-254, Clearinghouse No. 41,259 (D. Conn. Nov. 14 1985),

---

[9] *See* NATIONAL CONSUMER LAW CENTER, TRUTH IN LENDING § 11.5.4 (10th ed. 2019) for a discussion of alternate standards for determining actual damages for disclosure violations.

[10] *Price v. Berman's Automotive, Inc.*, 2015 WL 5720429 (D. Md. 2015).

the court found that the forgery of the debtor's signature on a retail contract and the creditor's failure to accurately disclose financing terms had caused actual damages in the form of "emotional trauma and unnecessary aggravation." Thus, the court awarded the plaintiff $2,000 in damages.

5. CREDITOR DEFENSES

a. Assignee Liability

Consumer credit sales frequently involve the assignment of a credit seller's rights against the consumer to a separate financial service provider. Under the Regulation Z definition of "creditor," only the party "to whom credit is initially payable on the face of the note or contract" has the obligation to make disclosures. 12 C.F.R. § 1026.2(a)(17)(i). Therefore, as a general rule, the consumer may only recover against the credit seller or the original creditor for TILA violations.

On the other hand, the section on "Liability of Assignees," 15 U.S.C. § 1641(a), provides that an action for a TILA violation which may be brought against a creditor may also be brought against an assignee, but only if the violation is evident on the face of the loan documents.[11] The rationale behind this provision is that a purchaser of loan paper should at least be expected to read the terms of the documents purchased and bear responsibility for obvious violations. However, this provision does not

---

[11] Rescission is available against assignees regardless of whether the violations were apparent on the face of the documents.

entitle a consumer to separate statutory damages from both the creditor and the assignee. Indeed, in *Greenlee v. Steering Wheel, Inc.*, 693 F. Supp. 1396 (D.Conn.1988), where the plaintiff sought damages from both the creditor and assignee, the court held that this provision did not alter the rule that assignees and creditors are jointly and severally liable.

Consumers have also attempted (unsuccessfully) to argue that assignees are liable for damages under the so-called FTC "Holder Rule," officially entitled Preservation of Consumers' Claims and Defenses, discussed fully in Chapter Ten, *infra*. 16 C.F.R. Part 433. The argument for the consumer is that the rule ensures that any legal rights that the buyer has against the seller arising out of the transaction are also valid against subsequent holders. The rule requires that consumer contracts contain a "notice" stating specifically that the "holder" of the consumer contract is subject to all claims and defenses which the debtor could assert against the original seller. Most courts who have addressed this question have held that to the extent the "Holder Rule" conflicts with TILA's "Liability of Assignees," TILA takes precedence, even when the FTC notice is actually included in the contract.[12] Thus, the assignee is only subject to TILA liability to the extent the violation is evident on the face of the loan documents.

---

[12] *See Ramadan v. Chase Manhattan Corp.*, 229 F.3d 194 (3d Cir. 2000); *Taylor v. Quality Hyundai, Inc.*, 150 F.3d 689 (7th Cir. 1998); *Ellis v. General Motors Acceptance Corp.*, 160 F.3d 703 (11th Cir. 1998).

In the case of high cost (HOEPA) mortgages, however, the assignee *is* liable for all claims and defenses that the consumer could assert against the original lender. 15 U.S.C. § 1641(d)(1). Due to the predatory nature of many HOEPA loans, and the fact that third party financers were either working with the original mortgage brokers or would be in a position to police them, one court said that "it is clear that Congress intended to subject assignees of HOEPA loans to a more expansive standard of liability than is normally applied under TILA." *Bryant v. Mortgage Capital Resource Corp.*, 197 F. Supp. 2d 1357, 1364 (N.D. Ga. 2002). HOEPA loan assignee liability is limited to situations in which a "reasonable person exercising ordinary due diligence" could ascertain that the mortgage was subject to HOEPA. Anyone who sells or assigns such mortgages is supposed to include a prominent notice of this potential liability. Also, assignee damages under the HOEPA rule are limited to TILA statutory damages plus other damages up to a ceiling of the amount of the remaining consumer indebtedness and the amount already paid by the consumer. 15 U.S.C. § 1641(d). Despite these limitations, the expanded scope of HOEPA that became effective with the 2010 Dodd-Frank legislation, discussed in the previous chapter, may well mean that more assignees will be liable for TILA damages.

b. Statute of Limitations

One of the more common defenses asserted in a Truth in Lending action is that the consumer's claim is time barred based on the statute of limitations. 15

U.S.C. § 1640(e) provides that TILA claims may be raised "within one year from the date of the occurrence of the violation." There are some exceptions, however. For instance, as a result of the Mortgage Reform and Anti-Predatory Lending Act of 2010, actions for violations of certain mortgage loan-related provisions of TILA enjoy an extended statutory limit of up to three years from the date of the occurrence of the violation.

Most courts will consider arguments that the TILA time limits for filing suit should be subject to "equitable tolling." This doctrine is applicable: (1) where there has been fraudulent concealment by the defendant respecting the plaintiff's cause of action; or (2) where the plaintiff in some extraordinary way has been prevented from asserting his or her rights, such as by virtue of a mental disability or dementia.

Because the limitation period is measured from the date of the occurrence of the violation, it is often important to determine that exact date. For violations involving a "private education loan," the period runs from the date on which the first regular payment of principal is due under the loan. 15 U.S.C. § 1640(e). In most other situations, such as when the alleged violation is a failure to make timely disclosures, the violation occurs at the time when the disclosures should have been made. This type of violation may be deemed "continuing" until a later point when the actual disclosures are made, however, thus extending the statute of limitations. This is particularly true in open end credit situations, where the same violation may be repeated (or not corrected) in periodic statements.[13]

Many if not most consumers do not discover a TILA violation within one year, but instead they will be unaware until they are sued in a collection action and seek the advice of legal counsel. Fortunately for such consumers, the one-year limitation does not bar them from alleging a TILA violation when a creditor brings a collection action. This is explicitly allowed under 15 U.S.C. § 1640(e), which states: "This subsection does not bar a person from asserting a violation of this title in an action to collect the debt which was brought more than one year from the date of the occurrence of the violation as a matter of defense by way of recoupment or set-off in such action, except as otherwise provided by State law." As amended by the 2010 Mortgage Reform and Anti-Predatory Lending Act, TILA also permits consumers to assert violations with regard to certain mortgage related provisions as a defense by recoupment or set off to either judicial or non-judicial foreclosures of residential mortgage loans, without regard for the normal time limit. 15 U.S.C. § 1640(k).

c. Creditor Error

Section 1640(c) provides a defense to the creditor that bars liability if the preponderance of the evidence shows that the violation was unintentional

---

[13] *See, e.g., Schwartz v. HSBC Bank USA, N.A.*, 160 F. Supp. 3d 666 (S.D.N.Y. 2016) (TILA statute of limitations runs from each instance of defendant's failure to make a required disclosure on the periodic statement).

SEC. C CONSUMER REMEDIES

and "resulted from a bona fide error notwithstanding the maintenance of procedures reasonably adapted to avoid any such error." Examples of such errors include clerical, calculation, computer malfunction, computer programming, and printing errors.[14] On the other hand, an error of legal judgment with regard to one's TILA obligations is not a bona fide error. The bona fide error defense is difficult to prove and is more often than not rejected by the courts.

The statute also allows a creditor to escape liability for a TILA disclosure violation if that creditor makes a timely correction of the error. 15 U.S.C. § 1640(b). The creditor must act to correct the mistake within 60 days after first discovering the error and before the consumer gives notice of the error or brings an action for a TILA violation. While some courts have held that this error correction provision applies only to clerical or mathematical type errors, others have found that the 60-day window is not so limited, allowing the creditor to correct any type of error, including timing requirements, as long as the statutory requirements are met.[15]

---

[14] *See, e.g., Messineo v. Ocwen Loan Servicing, LLC*, 2017 WL 733219 (N.D. Cal. 2017) (software "bugs" could potentially be considered a bona fide error).

[15] *Compare Thomka v. A.Z. Chevrolet, Inc.*, 619 F.2d 246, 251–52 (3d Cir. 1980) (provision applies only to clerical errors, otherwise creditors would have incentive to delay disclosures) and *Baker v. Sunny Chevrolet, Inc.*, 349 F.3d 862, 869–71 (6th Cir. 2003) (wording of statute did not limit 60-day correction period to clerical errors).

6. ATTORNEY'S FEES

The Truth in Lending Act provides that a successful consumer claimant shall be entitled to recover from the creditor "the costs of the action, together with a reasonable attorney's fee as determined by the court." 15 U.S.C. § 1640(a)(3). This provision may not be applicable to attorneys representing themselves, however, especially if the fee requested appears unreasonable. *See, e.g., Kurz v. Chase Manhattan Bank USA, NA.*, 324 F. Supp. 2d 444 (S.D.N.Y. 2004).

Courts in TILA cases follow the same guidelines in determining an appropriate fee award as they would in other cases involving statutory attorney's fees, such as time spent on the case, skill required, and the prevailing hourly rate for similar work. Trial courts may reduce the requested fee, may decline to award fees for aspects that were not successful, or for time spent on non-TILA claims for which no statutory fee award was applicable. Normally, the judgment of the trial court as to attorney's fees will not be overturned unless there is a showing of abuse of discretion.

7. CLASS ACTIONS AND ARBITRATIONS

Class actions are permitted under TILA, but liability is limited to the lesser of $1,000,000 or 1% of the net worth of the creditor. These limits, which have increased since lower limits were originally imposed in 1974, are meant to eliminate the potential for unjustifiably large recoveries based on statutory minimum damages multiplied by large numbers of consumers affected. The ceiling applies to a single class action or to a "series of class action suits arising out of the same failure to comply by the same creditor." 15 U.S.C. § 1640(a)(2)(B).

If the class is certified and the plaintiffs prevail in a TILA class action, the court must consider the following factors in determining the amount of the award: (1) the amount of any actual damages; (2) the frequency and persistence of failures of compliance by the creditor; (3) the resources of the creditor; (4) the number of persons adversely affected; and (5) the extent to which the creditor's failure of compliance was intentional. 15 U.S.C. § 1640(a). Class actions are not precluded simply because there are no actual damages. *Adiel v. Chase Federal Sav. & Loan Ass'n*, 810 F.2d 1051 (11th Cir. 1987).

To be certified as a class action, a TILA case must fulfill the prerequisites of Rule 23 of the Federal Rules of Civil Procedure or the equivalent state rule if filed in state court. Class actions under TILA must also comply with the Class Action Fairness Act of 2005, which expands federal court jurisdiction over class actions. 28 U.S.C. § 1332.

TILA class actions are most likely to be successful in situations based on documentary violations contained in preprinted forms, because this lowers the individual proof required and buttresses the commonality of the claims. For instance, in a case where the class plaintiff alleged a failure to disclose negative amortization in an adjustable rate mortgage, and where the creditor had used only one version of the loan documents, the case was deemed suitable for class action. *Lymburner v. U.S. Financial*

Funds, Inc., 263 F.R.D. 534 (N.D. Cal. 2010). TILA cases involving standard procedures of the creditor are also good candidates for class actions.

The number of TILA class actions brought in court may be declining due to the prevalence of binding arbitration clauses, accompanied by class action waivers, which are becoming increasingly common in consumer credit contracts. Since the mid-1990s, most consumer credit contracts, including pay day loans, credit card agreements, mobile phone contracts, home equity loans, and automobile financing contracts, mandate that all disputes arising under the contract be resolved by binding arbitration. These contracts also typically bar the claim from being brought on behalf of a class. Based on the policy contained in the Federal Arbitration Act, the U.S. Supreme Court has enforced most arbitration clauses against consumer challenges, including in a case involving a TILA claim. *Green Tree Financial Corp.-Alabama v. Randolph*, 531 U.S. 79 (2000). The Supreme Court has also held specifically that class action waivers contained in an arbitration clause will be enforceable because class arbitration would be inconsistent with the Federal Arbitration Act. *AT&T Mobility LLC v. Concepcion*, 563 U.S. 333 (2011).

As noted in the Chapter Seven, mandatory pre-dispute binding arbitration clauses are banned in credit contracts secured by an interest in the consumer's home. 15 U.S.C. § 1639c(e)(1). They are also banned in certain loans made to military service members. 10 U.S.C.A. § 987(e)(3); 32 C.F.R. § 232.8(a)(3). The Consumer Financial Protection

Bureau early on conducted a study of pre-dispute arbitration agreements between consumers and financial service providers, and proposed a regulation that would have banned class action waivers in arbitration clauses. This regulation was vetoed by Congress in 2017.

D. RIGHT OF RESCISSION

TILA gives consumers a three-day right to rescind a credit transaction in which a non-purchase lien or security interest is or will be placed, on the consumer's principal dwelling. 15 U.S.C. § 1635. This "cooling-off" type provision was meant to give consumers the chance to reconsider a transaction that would encumber their home ownership rights. Note that a right to rescind applies after consummation, and is not the same as the three-day waiting period between the provision of the "Closing Disclosures" and the actual closing, applicable to credit transactions secured by a consumer's dwelling, as discussed *supra*, Chapter Seven. The right to rescind applies to both closed-end and open-end transactions that otherwise meet the prerequisites.

Section 1635 is different from most other TILA provisions. It is not primarily a disclosure provision. Instead, it creates an affirmative right to rescind. Rescission under TILA is not a penalty for nondisclosure. Even though a creditor makes all required disclosures, the consumer will have the three-day right to rescind if the transaction comes within 15 U.S.C. § 1635.

To determine whether a consumer credit transaction qualifies for the right to rescind, one should ask the following questions:

(1) Will the transaction result in a lien on any property that the consumer uses as his or her dwelling?

The lien may be either a consensual lien, such as a mortgage or deed of trust, or it may be a statutory lien, such as a mechanic's or materialmen's lien. For example, almost all home repair work done on credit involves a statutory lien and thus gives rise to a right to rescind. Even if the contractor waives all of his or her liens, the consumer still has the right to rescind if the contractor's suppliers, subcontractors, employees, etc. might acquire liens for materials that go into the house or work on it.

(2) Is this property that the consumer uses as his or her dwelling also used or expected to be used as the consumer's principal residence?

The right of rescission is restricted to transactions resulting in liens on a "principal dwelling." The right of rescission would not apply, therefore, if the real property encumbered is a vacation home.

(3) Is the lien a first lien securing the costs of the dwelling or the construction of the dwelling?

The right of rescission does not extend to first liens to secure the acquisition or construction of the dwelling. The rationale for this exclusion is that most

SEC. D RIGHT OF RESCISSION

borrowers will realize that when they secure a mortgage to purchase a home, that it would be subject to foreclosure if they default, and thus would not need the three day cooling-off period.

The right of rescission also does not apply to a refinancing of an existing loan by the same creditor (with no new advances), 15 U.S.C. § 1635(e), nor would it apply to the reacquisition of a previously owned property. *See Barnes v. Chase Home Finance, LLC*, 934 F.3d 901 (9th Cir. 2019).

If, then, you are able to answer the first two questions "yes" and the third question "no," then the transaction comes within 15 U.S.C. § 1635.

In a contract subject to rescission, the creditor must deliver to each owner two copies of a notice of the right to rescind and one copy of the TILA disclosure statement containing material disclosures. 12 C.F.R. §§ 1026.15(b) and .23(b). The CFPB provides model forms for the notice of the right to rescind, and use of such forms provides a "safe haven" for creditors against challenges on the adequacy of the form of disclosure. 15 U.S.C. § 1635(h).

The three-day right of rescission in closed end credit transactions arises at the latest of three events: (1) consummation of the transaction; (2) consumer's receipt of the notice of the right to rescind; or (3) consumer's receipt of all material disclosures as required. 12 C.F.R. § 1026.23(a)(3)(i). If the notice of the right to rescind or the material disclosures are not properly made, the three day right to rescind may actually come into play much later than when the transaction was initially concluded, as would occur in the event the consumer does not receive all material disclosures. Material disclosures do not include all required TILA disclosures but are limited to certain terms specified in the regulation, including annual percentage rate, finance charge, amount financed, total of payments and the payment schedule. For purposes of rescission-related material disclosures, the amount disclosed as finance charge can vary by up to one-half of one percent of the total amount of credit extended. 15 U.S.C. § 1605(f). For rescission rights exercised after the initiation of foreclosures, however, the error tolerance is no more than $35 understated. 15 U.S.C. § 1635(i)(2).

For open end credit secured by the consumer's principal dwelling, the right of rescission arises at the latest of the following events: plan opening; a security interest in the consumer's principal dwelling is added to secure an existing plan; or the credit limit on the plan or the security interest is increased. 12 C.F.R. § 1026.15(a)(1). Thus, for either open or closed end credit transactions, the three-day right of rescission can arise well after the original transaction is consummated if the creditor fails to provide the required notices or the material disclosures. There is an absolute three-years from consummation limit on the right to rescind, however, that has been strictly enforced, even in cases where the consumer is being sued on the debt and wishes to assert rescission by way of defense. 15 U.S.C.

§ 1635(f), as applied in *Beach v. Ocwen Federal Bank*, 523 U.S. 410 (1998).

If the transaction comes within 15 U.S.C. § 1635, the creditor must be reasonably satisfied that the consumer has not elected to rescind in a timely manner before disbursing any money other than in escrow, making any physical changes in the property, performing any work or service for the consumer, or making any deliveries to the consumer's residence. 12 C.F.R. §§ 1026.15(c) and .23(c).

The importance of delaying performance is evident by considering the possible consequences of rescission. Upon rescission, the consumer is immediately relieved of all liability for finance or other charges, and the lien retained by the creditor is automatically void. The creditor must, within twenty days after receipt of the notice of rescission, take whatever action is necessary to cancel the lien on the public records. The creditor also has twenty days to return down-payments in cash or by way of trade-in, with charges and fees collected in connection with the transfer.

It is only after the creditor has fulfilled these obligations that the consumer is required to tender property that the creditor has previously delivered. At the consumer's option, the tender may be made at the site of the property or at the consumer's residence. If the creditor fails to take possession of the property within twenty days after tender, then the property becomes the consumer's, without obligation on his or her part to pay for it. 12 C.F.R. §§ 1026.23(d) and .15(d). In situations where rescission comes well after loan proceeds have been disbursed or home repair services have been rendered, however, courts may alter these procedures and require that the consumer tender back the money or reasonable value of services before the creditor is required to relinquish its security interest and return the consumer's payments.[16]

A consumer may waive the right to rescind in "emergency" situations. 15 U.S.C. § 1635(d); 12 C.F.R. §§ 1026.23(e) and .15(e). To modify or waive the right, the consumer must give the creditor a dated, written statement that describes the emergency, that specifically modifies or waives the right to rescind, and that bears the signature of all the consumers entitled to rescind. An emergency situation occurs when the extension of credit is needed in order to meet a bona fide personal family emergency, such as financing a heating or plumbing repair.

E. RELATED STATUTES

1. TRUTH IN SAVINGS ACT

While Congress enacted TILA in order to provide consumers with the real cost of credit, the Truth in Savings Act (TISA) was enacted in 1991 in order to provide consumers with essential information about accounts at depositary institutions. TISA (12 U.S.C. §§ 4301 et seq.) covers checking, savings and time accounts held by an individual primarily for a

---

[16] 15 U.S.C. § 1635(b) ("The procedures prescribed by this subsection shall apply except when otherwise ordered by a court").

personal, family or household purpose. A depositary institution is one that is either federally insured or is eligible to apply for such insurance.

The implementing regulation for TISA is Regulation DD and a concurrent regulation for credit unions. 12 C.F.R. Part 1030 (Regulation DD); 12 C.F.R. Part 707 (credit unions). The disclosure requirements under TISA and Regulation DD aid comparison shopping on the savings side, just as TILA and Regulation Z do on the borrowing side. The essential disclosures TISA requires include fees, the "annual percentage yield" (APY), the interest rate and other terms. Interest must be paid on the full balance in the account each day, based on one of two methods for calculating the balance.

The disclosures required by TISA include:

(1) A description of all the charges that can be assessed against an account holder and the circumstances under which each charge can be imposed;

(2) The amount of such charges, or the method by which the amount is calculated; and

(3) Minimum balance requirements, including how the balance is calculated and the consequences of falling below the minimum.

Depositary institutions must maintain a current schedule of the terms and conditions applicable to each class of accounts that is offered. These account schedules must be written in clear and plain language, and be available upon request to any person.

The account schedules must include:

(1) The annual percentage yield (APY);

(2) The period during which the APY will be in effect;

(3) The annual rate of simple interest;

(4) The frequency with which interest is compounded and credited;

(5) The method used to arrive at the account balance;

(6) Any minimum account balance requirements to realize yields;

(7) Any minimum time requirements to realize yields;

(8) Any early-withdrawal penalties; and

(9) Any other occurrence which can cause a reduced payment.

12 C.F.R. § 1030.4.

2. CONSUMER LEASING ACT

Part E of the Truth in Lending Act is the Consumer Leasing Act (CLA). 15 U.S.C. § 1667. The CLA mandates the clear disclosure of a number of lease terms and contains a private right of action as provided under TILA. As is true with other parts of TILA, the CLA is supplemented by a regulation

(Regulation M), and an Official Staff Commentary. 12 C.F.R. Part 1013.

The CLA applies to leases of greater than four months duration. If the lease is terminable without penalty during the first four months, the CLA does not apply. Because rent-to-own transactions are terminable without penalty at any time, they are not subject to the CLA. Typically the rent-to-own industry is subject to state disclosure laws, which disclose the terms of the lease, and may contain some limitations on repossession and rights of the consumer to "reinstate" the lease after default. *See, e.g.*, Maryland Rental-Purchase Agreement Act, Maryland Annotated Code §§ 12–1101 to 1111.1.

The CLA does not apply to leases where the total contractual obligation exceeds $50,000 (adjustable for inflation). The total contract obligation includes the total of payments due under the lease, plus any trade-in or initial payment. It does not include an option price stated in the contract for a consumer to purchase the item, or the residual value at the end of the term, which is what the item is expected to be worth.

The CLA applies only to "consumer leases," defined as being primarily for personal, family or household purposes. Lessees are not covered where they are a corporation or other business organization. For most consumers the most important application of the CLA is in automobile leases. Only personal property leases are covered by the CLA. Real property leases are not covered by the CLA.

Under the CLA, as with TILA, enumerated disclosures must be segregated from other required disclosures. The segregated disclosures must be separate from other information and shall contain the following information:

(1) The amount due at lease signing;

(2) The payment schedule and total of periodic payments;

(3) Other charges;

(4) Total of payments;

(5) An eleven-step payment calculation;

(6) A notice that the charge for early termination may be substantial;

(7) An "early termination warning," telling consumers that "you may have to pay a substantial charge if you end this lease early";

(8) Amount or method of determining the charges for excessive wear and tear;

(9) The end of term purchase option price; and

(10) Rent and other charges paid by the lessee.

Other disclosures can be made separately from the segregated disclosures. 12 C.F.R. §§ 1013.3 and .4.

The early termination warning was added in 1997, due to the fact that many consumers do not realize that for most long term automobile leases there may be a substantial early termination fee that is difficult to determine ahead of time. For example, in one case the contractual formula in the lease would have required the lessees to pay $5,336.95 for paying off a $267 per month lease only one month early.[17] The statute requires that the amount of the early termination penalty be reasonable. 15 U.S.C. § 1667b(b).

Although many consumers may consider automobile leases as an alternative to purchasing a vehicle on credit, the CLA disclosures basically only help make comparisons between different lease deals. There is no disclosure of an equivalent APR under the lease disclosures, because a lease transaction is not equivalent to a credit purchase, and it was felt that any attempt to determine an APR equivalent for a lease transaction would be easily manipulated by the lessor.

3. INTERSTATE LAND SALES FULL DISCLOSURE ACT

The Interstate Land Sales Full Disclosure Act, 15 U.S.C. §§ 1701–1720, is patterned after the Securities Act of 1933. It requires that anyone selling or leasing 100 or more lots of unimproved land as part of a common promotional plan in interstate commerce must first file a "statement of record" with the Director of the Consumer Financial Protection Bureau (prior to 2011, statements were filed with the Department of Housing and Urban Development).

---

[17] *Miller v. Nissan Motor Acceptance Corp.*, 362 F.3d 209 (3d Cir. 2004) (case dismissed because the leasing company agreed to accept $267 as payoff).

The requirements for the statement of record are set out in 12 C.F.R. Part 1010. The statement of record contains very detailed information about the land and the developer. Preparing the statement is similar to preparing a registration statement for the Securities and Exchange Commission. Electronic submission of the required filings under the ILSFDA is permitted. Section 1702 of the Act and §§ 1010.10–1010.13 of the regulations list the transactions that are exempt from the application of the Act. The most important exemption is intrastate land offerings (as the title of the Act indicates).

After the statement of record is approved as being accurate on its face and as containing the required information, a developer may then offer land for sale or lease. The developer must also furnish each purchaser a "property report" before signing any contract or agreement.

The Act provides the right to sue for relief in an action at law or in equity against a developer or agent if the sale or lease was made in violation of the Act. The relief available includes:

> damages, specific performance, or such other relief as the court deems fair, just, and equitable. In determining such relief the court may take into account, but not be limited to, the following factors: the contract price of the lot or leasehold; the amount the purchaser or lessee actually paid; the cost of any improvements to the lot; the fair market value of the lot or leasehold at the time relief is determined; and

SEC. E *RELATED STATUTES* *285*

the fair market value of the lot or leasehold at the time such lot was purchased or leased.

15 U.S.C. § 1709(a).

Criminal penalties are set forth in 15 U.S.C. § 1717 for willful violations of the Act. Upon conviction, a person may be fined not more than $10,000 or be imprisoned for not more than five years, or both.

The most important remedy under the Act is a purchaser's right of rescission. Three different provisions of the Act create this right. First, a purchaser who did not receive the property report required by the Act *prior to* signing a contract has a right to rescind for two years from the date of signing the contract. The land sale contract must clearly disclose this right of rescission. 15 U.S.C. § 1703(c).

Second, there is also a two-year rescission period if the sales contract does not contain the disclosures required by 15 U.S.C. § 1703(d). The purchaser loses this right of rescission if he/she receives a warranty deed within 180 days of signing the contract.

Third, there is an absolute seven-day right of rescission that exists regardless of the disclosures that the seller makes. During this limited time period, the right to rescind is absolute. The sales contract must clearly disclose this right of rescission. 15 U.S.C. § 1703(b).

In addition to these rescission rights under the Interstate Land Sales Full Disclosure Act, consumers also have the right to rescind under TILA, 15 U.S.C. § 1635, to the extent that it applies. There is nothing in either statute that precludes or preempts the operation of the other. A number of transactions will be covered by both Acts. If an individual is acquiring land in an "interstate land sale" on credit for consumer purposes, both Acts will cover the transaction. As always, the right of rescission under TILA will only apply if the property so acquired is used or is to be used as the consumer's principal residence.

4. REAL ESTATE SETTLEMENT PROCEDURES ACT

Since 1975, some real estate transactions have been governed by yet a third federal disclosure statute: the Real Estate Settlement Procedures Act ("RESPA"). 12 U.S.C. §§ 2601–2614. The Act was passed

> [to] insure that consumers throughout the Nation are provided with greater and more timely information on the nature and costs of the settlement process and are protected from unnecessarily high settlement charges caused by certain abusive practices that have developed in some areas of the country.

12 U.S.C. § 2601(a). Prior to the passage of RESPA, some consumers were uninformed and unprepared for the sometimes substantial costs payable at settlement.

This Act applies to all "federally related mortgage loans." The definition of "federally related" focuses on: (1) the lender and (2) the nature of the property encumbered.

Virtually all mortgage lenders taking a first lien on residential real property are covered: banks, savings and loan associations, and other lenders insured or regulated by a federal agency. State chartered lenders who make more than $1 million in "residential real estate loans each year" are also covered.

The Act is much broader than TILA. To be covered by RESPA, the property offered for security must be residential real property on which is built a one to four family residential dwelling. RESPA coverage is not limited to loans securing the consumer's principal dwelling. There is no inquiry into the nature of the debtor, but there is an exemption from coverage for business purpose loans. 12 C.F.R. § 1024.5(b)(2).

The primary burden of complying with the requirements of RESPA falls on lenders. When someone applies for a "federally related mortgage loan," the lender must deliver to the applicant a copy of the Special Information Booklet prepared by the Consumer Financial Protection Bureau (formerly by HUD) to explain the nature and costs of real estate settlement services. The lender must supply the Booklet by delivering it or placing it in the mail to the applicant not later than three days after the borrower's loan application is received. 12 C.F.R. § 1024.6(a)(1).

Until some important changes in the disclosure process became effective in 2015, RESPA required the lender to provide an early good faith estimate of the amount or range of charges for specific settlement services the borrower is likely to incur in connection with the settlement, which was separate from the TILA early cost of credit disclosures, and were provided to consumer in the same time frame. There was also a HUD-1 form showing the final settlement costs which was given on or before the settlement, along with separate final TILA disclosures. Pursuant to a directive in the Dodd-Frank Act of 2010, however, the CFPB was charged with issuing regulations that would combine or unify these two sometimes overlapping and somewhat confusing sets of disclosures. Now there is a combined RESPA/TILA "Loan Estimate" disclosure provided within three days of the receipt of the loan application, and a second combined "Closing Disclosure" given three days prior to closing. These combined disclosures were discussed in the prior chapter, in the section on real estate related TILA provisions.

The Real Estate Settlement Procedures Act is not a pure disclosure statute. The Act contains a number of substantive regulations. A seller may not require a buyer to purchase title insurance from any particular company. Kickbacks and unearned fees are prohibited. For example, a title insurance company may not pay a referral commission to the lender's attorneys. Advance deposits in escrow accounts are limited. In addition, RESPA prohibits lenders from charging fees for the preparation of disclosure statements that it and TILA require.

RESPA's provisions are enforced by the CFPB, which has been quite active in enforcing the anti-kickback provisions. Most private actions to enforce the disclosure provisions are precluded, but the statute specifically authorizes a private right of action for the anti-kickback and escrow account limitations. 12 U.S.C. § 2614. There is also a private right of action to enforce certain duties of mortgage servicers, including responding to written requests for information. 12 U.S.C. § 2605. This section authorizes actual damages and a small discretionary amount up to $2,000 per individual but does not include mental anguish. *Moore v. Wells Fargo Bank, N.A.*, 908 F.3d 1050 (7th Cir. 2018).

CHAPTER NINE
REGULATING THE COST OF CREDIT

A. HISTORY OF RATE REGULATION

Although it may be difficult for some people to embrace, the making of a loan is really just the sale of dollars, for a price. The price is generally referred to as the "interest" on a loan. Lenders note that they are in the business of selling and "moving" money, and that sales volume is as critical to them as it is to any retailer of goods. In many ways, selling money is no different than selling beer, where some people are willing to pay an exaggerated price, in what is becoming an increasingly deregulated market for the cost of credit. A six-pack purchased at a convenience store or ski resort grocery may sell for twice as much as it does at a large grocery store in the suburbs, but people pay the price because the convenience outweighs the cost, or no other alternative is available. Some people shop for credit facing similar constraints.

However, people do not view money and beer in the same way. Were the sale of money viewed by most people as the sale of six-packs, we would not have the mountain of consumer credit regulations we have today, including some of the usury laws that regulate the cost of credit. When it comes to money, people generally do not like high rates and are tolerant of more regulation. However, although it is true that today there are more disclosure requirements in consumer credit than at any other time in our history, many of the laws regulating the cost of that credit have been swept away or preempted by federal laws that moved us to a more deregulated market.

But some usury laws remain and are as controversial now as they were long ago. The issue of whether to impose usury laws has long been debated. A detailed history of usury laws, however, is beyond the scope of this nutshell.[1] Nonetheless, there are two important influences on usury laws that aid in understanding the current status of usury laws.

One part of the history which is of practical significance is the influence of the Bible. Phrases such as "Take thou no usury of him, or increase: but fear thy God; that thy brother may live with thee," teaches us that extracting interest is wrong. Also, as early as 2000 B.C. the law limited the rate of interest that could be charged on loans of money.

The other important influence on our usury laws is from Europe. In 1545, Henry VII allowed taking interest legally for the first time in England. Following that path, Massachusetts enacted the first usury statute in the colonies in 1661, which allows interest to be charged up to a ceiling imposed by the law.

Consumer credit, however, has a much shorter history; it became common only at about the turn of the 20th century. A jeweler started it all. Frank Macker began offering unsecured personal loans to

---

[1] An excellent brief history of usury laws can be found in CHRISTOPHER L. PETERSON, TAMING THE SHARKS, TOWARDS A CURE FOR THE HIGH-COST CREDIT MARKET, Chapter Two (U. Akron Press 2004).

average income consumers in order to support the purchase of his jewelry. Soon after, in 1878, Household Finance Company started as the first of many companies to tap this credit market.

Until that time, most people were farmers rather than wage earners. But in the late 19th century, the United States economy began to see a change from a purely agrarian society to an industrialized society. With industry and the mass production of consumer goods, the average citizen needed some sort of credit system to purchase the goods being produced. In some cases, banks and finance companies provided the flow of credit needed to support a consumer economy.

Still, there were impediments to consumer finance companies. The usury laws in many places prohibited lenders from charging more than 6% per annum. There was no way profit could be made at that rate. These artificially low rates caused people to look elsewhere, including illegal loan shark markets.

The rise of loan sharks who charged abusive interest rates and the lack of legitimate consumer credit prompted a study by the Russell Sage Foundation in 1907. This led to the adoption of the Uniform Small Loan Law, which was drafted in 1916. The effect of this law was to mandate an all inclusive fee to prevent hidden charges and raise the usury ceiling to make small lending more profitable. Small loans were defined as loans of $300 or less and the maximum charge for such loans was set at no more than 3 ½ percent per month.

The Uniform Small Loan Law is only one of the exceptions to general usury statutes that have been created for consumer credit transactions, allowing higher rates for smaller loans. As other lenders entered into the consumer credit market, other statutory exceptions developed. For example, the regulation of retail sales where the seller provided credit resulted in still more statutes regulating the amount of finance charges a seller can impose when goods are purchased "on time."

Effectively, the Uniform Small Loan Law legitimized the consumer finance industry, which included banks, retail stores, and finance companies affiliated with automobile manufacturers. This led to a host of other regulations at both the local and national level. The National Commission on Consumer Finance used the word "hodgepodge" to describe the array of usury laws in place. Thus, as creditors got more creative in their lending policies, the legislator responded with further regulation.

B. SHOULD THERE BE RATE CEILINGS?

The consumer finance industry is one of the most heavily regulated industries today. In addition to the federal statutes, such as TILA (consisting mostly of disclosure requirements), most states have consumer credit laws, some of which actually set ceilings on the cost of consumer credit. Most of the ceilings are on small loans and credit sales. The common law doctrine of unconscionability is also a possible source of discipline on excessive loan rates but is difficult to prove and thus has not often been successful. *See De La Torre v. CashCall*, 422 P.3d 1004 (Cal. 2018).

Critics of rate regulation make a two-fold argument: (1) let basic principles of the free market control, and (2) regulation decreases many consumers' ability to get credit. The first argument is that in the United States, government price control is resorted to only in abnormal or emergency situations. The market, not the state, controls the cost of beer; therefore, the market, not the state, should control the cost of cash. Market control of price is thought to result in the most efficient and beneficial price level, without a distortion of supply and demand. There is nothing inherent in the consumer credit market that makes it any less competitive than any other market. Second, critics argue that usury statutes hurt, rather than help consumers. The effect of regulating the finance charge in loans is to determine which consumers can obtain cash from legitimate lenders i.e., only consumers with favorable credit.

State legislatures have historically favored usury laws because these laws gave them power over the credit industry, and voters tend to favor usury laws that keep rates low. High interest rates are easy to hate. Thus, access to affordable credit will always be a popular political platform. In addition, like other advocates of usury laws, legislatures feel that regulation is necessary to prevent economic disaster and consumer exploitation. These laws are necessary to prevent lenders from engaging in such evils as discriminating or overcharging.[2] The need for some regulation may be particularly strong where many of the consumers are poor, illiterate and without political power.[3] On the other hand, since the 1980s, many states have deregulated consumer credit prices in an effort to attract large credit card issuers and other consumer lenders to their state. In addition, due to the effect of the U.S. Supreme Court decision in *Marquette National Bank v. First of Omaha*, 439 U.S. 299 (1978), to be discussed in more detail later in this chapter, many state usury laws have been rendered ineffective due to federal preemption.

C. PROBLEMS IN PROVING USURY

Although the cost of consumer credit has been significantly deregulated, usury laws continue to govern many consumer credit transactions, particularly for small loans and credit sales. So, how are usury laws applied?

Interest is the price of using someone else's capital. This price is dependent on such factors as the term of the loan, the cost to the creditor of servicing the loan, the risk that the creditor will not be repaid, the amount of the loan and the credit rating of the individual borrower. As discussed at the beginning of this chapter, usury was defined during Biblical times

---

[2] *See* Paul Hayeck, *An Economic Analysis of the Justifications for Usury Laws*, 15 Ann. Rev. Banking L. 253, 1996.

[3] *See* Gene A. Marsh, *A Practitioner's Guide to the New Alabama Mini-Code*, 48 Ala.L.Rev. 957 (1997) (noting that low income and high illiteracy rates lead to the need to protect the public in consumer credit markets).

as *any* interest. Today, however, usury is "the exaction of a greater sum for use of money than the highest rate of interest allowed by law." *Foreign Commerce v. Tonn*, 789 F.2d 221 (3d Cir. 1986).

There are generally four elements of usury:

(1) a loan of money or forbearance of debt;

(2) an agreement between the parties that the principle shall be repayable absolutely;

(3) the exaction of a greater amount of interest or profit than is allowed by law; and

(4) the presence of an intention to evade the law at the inception of the transaction.

Several matters related to the elements of usury are discussed below.

1. INTENT

The intent element of usury does not require the plaintiff to show that the defendant lender had a specific intent to commit usury. The lender's subjective intent is often viewed as irrelevant in a usury case. If the loan is usurious on its face then the courts will impute a usurious intent on the parties. "Intent in usury cases does not mean intent to charge a usurious rate of interest. Rather, it means intent to make the bargain made. The subjective intent of the lender is irrelevant if, in fact, the lender has contracted for, charged or received interest on a loan in excess of the maximum permitted by law." *Najarro v. SASI Int'l, Ltd.*, 904 F.2d 1002 (5th Cir.1990). In other words, the intent of the parties is presumed to be reflected in the documents which they signed.

2. SHOULD LOANS AND CREDIT SALES RECEIVE DIFFERENT TREATMENT?

Traditionally, general usury statutes have been applied only to loans. In the past, credit sales were sometimes viewed as exempt from provisions of general usury statutes because of a judicially created rule, commonly referred to as the time-price doctrine.

Essentially, the time-price agreement depends on the presentation of two prices to the purchaser: (1) a cash price and (2) a time-price. Under the time-price doctrine payments are to be made over a period of time, but the difference in amounts between the two prices was not considered as interest. *Whitaker v. Spiegel, Inc.*, 95 Wash.2d 408, 623 P.2d 1147 (Wash. 1981). This judicially created exception to the usury law applies to bona fide installment sales.

This is the usual justification of the time-price doctrine: that usury only applies where there is a loan or forbearance of money, and that a sale of property does not involve such a loan or forbearance. That is a narrow construction of the loan or forbearance language in usury statutes.

In modern times, the time-price doctrine is generally viewed as a legal fiction and most jurisdictions no longer apply the doctrine to consumer credit transactions for usury purposes. Thus, since courts have recognized that a modern credit sale is not logically distinguishable from a loan by the seller to the buyer, most usury laws apply to the difference between the cash price and the total of payments over time.

3. HAS THE MAXIMUM LEGAL RATE BEEN EXCEEDED?

Determining whether a creditor is charging more than the legal rate of interest is often a complex process involving a number of separate issues and problems. Lawyers working in these cases are wise to employ accountants who may do the "credit math" analysis to see if the creditor's compensation exceeds the legal limit. The process becomes even more complex as creditors' lending practices become more and more diverse. Not only is a borrower unsure whether the maximum legal rate has been exceeded, but courts have to decide whether interest has been charged at all. A detailed discussion on how to identify and compute interest for usury litigation purposes is beyond the scope of this volume.

D. FEDERAL PREEMPTION

State law is not the only regulator of interest rates. Federal law may preempt state usury laws in several different ways and areas. Under the National Bank Act, 12 U.S.C. § 85, a national bank may charge "interest at the rate allowed by the laws of the State . . . where the bank is located." The U.S. Supreme Court in *Marquette Nat'l Bank of Minneapolis v. First of Omaha Service Corp.*, 439 U.S. 299 (1978) held that this language in the National Bank Act meant that a national bank headquartered in one state, can "export" that home state's credit regulations to customers in any state in the nation. The Court reasoned that "if the location of the Bank were to depend on the whereabouts of each credit transaction, the meaning of the term 'located' would be so stretched as to throw into confusion the complex system of modern interstate banking. A national bank could never be certain whether its contracts with residents of a foreign state were sufficient to alter its location for purposes of § 85." *Marquette*, 439 U.S. at 312.

Thus, under *Marquette*, a national bank can charge the highest rate of interest allowed by the laws of the state where it is located. That means that a bank located in Nebraska may charge its cardholders the highest maximum rate of interest under Nebraska law even if its cardholders live in Minnesota and are dealing with Minnesota merchants, and even if the maximum interest is Nebraska is higher than the maximum interest in Minnesota. Furthermore, the term "interest" under the National Bank Act includes flat-rate fees charged on credit cards such as annual fees, late payment fees, returned check charges and over-the-limit fees, as well as percentage-based charges. 12 C.F.R. § 7.4001(a); *Smiley v. Citibank (South Dakota), N.A.*, 517 U.S. 735 (1996); *Richardson v. Citibank*, 908 P.2d 532 (Colo.1995) (the court held that the charge of a late fee was not prohibited where the bank was a national bank and the fee was an interest charge under 12 U.S.C. § 85 despite the fact that Colorado's law prohibited such fees.)

SEC. D   FEDERAL PREEMPTION

Shortly after the *Marquette* decision, South Dakota and Delaware eliminated their usury laws completely in order to enjoy the economic benefits that would ensue from having large national credit card issuers located in their states. Since other states could no longer control the credit rates imposed on their residents by out-of-state national banks, many states enacted "parity" laws that would allow state banks to charge whatever rates the out-of-state banks could charge. Thus, most state usury laws have become illusory due to the combination of federal preemption and changes in state laws.[4]

Federal law may also preempt state usury laws by allowing state-chartered institutions as well as national ones to charge on certain types of loans an interest rate which exceeds local ceilings. For example, the Veterans Housing Amendments Act of 1976 rendered inapplicable to certain federally insured loans and mortgages any state constitutional provision "expressly limiting the rate of interest which may be charged, taken, received or reserved by certain classes of lenders." 12 U.S.C. § 1709–1a.

Another good example of federal preemption is Title V of the Depository Institutions Deregulation and Monetary Control Act of 1980 (DIDMCA). That Act exempts mortgages or loans "secured by a first lien on residential real property" from state laws "expressly limiting the rate or amount of interest, discount points, finance charges or other charges." 12 U.S.C. § 1735f–7a(a)(2). DIDMCA also amended the

---

[4]   James J. White, *The Usury Trompe l'Oeil*, 51 S.C. L. Rev. 445 (2000).

Federal Deposit Insurance Act to give state-chartered banks the same power to export interest rates as federally chartered banks. 12 U.S.C. § 1831d(a).

In the 2000s, some states sought to stem the tide of predatory home mortgage loans by enacting anti-predatory loan statutes. These laws contained substantive restrictions on high-cost loans, including bans on balloon payments, negative amortization, increased interest rates after default, and on lending without regard to the debtor's ability to repay. *E.g.*, North Carolina Predatory Lending Act, N.C. GEN. STAT. § 24–1.1E and Georgia Fair Lending Act, GA. CODE ANN. §§ 7–6A–1 to –11. While these laws were not classic usury laws, they did attempt to provide some curbs on the cost of credit to consumers by imposing more protections on particularly high cost loans, in a manner similar to the federal Home Owners Equity Protection Act (HOEPA), discussed *supra* Chapter Seven. The reaction of the federal bank regulators, especially the Office of the Comptroller of the Currency (OCC) and the Office of Thrift Supervision, was to move to preempt such state laws if they were found to "obstruct, impair, or condition" a national bank's exercise of its powers under the National Bank Act. The U.S. Supreme Court upheld the OCC's authority to preempt state law not only with regard to federally-chartered banks, but also with regard to their nonbank subsidiaries. *Watters v. Wachovia Bank*, 550 U.S. 1 (2007).

The OCC's restrictive federal preemption policies were superseded by the provisions of the Dodd-Frank Act passed in 2010. That Act created the Consumer Financial Protection Bureau or CFPB, and empowered that agency with the authority, through rulemaking, enforcement and oversight, to regulate banks and other financial service providers that may be engaged in unfair, deceptive or abusive practices. The law also cut back on the federal preemption of state consumer financial laws, stating that such laws can be preempted only if the application of a state consumer financial law would have a discriminatory effect on national banks. 15 U.S.C. § 25b(b). Furthermore, nonbank subsidiaries of federally chartered banks no longer automatically enjoy any preemption from state law that the parent institution may have. 15 U.S.C. § 25b(e) & (h). It remains to be seen how this more state-friendly preemption approach may affect the future of state usury laws which, as noted above, had been considered effectively abolished by the effects of the National Bank Act and its interpretation by the Supreme Court.

The patchwork quilt of usury laws in place across the country may require a search of state and federal law, and in some cases several state statutes may need to be consulted. Although rate ceilings may be established in a general state usury law provision, those provisions may be overridden by separate statutory provisions that deal with pawnshops, payday loan shops, rent-to-own stores and even finance companies. The search for the appropriate usury law rarely lends itself to one-stop-shopping among the various provisions of state law.

E. TYPES OF LENDERS AND CREDIT COVERED BY RATE REGULATION

Most states have established numerous exemptions or exceptions to general usury rates and provide special ceilings with respect to finance charges. These exceptional or special rates vary depending on who the lender is or what type of credit is being extended. The most common statutes are based on the size and type of credit.

For example, virtually every state has a specific regulation for "small" loans. These "small" loans are consumer loans which in some states may be as large as $5000 while in other states as small as $2000. In addition to special rate provisions, small consumer lenders are usually also required to be state-licensed. With the resurgence of payday loans, discussed *infra*, some states have excepted payday loans from their small loan acts and provide for a separate, much higher set of usury limitations.[5] It is also very common to have separate statutes which permit very high rates on pawnshop transactions, including auto-title-pawns.

Small consumer loans made by online direct lenders are becoming more widespread. These "fintech" lenders are not banks and would normally

---

[5] Some examples of rates on payday loans established by some states for a 14 day loan are: California—625%, Iowa—391%, Florida—261%.

be subject to usury laws, state small loan regulation and licensing requirements. However, the OCC, the CFPB and some state legislatures, wishing to support innovation in consumer finance, have proposed to allow some regulatory leeway for these relatively new types of lenders to develop, through the use of "regulatory sandboxes," "no-action letters," and special federal charters. These proposals, if enacted, have the potential to free the fintech consumer financial services sector from state regulation, including interest rate ceilings.

In some states there are exceptions to general usury statutes which establish maximum rates of interest on loans secured by real estate, especially home mortgages. Additionally, most states have special legislation regulating interest charges on loans to be repaid in installments and finance charges imposed in connection with the retail installment sales, with automobiles occasionally treated separately. As noted above, during the 2000s, some states passed "anti-predatory lending" statutes with regard to high cost residential mortgage loans but were met with resistance in the form of federal preemption by the federal bank regulatory agencies.

The federal government took some significant steps in the direction of more direct substantive regulation of the cost of credit at the beginning of the 21st century, swinging the pendulum in the opposite direction of the deregulatory era of the 1980s. Thus, in 2006, Congress passed a law, the Military Lending Act, that, among other things, bars creditors from lending to military personnel or their dependents at

APRs greater than 36%. 10 U.S.C. § 987. Military service members were thought to be particularly vulnerable to short-term, high-cost loans, such as payday loans or car title loans, due to their relative youth and inexperience, isolation from friends and family, steady but modest income, and the military discipline imposed on service members who default on their loans. In 2015, the regulations were amended to broaden the coverage to include all consumer credit covered by TILA, to the extent such credit is offered to covered military borrowers. Home mortgage loans and automobile purchase loans are exempted. The CFPB and the FTC have enforcement authority for these provisions and there is also a private cause of action for military consumers. 32 C.F.R. § 232.

Nonbank lenders such as payday lenders, in theory should be subject to state usury laws regardless of the effects of federal preemption with regard to national and state chartered banks as outlined above. There is a potential exception, however, for nonbank lenders who are acting as agents for out-of-state banks who themselves have the ability to charge their home state rates, as long as the agents do not receive a "predominant economic interest" in the loan revenues. 12 U.S.C. § 1831d(a). Thus, an out-of-state bank that could legally engage in payday lending at rates that exceeded the state limits by virtue of federal preemption, could also empower a local payday lender to act as the out-of-state bank's agent, thus exempting the agent from the state usury limit as well. But courts will not tolerate schemes that tend to abuse the national bank agency exception. Thus, in a case where the local payday lender agent did all the loan processing, the out-of-state bank had no physical presence in the state, and the agents received roughly 80% of the loan revenues, a federal court declined to enjoin enforcement of a strict Georgia anti-payday lending law. The case noted the concern in some quarters that banks may be "renting out" their charters in order to allow local lenders to evade state usury laws. *Bankwest, Inc. v. Baker*, 324 F. Supp. 2d 1333 (N.D. Ga. 2004). State regulators have pursued similar cases against online lending platforms that partner with banks in order to offer usurious loans or avoid state licensing. These cases, alleging that the nonbank partner is the "true lender," have met with mixed success.[6]

Relatively new in the market currently served by payday lenders are so-called "earned wage advance" or "earned wage access" products, part of the "fintech" sector of financial services. These are Internet-based companies that work with employers and employees to allow employees to have access prior to the regular payday to wages already earned. The employees agree to have those advances repaid by a deduction from their paychecks. Because this is an automated service and repayment is virtually automatic, the fees are relatively low compared to store front payday lenders. These are nonbank entities not subject to state or federal bank

---

[6] *Meade v. Avant of Colorado, LLC*, 307 F. Supp. 3d 134 (D. Colo. 2018); *Meade v. Marlette Funding, LLC*, 2018 WL 1417706 (D. Colo. 2018) (in both cases, the Colorado Uniform Consumer Credit Code Administrator succeeded in at least avoiding federal preemption and removal to federal court).

regulation, and it is also unclear whether they are even subject to other consumer credit laws, including usury laws, since technically they are not charging "interest" on a "loan," even though they seem to function very similarly to payday loans.[7]

Other types of third parties may be subject to state usury laws, despite the widespread cloak provided by the National Bank Act (NBA). Thus, a third party debt collector that had actually purchased the consumer debt outright from a national bank was not able to convince the Second Circuit Court of Appeals that it could avail itself of the preemption available to national banks for its interest charges in excess of applicable state law. Since the bank no longer had any ownership or other interest in the debt, and the debt collector was not itself a national bank nor a subsidiary of a national bank, nor acting on behalf of a national bank, it had no federal preemption defense under the NBA to the state usury charges. *Madden v. Midland Funding*, LLC, 786 F.3d 246 (2d Cir. 2015).

The CFPB issued a rule in 2017 to regulate on a federal level certain fringe, nonbank lenders, such as payday lenders, car title lenders and pawn shops. That rule was substantially cut back by a rule amendment issued by the CFPB in July, 2020. The revoked portion of the regulation, while not directly regulating the cost of credit, would have required lenders of these types of loans to make an initial determination of the borrower's ability to repay the

---

[7] *See* Jim Hawkins, *Earned Wages Access and the End of Payday Lending*, 101 BOSTON U. L. REV. (forthcoming 2020).

loan in full when it is due. The rationale is to avoid debtors being trapped in a cycle of borrowing. Additional loans by the same lender to refinance the same debt would have been restricted. These aspects of the regulation were eliminated by the 2020 amendments, based on further consideration. The portion of the 2017 regulation that limited repeated attempts by lenders to collect payment from consumers' empty bank accounts was retained. Such automatic withdrawal attempts were made subject to notice requirements and limited to two unsuccessful attempts without borrower authorization.[8]

Some have suggested that the 36% usury limits contained in the Military Lending Act, discussed above, could be extended to all consumers under federal law, or that the MLA could be used as a template for further state or federal usury regulation.[9] This approach could provide an alternative to the now-sidelined CFPB payday lending regulation, to help consumers avoid excessive interest rates imposed by payday and similar small dollar lenders.

---

[8] This aspect of the final amended regulation is currently codified at 12 C.F.R. § 1041.7–.9.

[9] Paul E. Kantwill & Christopher L. Peterson, *American Usury Law and the Military Lending Act*, 31 LOY. CONSUMER L. REV. 500 (2019).

CHAPTER TEN

HOLDER IN DUE COURSE AND WARRANTIES

A. THE HOLDER IN DUE COURSE DOCTRINE

1. INTRODUCTION

In the mid-20th century, retailers often arranged for financing of the sale of most consumer goods. Although some retailers kept their installment sales contracts and collected the monthly payments themselves, most retailers sold the product but assigned (sold) the installment sales contract to a finance company or bank. By the turn of the 21st century, however, most retailers of goods and services abandoned installment sales contracts in favor of credit card sales (or for low income customers, rent-to-own), with the exception of motor vehicles, which are still financed through the dealer. One of the big drawbacks of installment sales contracts for consumers was that when consumers had trouble with the product or had a legal claim against the seller, they often faced an assignee/finance company that demanded to be paid and legally could be kept out of any dispute between the consumer and the retailer.

Prior to the development of the FTC Rule, discussed in the next section, consumers would often find themselves obligated to pay the holder of the note financing a sale even though they might have had a valid defense against the original seller. This was due to the ancient doctrine protecting the "holder in due course" of negotiable instruments. The purpose underlying this doctrine was first stated in the eighteenth century and was usually described as being needed to promote "the growth of commerce by assuring liquidity of commercial paper."[1] That is, individuals are normally willing to finance and purchase paper only if payment is reasonably certain, or at least not subject to common disputes which occasionally arise between the buyer and seller of the goods.

The principles of the Holder in Due Course (HDC) doctrine were incorporated in the Uniform Commercial Code (UCC), which is now the statutory source of the doctrine. Through the application of several sections of the UCC, a "negotiation" (usually a sale) of a promissory note to a holder in due course separated the buyer's obligation to pay from the seller's obligation to perform. According to the UCC, a holder in due course is a holder who takes the instrument:

(a) For value; and

(b) In good faith; and

---

[1] *See* Thomas J. Grendell, *Let the Holder Beware! A Problematic Analysis of the FTC Holder in Due Course Rule*, 27 Case W. Res. L. Rev. 977, 979 (1977) (containing an excellent historical analysis of the holder in due course doctrine and the development of the FTC Rule).

(c) Without notice that it is overdue or has been dishonored or of any defense against or claim to it on the part of any person.[2]

Because holder in due course status shields the holder from defenses most commonly raised by consumers who were sold defective goods or services, the status of a holder in due course has sometimes been described as that of a "superplaintiff."[3] The same defense-free status could also be achieved by mere contract assignees, who normally would be subject to claims against the original seller, due to the inclusion of a "waiver of defense" clause by which the consumer "agreed" to raise their claims and defenses only against the immediate seller, and not against the assignee.

Prior to the passage of the FTC regulation, the issue was stated succinctly by contracts scholar Grant Gilmore:

> It is hard, and it becomes each year harder, for counsel to explain convincingly why "the law" requires that a hard-pressed wage-earner who has been bilked by a now-insolvent seller into buying junk masquerading as a television set or a washing machine must pay the full price to a bank or finance company whose own

---

[2] UCC § 3–302(a).

[3] *See* James J. White & Robert S. Summers, Uniform Commercial Code 613 (3d ed. 1988).

relationship with the fraudulent seller has been intimate, long-continued and profitable.[4]

Dissatisfaction with the harsh operation of the holder in due course doctrine (and the related "waiver of defense" clauses) in consumer transactions caused reaction on several fronts. During the 1960s and early 1970s, some courts concluded that particular buyer-transferees of consumer paper were too closely connected to the seller-transferor to be protected by HDC status.[5] For example, in *United States Finance Co. v. Jones*, 229 So.2d 495 (Ala.1969), where the homeowner received tar paper sprayed with paint instead of aluminum siding, the Alabama Supreme Court upheld the trial court's denial of holder in due course status, citing the steep discount in the purchase price of the note and the fact that the mortgage and certificate of completion of the work were signed on the same date. The court focused on the "good faith" element of the holder in due course test, but noted that the number of transactions between the contractor and lender, along with the knowledge the lender had of the contractor's business, made it difficult to view the lender as an innocent purchaser for value without notice.

During the same period, some 40 states enacted anti-holder-in-due course legislation, at least as it affected consumer transactions. For example, in

---

[4] Grant Gilmore, *The Commercial Doctrine of Good Faith Purchase*, 63 Yale L.J. 1057, 1098 (1954).

[5] Most commentators cite Unico v. Owen, 232 A.2d 405 (N.J.1967), as the landmark decision in what is now called the "closely connected" doctrine.

Alabama, a section of the Alabama Consumer Credit Act (the Mini-Code), adopted in 1971, makes either a holder or an assignee subject to all claims and defenses of the buyer arising out of a consumer credit sale or consumer lease.[6] The Uniform Consumer Credit Code (UCCC), a model state law adopted in eleven states, also contains provisions that both prohibit the use of negotiable instruments in consumer credit sales, and make contract assignees subject to all claims and defenses of the consumer against the seller notwithstanding that the assignee is a holder in due course. UCCC §§ 3.307 and 3.404. However, the failure of all of the states to pass legislation to protect consumers, the ineffectual nature of some of the statutes, and the creative strategies used by some lenders to circumvent state regulation caused the Federal Trade Commission to respond.

2. THE LOSS OF HOLDER IN DUE COURSE STATUS IN CERTAIN CONSUMER LENDING

In 1975, the Federal Trade Commission promulgated its Trade Regulation Rule Concerning Preservation of Consumers' Claims and Defenses (FTC Holder Rule), codified at 16 C.F.R. Part 433. After an extensive review of selling and lending practices in many sectors of the economy, including major appliances, home improvements, and the sale of aluminum siding, the FTC concluded that unethical merchants and lenders were victimizing

---

[6] Ala. Code § 5–19–8.

consumers.[7] The operation of the holder in due course doctrine was viewed as inappropriate and outdated in consumer settings.

Under the HDC doctrine, consumers were relegated to private actions against the seller of goods, which were often fruitless because the retailers were frequently on the move and judgment proof.[8] Further, many consumer claims were so small that attorneys would not take their cases. Consumers were thus viewed as lacking the economic muscle to enforce their rights against sellers.

In response to these considerations, the FTC Rule requires that most consumer credit contracts contain the following provision:

NOTICE

ANY HOLDER OF THIS CONSUMER CREDIT CONTRACT IS SUBJECT TO ALL CLAIMS AND DEFENSES WHICH THE DEBTOR COULD ASSERT AGAINST THE SELLER OF GOODS OR SERVICES OBTAINED PURSUANT HERETO OR WITH THE PROCEEDS HEREOF. RECOVERY HEREUNDER BY THE DEBTOR SHALL NOT

---

[7] *See* Michael F. Sturley, *The Legal Impact of the Federal Trade Commission's Holder in Due Course Notice on a Negotiable Instrument: How Clever Are the Rascals at the FTC?*, 68 N.C. L. Rev. 953, 955 (1990).

[8] Michael T. Lewis & Gregg L. Spyridon, *Preservation of Consumer Claims and Defenses: Miller's Tale Tolled By FTC (Or is it?)*, 47 Miss. L.J. 768, 781 (1976).

EXCEED AMOUNTS PAID BY THE DEBTOR HEREUNDER.

The inclusion of the FTC-required "notice" in the contract basically eliminates the holder-in-due course shield by agreement. The FTC Rule was adopted specifically to prevent the seller from making the consumer's obligation to pay independent of the seller's obligation to perform the contract and comply with consumer protection laws. The FTC supported the Rule with the explanation that if the seller was out of business or sold defective merchandise, then, as between the consumer and the assignee-lender, the latter was in the best position to protect itself against dealer misconduct, thus policing the consumer marketplace. Lenders had better access to information regarding the dealer and could resort to reserve or recourse agreements with the dealer in the event the consumer raised a legitimate defense. In crafting the dealer agreement, the lender could require the dealer to buy back the note if the consumer raised a defense to payment. Because the lender could transfer back to the dealer the costs of any "misconduct" that had occurred, the FTC described the Rule as one which would "internalize" the costs of the failed performance of the seller, removing that cost from the consumer.[9]

Although justification for the FTC Rule may be stated in terms of "internalization of costs," a more simply stated purpose is to indirectly drive dishonest

---

[9] FTC, Trade Regulation Rule, Preservation of Consumers' Claims and Defenses, Statement of Basis and Purpose, 40 Fed. Reg. 53,506, 53, 509, 53,522–23 (Nov. 18, 1975).

dealers out of the market. It was thought that lenders who experienced losses in paper purchased from a dealer would likely cut the dealer off and not finance new contracts made between that dealer and consumers. Because the lender is subject to consumer claims and defenses based on the underlying contract, buying paper from a bad dealer is buying trouble unless the lender is able to shift the loss back to the dealer through a provision in the dealer agreement.

The last sentence in the required notice under the FTC Rule purports to place a limit on the liability of the lender where the consumer is raising a claim or defense. The sentence reads: "[r]ecovery hereunder by the debtor shall not exceed amounts paid by the debtor hereunder." The origin of this language and its application in judicial decisions will be examined next.

3. SHOULD THE FTC RULE LIMIT AFFIRMATIVE RECOVERY?

The Federal Trade Commission developed the Rule anticipating a defensive use by consumers. By sweeping away the classic holder in due course doctrine in consumer transactions, the FTC expected that consumers would commonly use the FTC Rule to assert the right to avoid future payments, and even recover payments made, based on the claim that the seller had delivered defective goods or had otherwise breached the agreement. Nothing in the FTC Rule itself or the commentary surrounding the rule limits the effect of the Rule to contractual claims and defenses, however. The FTC expressly included fraud in the list of claims preserved in their Guidelines on the Rule.

There are a few judicial decisions interpreting the FTC Rule in cases where consumers have made a claim for an affirmative recovery. In *Eachen v. Scott Housing Systems*, 630 F. Supp. 162 (M.D.Ala.1986), the court held that under the FTC Rule consumers are *not* limited to asserting claims against lenders only by way of defense or set-off. The court noted that if the consumer has a legitimate defense and stops payment, he may be sued for the balance due by the third-party lender. The lender, however, may elect not to bring suit, especially if he knows that he would be unable to implead the seller and he knows the consumer's defenses may be meritorious. Thus, the consumer should be allowed to make an affirmative claim.

The Texas Supreme Court has held that a creditor's derivative liability for seller misconduct is limited to the amount paid by the consumer under the contract. The court stated the issue in *Home Savings Ass'n v. Guerra*, 733 S.W.2d 134 (Tex.1987), as whether an assignee of a retail installment contract can be held derivatively liable for the seller's misconduct in excess of the amount paid by the buyer. In finding a limit on the creditor's liability, the court traced the development of the FTC Rule and reasoned that a rule of unlimited liability would place the creditor in the position of an absolute insurer or guarantor of the seller's performance.

In a somewhat restrictive view of the consumer's right of recovery under the FTC Rule, the Massachusetts Supreme Court held that the consumer's affirmative recovery against a creditor not only is available only up to the amount already paid by the consumer, but also is limited to situations where the consumer would be entitled to rescission and restitution from the seller. *Ford Motor Credit Co. v. Morgan*, 536 N.E.2d 587 (Mass. 1989). *See also Irby-Greene v. M.O.R., Inc.*, 79 F. Supp. 2d 630 (E.D. Va. 2000).

Despite these cases, the language of the FTC Rule contains nothing that indicates that affirmative recovery is meant to be limited to only certain types of egregious claims against the seller, as long as the claims are meritorious. As stated by the FTC in a 2012 Opinion Letter, the only limit on affirmative recovery is that the recovery should not exceed the amount already paid by the consumer.

Punitive damages awards, as well as attorney's fees, are not considered "claims" against the seller, and thus cannot be raised against the holder who is only derivatively liable. An award of attorney's fees that went beyond the amount already paid by the debtor was precluded in a Nebraska case. *State ex rel. Stenberg v. Consumer's Choice Foods, Inc.*, 755 N.W.2d 583 (Neb. 2008). A California Court of Appeals case also held that any award of attorney's fees beyond the amount already paid by the debtor is precluded, not because it was not a claim against the seller, but because under the plain language of the Holder Rule, the consumer's recovery is limited to amounts already paid. *Lafferty v. Wells Fargo Bank, N.A.,* 25 Cal. App. 5th 398 (2018).

4. LIMITATIONS ON THE FTC HOLDER RULE'S COVERAGE

While the promulgation of the FTC Holder Rule has eliminated the issue of HDC protection for third party financers in the vast majority of consumer credit transactions involving the sale of goods or services, there are some gaps in its coverage. First, the FTC Rule does not cover residential real estate credit transactions, which are often financed using negotiable instruments, i.e., promissory notes, that can create holders in due course. The FTC Rule only covers credit sales or leases of goods and services. Second, the FTC Rule makes it an unfair trade practice for the seller to accept a consumer credit contract that fails to contain the required FTC Notice. It does not directly regulate the financer. Also, many third-party financers are banks, and banks are not within the jurisdiction of the FTC. Thus, if a consumer credit transaction that should have contained the FTC Notice in fact does not, the consumer may well have to fall back on state laws that effectively eliminate HDC status from holders of consumer contracts that should have contained the notice.

The Uniform Commercial Code itself, which as stated above is the statutory source of the HDC doctrine, may also be the source of the solution. In 2002, the drafters of the UCC proposed the addition of Article 3, Section 305(e), which basically states that if another law, such as the FTC Rule, requires the inclusion of a statement that the rights of a holder or transferee are subject to the claims or defenses of the original consumer, and that statement was not included, then the instrument has the same effect as if it had included the statement, and the consumer can assert claims and defenses against the holder or transferee. Only a minority of state legislatures have adopted this proposed amendment, however.

5. SPECIAL CASES OF THIRD-PARTY CREDITOR LIABILITY—CREDIT CARDS

There are some third-party financer liability situations that are dealt with outside of the FTC Holder Rule. For instance, as discussed previously in Chapter Eight, under Creditor Defenses in Truth in Lending, assignees of consumer credit contracts are only liable for TILA violations apparent on the face of the loan documents. This TILA provision prevails over the FTC Holder Notice. For the category of high cost HOEPA loans, however, assignees are liable for all TILA violations whether apparent or not.

As stated at the beginning of this chapter, most credit sales of consumer goods and services are now financed with credit cards, rather than through retailer-initiated installment contracts. But there is still a three party transaction involved in credit card sales, with the possibility of separating the consumer's duty to pay the third party credit card issuer from the seller's (or merchant's) duty to honor their warranties or to comply with other legal requirements. Some protection is provided to consumers in this situation under the Truth in Lending Act, as will be discussed below.

Consider the following example. Bob purchases a lawnmower from Sears on his Sears credit card. He takes the lawnmower home but is unable to get the mower to start. So, Bob returns the mower to Sears and demands a refund. The fact that Bob used the Sears card does not affect his rights as to Sears. But, what if Bob purchased the lawnmower with a bankcard, such as a VISA card? Now, there are three parties and three contracts involved.

The first contract is between Bob and the VISA card issuer, which arose when Bob applied for and accepted the VISA card. The credit card agreement between Bob and VISA authorizes VISA to pay money to Sears (or another merchant) when it presents VISA with a "sales slip." In exchange for this payment, the agreement also contains the terms upon which Bob is to repay VISA for the credit so extended, such as the finance charged involved, grace period and minimum payment, as discussed in Chapter Seven. The second contract is between VISA and Sears. That agreement, among other things, sets forth the terms and conditions whereby VISA will accept sales slips presented by Sears. The third contract is between Sears and Bob. That contract is contained in the sales slips which Bob signed for the purchase of the mower. Since there are three parties now, can Bob assert the same product defense against VISA, rather than against Sears? The Truth-in-Lending Act say yes in certain situations.

Under 15 U.S.C. § 1666i, consumers can assert product defenses against a credit card issuer if the merchant is located in the same home state as the cardholder or within 100 miles of his address. This geographic limitation, however, may be considered as waived by the issuer if it agrees to assist a cardholder in a dispute with a foreign merchant. *See Hyland v. First USA Bank*, 1995 WL 595861 (E.D.Pa.) In mail-order cases the question of where a particular transaction took place is determined according to the applicable state law. *See Izraelewitz v. Manufacturers Hanover Trust Co.*, 465 N.Y.S.2d 486 (NY Civ. Court. 1983). Although the geographic limitation may seem harsh, especially, when card holders use credit cards for purchases made while traveling out of state or even out of the country, courts have declined to make any such exception to the statute. *See Singer v. Chase Manhattan Bank*, 890 P.2d 1305 (Nev.1995).

Additionally, before the cardholder can assert any defense against the issuer he must make "a good-faith attempt to resolve the dispute with the person honoring the credit card."[10] And, the purchase price must be greater than $50 because a transaction for $50 or less is treated as if it had been a cash transaction.

If a consumer has already paid the disputed balance, he loses any further rights to assert claims and defenses other than billing errors. The 60-day time limit for consumers to notify the card issuer of a

---

[10] Regulation Z, 12 C.F.R. § 1026.12(c)(3).

billing error, however, is not applicable to the right of the cardholder to assert claims or defenses against the card issuer. *See Citibank (South Dakota), N.A. v. Mincks*, 135 S.W.3d 545 (Mo. Ct. App. 2004). The merits of the claims and defenses available against the issuer because they are available against the seller, are determined by the applicable state law.

The other limitation placed on consumers by the Truth in Lending Act is that the cardholder may only withhold payments up to the amount of credit outstanding from the property or services that gave rise to the dispute and any finance or other charges imposed on such amount. That amount is determined at the time the cardholder first notifies the card issuer or the person honoring the card of the existence of a claim or defense. If a consumer withholds a disputed amount, the card issuer may not issue an adverse credit report or begin collection of the disputed amount until after the matter has been investigated. 12 C.F.R. § 1026.12(c)(2).

In most cases, rather than going after the cardholder for non-payment of a disputed purchase, the issuer has a much quicker remedy against the merchant. Generally, issuers, particularly issuers of general bank credit cards, have agreements with merchants whereby the issuers may charge-back the merchant's account for charges made where the purchaser disputes the sale of merchandise or services performed or for the non-delivery or the return of merchandise. The charge-back simply involves the issuer bank pulling the merchant's account and reversing the credit originally given by the bank on receipt of the "sales slip" signed by the consumer.

B. WARRANTIES

1. UNIFORM COMMERCIAL CODE—ARTICLE TWO

Warranties accompanying the sale of consumer products are governed by the Uniform Commercial Code (UCC).[11] The UCC applies to both commercial and consumer transactions, and is premised on the philosophy of freedom of contract between equal parties. State and federal law has overlaid some special protections for consumers with regard to warranties, but the UCC, a uniform state law that has been enacted in every state, remains the foundation.

The warranty provisions that may affect consumer purchases of goods are contained in Article Two of the UCC. This article underwent a prolonged and controversial amendment process in the late 1990s and at some points included a few pro-consumer proposed amendments in the warranty provisions. Ultimately the amended Article Two was fairly weak, was not adopted by any state legislature and was withdrawn from consideration by the Code drafters in 2011. Thus, the provisions of Article Two remain

---

[11] For a detailed treatment of UCC warranties, lemon laws and the Magnuson-Moss Warranty Act, *see* Dee Pridgen, Richard M. Alderman & Jolina Cuaresma, *Consumer Protection and the Law*, Chapters 14–18 (2019–2020 ed.); National Consumer Law Center, *Consumer Warranty Law* (5th ed. 2015).

SEC. B   WARRANTIES

for the most part as they stood when originally adopted in the 1960s.

Three warranties under the Code have the broadest impact on consumer transactions: express warranty, implied warranty of merchantability and implied warranty of fitness. While these warranties provide some benefits to consumers, other Code provisions, such as warranty disclaimers and remedy limitations, have been used to severely limit the usefulness of the UCC warranties with respect to consumer transactions.

Section 2–313 describes a number of actions of the seller which may result in an express warranty. Of course, an express warranty may be created as a result of a statement made by the seller to the buyer. The statement need not include the words "warrant" or "guarantee." For example, a statement by a boat dealer that a boat is new constitutes an express warranty. The statement need not be in writing, although oral statements present obvious parol evidence problems. The statement must be an "affirmation of fact" or "promise" as contrasted with an "affirmation of value," "opinion" or "commendation." Phrases such as "perfect condition," "last a lifetime," and "as good as anyone's" have been regarded as "puffing" rather than warranties.

Under section 2–314, a warranty of merchantability is implied in every sale of goods by a merchant seller. Section 2–314(2) sets out a nonexclusive listing of the attributes of merchantability. The key concept is that the goods must be "fit for the ordinary purposes for which such goods are used." For example, there is an implied warranty of merchantability that an automobile will be able to provide basic transportation. Failure to satisfy this standard is the usual claim in merchantability litigation.

Section 2–315 contains the implied warranty of fitness for a particular purpose. This warranty arises whenever any seller, merchant or not, has reason to know (1) the *particular* purpose for which the goods are to be used and (2) that the buyer is relying on the seller's skill and judgment to select suitable goods. For example, if customer describes his needs to seller, failure of the hot water heater recommended by seller to produce sufficient hot water is a breach of warranty.

The standard remedies for breach of warranty under the UCC include damages, § 2–714, rejection of goods that do not conform to the warranty, § 2–601, and revocation of acceptance and return of the defective goods leading to a refund of the purchase price, § 2–608. Since most consumers are not in a position to resell defective goods, the remedy of keeping the goods and collecting damages for the loss in value caused by the breach is not very useful. The remedy of rejection is only available if the buyer acts very quickly. In the typical consumer case, however, the buyer will keep the product for a period of time while trying to obtain a repair or a refund from the seller, so that rejection may no longer be available. The best UCC remedy for most consumers is revocation and refund, *i.e.*, returning the product and getting their money back. But that remedy has been difficult for consumers to obtain due to various barriers that are allowed by the UCC, including the fact that 2–608 is usually not applicable to manufacturers who did not deal directly with the consumer.

To recover on an implied warranty theory and/or to obtain the remedy of revocation and refund, a consumer may have to show, among other things, privity of contract, *i.e.,* a direct contractual relationship between the injured plaintiff and the defendant. This requirement eliminates the possibility of a direct suit against a manufacturer who sells through a retail dealer. Most states have long eliminated the privity requirement in warranty actions for personal injuries. A growing number also waive the privity requirement for consumer claims against a manufacturer for breach of the implied warranty in cases involving purely economic loss. *See, e.g., Hyundai Motor America, Inc. v. Goodin,* 822 N.E. 2d 947 (Ind. 2005).

Another barrier to consumers seeking the preferred remedy of revocation and refund has been the standard remedy limitation, limiting the consumer suffering a breach of warranty to the remedy of repair or replacement of defective parts. UCC § 2–719. Such remedy limitations resulted in classic "lemon" situations, where the consumer is caught in an endless cycle of repairs and replacements that never seem to result in a defect-free car. In this situation, the consumer would rather just return the "lemon" and receive a refund. UCC § 2–719(1)(b), allows a claim that the limited remedy had "failed of its essential purpose," but that approach, while successful in some cases, has proven arduous and costly.

Under Section 2–719(3), a limitation of consequential damages for personal injury caused by consumer goods is considered prima facie unconscionable. This presumption of unconscionability does not apply to situations where the defective product causes only economic loss, however. Thus it is not applicable in the vast majority of cases where the consumer seeks a remedy for breach of warranty in consumer goods.

The state lemon laws are aimed at addressing this issue of limited remedies for breach of warranty, and will be discussed later in this chapter.

Warranty disclaimers are another obstacle faced by consumers in their quest for a remedy under the UCC for defective products that cause economic loss. *Express* warranties are very difficult to disclaim. The disclaimer must be express and must *not* be inconsistent with the express warranty. However, UCC § 2–316 allows for easy elimination of *implied* warranties. Under § 2–316(2) a disclaimer of an implied warranty of merchantability must mention merchantability and, *if in writing*, must be conspicuous. A term or clause is conspicuous when it is so written that a reasonable person against whom it is to operate ought to have noticed it. UCC § 1–201(10). For example, "SELLER MAKES NO WARRANTY OF MERCHANTABILITY WITH RESPECT TO GOODS SOLD UNDER THIS AGREEMENT," would probably be sufficient to disclaim the implied warranty of merchantability under this standard.

Section 2–316(2)'s requirements for disclaimer of warranties of fitness are quite different. The disclaimer *must be in writing* and conspicuous but need not specifically mention fitness. For example, "THERE ARE NO WARRANTIES WHICH EXTEND BEYOND THE DESCRIPTION ON THE FACE HEREOF" could be adequate to disclaim the implied warranty of fitness.

Despite the specific and different requirements just described, § 2–316(3) provides for the effective disclaimer of *all* implied warranties by words of general disclaimer. The words of general disclaimer include "as is," "with all faults" or similar language which "calls the buyer's attention to the exclusion of warranties and makes plain that there is no implied warranty." In a Minnesota case, however, the state supreme court held that a seller's fraudulent statements about a vehicle's condition and fitness prevented the seller from enforcing such an "as is" disclaimer. *Sorchaga v. Ride Auto*, LLC, 909 N.W.2d 550 (Minn. 2018).

Where a warranty has been successfully disclaimed under the UCC, or the remedy for breach has been limited, the buyer's cause of action for a breach of that warranty may be stymied. In such situations, the federal Magnuson-Moss Warranty Act, as well as certain state laws such as the new car lemon laws, may step in to supplement the UCC and provide the consumer with better remedies.

2. THE MAGNUSON-MOSS WARRANTY ACT

a. Overview

The Magnuson-Moss Warranty Act (MMWA) was passed by Congress in 1975, and is codified at 15 U.S.C. §§ 2301–2312. This legislation was aimed at several consumer issues regarding product warranties that were prevalent at the time, namely: (1) consumers did not understand the language and complex provisions of most warranties; (2) many warranties merely gave the appearance of meaningful protection against defects, but contained hidden qualifications or proviso's that made the warranties less than expected; and (3) consumers who felt victimized by warranty breaches did not have meaningful access to the courts or other methods of enforcing their rights under the warranties. The statute was designed primarily as a disclosure regime to promote consumer understanding of warranties, which would in turn promote competition among sellers to provide better warranties. The law also contains some important substantive protections for consumers, however.

Like most consumer protection statutes, the Magnuson-Moss Warranty Act is limited in scope. It applies to manufacturers and sellers of "consumer products" who make express "written warranties." "Consumer product" is defined as "any tangible personal property . . . which is normally used for personal, family, or household purposes." 15 U.S.C. § 2301(1). Thus, the particular buyer's subjective purpose in buying the product is irrelevant, but rather the "normal" type of use is what determines where or not it is a consumer product under the MMWA. Also, due to the definition of "consumer product," the statute does not cover real estate. The phrase "written warranty" is another term that limits the scope of the MMWA. "Written warranty" is not exactly the same as an express warranty under the UCC, although it is very similar. This definition applies to most written promises that a product will be defect-free, as well as most promises to repair or take other remedial action. 15 U.S.C. § 2301(6). Dealers who make no written promises of their own but simply pass on the manufacturer's written warranty may not be covered.

As consumer leases, particularly of motor vehicles, have risen in popularity, the issue has come up as to whether the MMWA applies to consumer products that are leased by the consumer, rather than purchased outright. While the statute and regulations do not address the issue directly, the current trend in judicial interpretations is to include leases within the coverage of the MMWA. *See, e.g., Peterson v. Volkswagen of America, Inc.,* 697 N.W.2d 61 (Wis. 2005); *Ryan v. American Honda Motor Co., Inc.,* 896 A.2d 454 (N.J. 2006). This result has been achieved through intensive analysis of the statutory terms, especially the term "consumer," which can include any person to whom the product is "transferred" during the warranty term, or to any person "entitled to enforce" the warranty. 15 U.S.C. § 2301(3).

b. Disclosure Requirements

The MMWA is basically a disclosure statute. Sellers and manufacturers are not required to make any warranties at all. If, however, a "supplier" issues a "written warranty" it must comply with the disclosure requirements of the Act as supplemented by rules promulgated by the Federal Trade Commission. 16 C.F.R. Part 700. The disclosure provisions of the Act are mainly enforced by the FTC. Under the MMWA, a violation of any of the Act's warranty requirements is a violation of section 5 of the Federal Trade Commission Act. 15 U.S.C. § 2310(b).

Any "supplier", *i.e.*, manufacturer or seller, using a written warranty in connection with sale of a product costing more than $15 must, to the extent required by FTC rules, "fully and conspicuously disclose in simple and readily understandable language the terms and conditions of such warranty." The contents of the warranty disclosure and the topics that must be covered are set out in 16 C.F.R. § 701.3. The provision that the language be "simple and readily understandable," however, has proven more difficult to enforce in any specific way.

In order for consumers to be able to understand and compare warranties, the MMWA requires that the text of all written warranties must be available to consumers before they buy. 15 U.S.C. § 2302(b)(1)(A); 16 C.F.R. § 702. This so-called "pre-sale availability" rule was meant to allow consumers to comparison shop for the best warranties, in the same way that TILA, by requiring prior disclosure of the costs of credit, was meant to create more competition in the consumer credit market. However, the retailer has considerable flexibility in terms of how to carry out this requirement. The retailer could make its warranties available on its website, or simply on request. It is unclear whether many consumers are inclined to seek out and compare warranty terms prior to purchase.

In addition to pre-sale availability, another way that the MMWA sought to promote comparison shopping for the best warranties was to mandate the use of standardized labels. Thus, the statute requires that all written warranties of consumer products costing more than $10 be clearly and conspicuously designated as either "full" or "limited." 15 U.S.C. § 2303. The MMWA drafters may have surmised that this kind of labeling might create more of a demand for "full" warranties, which are clearly more pro-consumer than most limited warranties.

The "full" warranty is a very good warranty for consumers and if available, could provide consumers with good remedies for products that turn out to be lemons. A warranty can be designated "full" only if it completely complies with the requirements of 15 U.S.C. § 2304.[12] A "warrantor" who gives a "full" warranty must fix a product that is defective or otherwise fails to conform to the written warranty

---

[12] 15 U.S.C. § 2304, setting forth the standards for the "full" warranty designation, is confusingly titled "Federal Minimum Standards for Warranties," thus leading some to conclude, erroneously, that these requirements apply to all warranties, rather than only to those that choose to use the "full" warranty label.

within a reasonable time and without charge. Under a "full" warranty, if repeated repair efforts fail to remedy the product, the consumer must be given a choice of a refund or replacement without charge. In essence, this aspect of the MMWA is an anti-lemon provision. The protection of a "full" warranty extends to "each person who is a *consumer* with respect to the consumer product," which in effect eliminates the privity requirement discussed above in the UCC section, at least for these warranties. "Consumer" is a statutorily defined term that includes second buyers and bailees. 15 U.S.C. § 2301(3).

Unfortunately for consumers, in the decades following the passage of the MMWA, very few manufacturers have actually offered "full" warranties as defined. Remember, Magnuson-Moss does not require a manufacturer or a seller to make a written warranty of any kind, either full or limited. If no written warranties are issued, Magnuson-Moss does not apply. Yet warranties are attractive to consumers, and a supplier can offer a warranty and avoid complying with the "full" warranty requirements by designating the warranty as "limited." It appears that the vast majority of consumer product warranties post-MMWA have been "limited" warranties, so the idea that the standard labels could help consumers distinguish broad categories of warranties has not been fulfilled.[13]

---

[13] *See* Janet W. Steverson & Aaron Munter, *Then and Now: Reviving the Promise of the Magnuson-Moss Warranty Act*, 63 U. Kansas L. Rev. 227 (2015).

c. Substantive Requirements and Provisions

The MMWA also helps address some of the other consumer issues with warranties, namely the disclaimers and remedy limitations that take away warranty protections, and the lack of access to meaningful enforcement. If suppliers offered "full" warranties as envisioned, such warranties would indeed get rid of the remedy limitation issues encountered by many consumers. As noted above, however, not that many "full" warranties are being offered.

Another problem with consumer warranties pre-MMWA was that a written warranty might appear to provide protection, but in fact was quite limited in duration, scope or in other ways. In that situation, a consumer might want to fall back on the underlying implied warranty of merchantability or fitness, but implied warranties can be easily disclaimed under the UCC. The MMWA addressed this by declaring, under 15 U.S.C. § 2308, that suppliers who make "written warranties," as defined in the Act, either full or limited, *cannot disclaim* implied warranties. A supplier who gives only a limited warranty, however, although it cannot completely disclaim the implied warranty, can restrict the duration of implied warranties. Such duration limits on the implied warranty are allowed if the following three requirements are satisfied: (1) such limitation is conscionable, (2) is in clear and unmistakable language and prominently displayed on the face of the warranty, and (3) the duration is reasonable.

Another important and often overlooked aspect of the MMWA is that § 2310(d) gives consumers the right to bring private actions for breach of written warranty, implied warranty, or service contract covered by the Act in state or federal court and receive attorney's fees and other litigation costs from the defendant if the consumer prevails. This is very beneficial to consumers who would not otherwise be entitled to attorney's fees and costs in a UCC breach of warranty action that was not pled under the MMWA.

Consumers can also bring an action to enforce the disclosure provisions of the MMWA. Since there are no statutory damages such as there are for TILA violations, however, there is not as much of an incentive to bring such an action as actual damages would likely be minimal. Access to federal court and to class actions is also quite limited.

In a breach of warranty action brought pursuant to the MMWA, the consumer can recover her litigation costs only if she "prevails" in her warranty claim and if she brings her action under 15 U.S.C. § 2310(d). Lack of privity might still be a problem for a consumer seeking to sue a manufacturer for a breach of the implied warranty of merchantability. The MMWA defers to state law for the definition of implied warranties, and if state law requires privity for an implied warranty action, then the MMWA right of action will be of no avail. *See, e.g., Voelker v. Porsche Cars N. Am., Inc.*, 353 F.3d 516 (7th Cir. 2003). As one court put it, "If state law requires vertical privity to enforce an implied warranty and there is none, then, like the yeastless soufflé, the warranty does not 'arise.' " *Feinstein v. Firestone Tire & Rubber Co.,* 535 F. Supp. 595, n. 13 (S.D.N.Y. 1982). As noted previously in the section on UCC warranties, however, many states have waived the privity requirement for breach of the implied warranty of merchantability in consumer cases. So the outcome will vary from state to state.

There are other restrictions on bringing private actions under Magnuson-Moss § 2310 (and thus on recovery of litigation costs by successful warranty claimants.) First, the warrantor must be "afforded a reasonable opportunity to cure" the breach of warranty, 15 U.S.C. § 2310(e). Second, if the warrantor has established informal dispute settlement procedures that comply with FTC regulations, the consumer plaintiff must first exhaust those procedures before seeking judicial redress under § 2310(d).

d. Informal Dispute Resolution and Arbitration Under the MMWA

One of the goals of the MMWA was to increase consumers' access to effective remedies for breaches of consumer product warranties. One way the Act attempted to achieve this goal was by encouraging warrantors (usually manufacturers) to establish informal dispute resolution mechanisms in-house that would provide an inexpensive and timely way for consumers to resolve their warranty complaints. The FTC prescribed rules governing these mechanisms, which are aimed at ensuring fairness and impartiality of the process. 16 C.F.R. Part 703. The use of these procedures is not mandatory, and manufacturers are not required to set them up, but if a conforming procedure is available and it is incorporated into the written warranty, the warrantor may require the consumer to use the mechanism prior to going to court to enforce their MMWA rights. 15 U.S.C. § 2310(a)(3). The establishment of MMWA informal dispute resolution mechanisms blossomed with the rise of state lemon laws. These laws, as discussed below, also required use of FTC Rule 703—complying procedures prior to consumers' going to court to enforce their lemon law rights. Since consumers were more likely to go to court over a new car lemon than most other products, automobile manufacturers set up these procedures shortly after the initial passage of the state lemon laws during the 1980s.

The FTC's implementing regulation, Rule 703, is detailed and complex, but basically tries to ensure a fair and speedy process for dispute resolution provided by the warrantors themselves. Some of the major provisions include: (1) consumers may not be charged a fee for using the mechanism; (2) the staff of the mechanism must be shielded from influence by the warrantor through various safeguards; (3) deadlines are provided for concluding the process; (4) informal methods of presentation are encouraged; and (5) decisions of the mechanisms, are not binding on the consumer, who is free to pursue their rights in court should they be dissatisfied with the decision.

Beginning in the 1990s, a strong trend began to develop toward the inclusion in consumer contracts, including warranties, of clauses requiring all disputes to be determined by binding arbitration. Such arbitration is not the same as the MMWA informal dispute resolution mechanisms, but instead is modeled on commercial arbitration. Under these mandatory arbitration clauses, the parties pay a private arbitrator of their choice to hear evidence and make a decision that is binding on both parties, thus precluding the consumer from going to court or appealing the arbitrator's decision. This is quite different from the FTC Rule 703 process, which requires that the process be free to the consumer and also nonbinding, thus preserving the consumer's right to go to court.

Although the FTC opined that binding arbitration clauses in warranty contracts are prohibited by MMWA, most courts that have considered the issue have ruled otherwise. Based on the policy of the Federal Arbitration Act (FAA) which strongly favors the enforcement of arbitration clauses, these courts have concluded that the FAA in effect "trumps" the MMWA even though both are statutes passed by Congress.[14] As warrantors switch from self-funded informal dispute resolution mechanisms to binding arbitration clauses, the availability of the more consumer-friendly processes encouraged by the MMWA may shrink.

---

[14] *See Walton v. Rose Mobile Homes, LLC*, 298 F.3d 470 (5th Cir. 2002); *Davis v. Southern Energy Homes, Inc.*, 305 F.3d 1268 (11th Cir. 2002).

3. LEMON LAWS

In the 1980s, the United States saw a wave of state legislation aimed at providing some relief to owners of new cars experiencing seemingly endless trips to the dealer for ineffective repairs of serious defects. Such cars are commonly referred to as "lemons," and the state laws addressing the issue have become known as "lemon laws." The state lemon laws were a reaction to the inadequacies of both the UCC and the Magnuson Moss Warranty Act in terms of providing adequate remedies to new car owners for warranty breaches. The lemon laws thus supplement the preexisting legal regime for the relatively narrow, but all important, category of new cars in private hands. Lemon laws have been passed in all fifty states and the District of Columbia.[15] There was no single "uniform" law model for the state lemon laws, so each one has slight variations. Nonetheless, there are some common basic features of all the state lemon laws, which will be discussed in this section.

Like most consumer protection statutes, the state lemon laws are limited in scope. Most of these laws cover new passenger vehicles meant for personal, family or household use, although some also include other types of vehicles such as light trucks, motorcycles and recreational vehicles. Most cover vehicles that are leased as well as those that are purchased. Also, lemon laws typically cover only "new" vehicles, but there is some variation as to what

---

[15] *See* Dee Pridgen, Richard M. Alderman & Jolina Cuaresma, *Consumer Protection and the Law*, Appendix 15 for a summary of the state lemon laws (2019–2020 ed.).

is considered "new." Many include vehicles that are still under the manufacturer's warranty. *See, e.g., Britton v. Bill Anselmi Pontiac-Buick-GMC, Inc.*, 786 P.2d 855 (Wyo. 1990). Others look to whether the car's ownership has changed after significant mileage has been put on it.

The typical state lemon law covers only problems that breach the warranty on the vehicle, and that result in substantial impairment of use, value or safety. There are also applicable time periods during which the consumer must discover and report the defect. Typically this would be within one year of purchase or during the period of the express warranty, whichever is earlier. While the coverage of lemon laws is relatively narrow, there has been quite a bit of litigation activity under them because a new motor vehicle is a relatively high cost product, and plays a very important role in the economic lives of most American consumers.

The goal of the lemon laws is to provide consumers with better remedies if they are among the unfortunate few who end up purchasing a new car suffering serious defects. The laws do this by providing the consumer with a direct cause of action against the manufacturer, thereby eliminating the privity barrier. To invoke this relief, consumers must provide the manufacturer with notice of the problem and allow the manufacturer an opportunity to attempt to repair.

All lemon laws overcome the barrier of "remedy limitation" clauses in warranties, as permitted by the UCC. Under the lemon law, if certain prerequisites are met, the car owner is entitled to a refund of the purchase price or a comparable replacement vehicle. These lemon law remedies supersede any remedy limitation contained in the warranty. There is no need to prove that the limited remedy of repair and replacement of defective parts has "failed of its essential purpose," as would be the case under Article 2 of the UCC. Rather, each state's lemon law provides that a specific number of failed repair attempts, or a specified number of days out of service, will presumptively constitute a "reasonable" opportunity to repair, thus entitling the consumer to the lemon law remedies of refund or replacement vehicle. The typical number of failed repair attempts allowed is three or four, and the typical number of days out of service is 30.

States are divided as to whether the vehicle can be eligible for "lemon law remedies" if the vehicle is ultimately repaired but the applicable presumptive number of repair attempts or days out of service has occurred. An Ohio case held that if the 30 day period had passed during which the vehicle was inoperable, the consumer could still demand a refund even though the repair was later completed successfully. As the Ohio court said, these specific time limits in the lemon laws of most states, are meant to provide a bright line demarcation of when "enough is enough." *Royster v. Toyota Motor Sales, U.S.A., Inc.*, 750 N.E.2d 531 (Ohio 2001).

The lemon law "remedies" are for the most part either a refund or a replacement vehicle. Some state laws say the initial choice between a refund or replacement is up to the consumer, some say it is up to the manufacturer, and some do not specify. There are variations among the states and in individual cases as to what constitutes a "comparable" replacement vehicle, and as to whether or not the consumer can "veto" a proffered replacement. As to the refund option, most state laws include taxes, registration and other charges in the refund amount. Most also allow a deduction from the refund for the value of the consumer's use of the car. Each state lemon law contains a formula or criteria for calculating the amount of this deduction.

Like the MMWA discussed in the previous section, the lemon laws also sought to encourage informal dispute resolution as an inexpensive and relatively speedy path to a remedy. To carry out this goal, most of the state lemon laws require that the consumer "exhaust" any available dispute resolution mechanism provided by the manufacturer, as long as that mechanism meets certain standards. Most states simply incorporated by reference the standards set forth by the FTC under the Magnuson Moss Act in 16 C.F.R. § 703. Faced with a possible deluge of lemon law court cases, most car manufacturers were inspired to set up such mechanisms. Some states require state certification of compliance with the FTC standards. A few, such as Connecticut, Vermont and Texas, set up their own state-run dispute resolution systems. As noted above in the MMWA discussion, many manufacturers now attempt to compel binding arbitration of lemon law disputes by including an arbitration clause in the consumer contract. In this situation, the federal statutory policy in favor of enforcing mandatory arbitration clauses may preempt the state lemon law.

Most state lemon laws provide that if the consumer is unable to satisfactorily resolve the dispute using the informal mechanism, that consumer may go to court seeking her lemon law remedies. If the consumer does go to court and prevails, she can recover attorney's fees and costs from the defendant.

Now that lemon laws have been on the books for decades, there have been many instances of consumers returning their "lemons" to the manufacturer, who then attempts to resell that vehicle. Since most consumers would not want to purchase a known "lemon," or at least would want to enjoy a substantial discount on such a vehicle, most state lemon laws provide for a disclosure or so-called "title branding" of the status of the vehicle that has been returned as a lemon. This allows the subsequent purchaser to have the relevant information before buying.

While the purchasers of new cars are protected by lemon laws, many low income consumers are relegated to the used car market, which is not subject to lemon laws except in a few states. The FTC Used Car Rule, promulgated in the early 1980s amid much controversy, provides some limited protection to used car buyers. The FTC Used Car Rule requires used car dealers to display the FTC Buyers Guide on the window of used cars offered for sale. The Guide includes disclosure of any applicable warranty coverage, an explanation of the meaning of the term "as is" (*i.e.,* no warranty), a warning to consumers to get all promises in writing, and a suggestion that consumers ask about the possibility of third party inspection. 16 C.F.R. § 455. The specifications regarding the Buyers Guide were amended effective 2018, by updating and improving the required disclosures.[16] There is no requirement that used car dealers disclose known defects, however. This relatively weak regulation is enforced solely by the FTC. There is no private right of action.

Since most used cars are sold without warranties, buyers will often have to fall back on common law fraud or on the state UDAP statutes prohibiting deceptive and unfair trade practices. A major obstacle in this approach is that most misrepresentations are made orally, whereas the contract of sale will likely contain a "merger" clause that effectively subsumes all oral representations. Hence the FTC's Buyer's Guide advises used car buyers to get all promises in writing.

Federal law provides a type of "warranty" protection with regard to the mileage or odometer reading on used vehicles. Rolling back odometers is a common type of fraud perpetrated on used car buyers. Because low mileage can significantly increase the value of a used car, any type of odometer tampering or setback can result in a major loss to the unwitting consumer. In response to this problem, Congress in 1972 passed the Motor Vehicle Information and Cost Savings Act, known informally as the "Odometer Act," codified at 49 U.S.C.

---

[16] 81 Fed. Reg. 81664 (Nov. 18, 2016), effective January 2018.

§§ 32701–32711. This law prohibits odometer tampering backed up by stiff penalties. It also requires that any transferor of a motor vehicle give the transferee a cumulative mileage disclosure or a disclosure that the actual mileage is unknown. These disclosures can provide a paper trail for detecting at what point in the chain of title odometer tampering occurred. Consumers have a private right of action with statutory damages and attorney's fees.

4. HOME WARRANTIES

Unlike the situation for consumer products, there is very little statutory warranty protection for consumers who purchase residential real estate. In this area, caveat emptor, or "buyer beware," still has some sway as a legal doctrine. This is somewhat dismaying, since as it is often said, a home is usually the largest single purchase that most consumers will make in their lifetime. Nonetheless, home buyers must rely on builders to voluntarily offer a homeowners' warranty, or on the judicial conferring of an "implied warranty of habitability," a doctrine that emerged from the slow process of common law development.

Starting in the late 1960s and early 1970s, and continuing through the 21st century, state courts gradually recognized and enforced an implied warranty of habitability running from the builder/seller to the original buyer of a new home. The courts recognized that after World War II single family homes were being built by developers on a mass production scale. At the same time, the ordinary home buyer was not in a position to discover defects that were not visible on the surface of the home, such as latent problems with plumbing, wiring or the foundation. *See, e.g., Tavares v. Horstman,* 542 P.2d 1275 (Wyo. 1975). Gradually, over time, courts in most states have applied the implied warranty of habitability in favor of first buyers who sued the builder/developer. This warranty has also been included in state legislation in some states. Basically, this warranty covers only latent or hidden defects that actually render the home "uninhabitable," or that at least are substantial. The implied warranty can cover off-site issues such as defective drainage systems, and in some cases can be invoked by homeowners' associations. *See Maronda Homes, Inc. v. Lakeview Reserve Homeowners Association, Inc.,* 127 So. 3d 1258 (Fla. 2013).

Since latent defects in a building, such as problems with the foundation, may not be discovered for a period of time, the question arose as to whether subsequent buyers had a cause of action against the builder/vendor. Less than half the states have been willing to extend such protection. The denial of such coverage is generally based on the lack of privity between the builder/vendor and the subsequent buyers. Also, no state implies a warranty from the seller of a used home who was not the original builder, due to the fact that a non-builder seller should not have to guarantee the work of the builder. A disappointed buyer in this situation will have to rely on common law fraud or a state UDAP statute, if applicable to real estate.

There are statutes in about a third of the states mandating warranty protection with regard to condominium buyers. Condominiums typically are developed from pre-existing apartment buildings and provide a way for buyers to own their own apartments while sharing some common facilities. These laws are typically derived from the Uniform Condominium Act or the Uniform Common Interest Ownership Act.

For those who rent rather than own their homes, many states have enacted landlord-tenant laws that aim to protect tenants from paying for uninhabitable housing. There have also been cases that have implied a warranty of habitability for tenants even in the absence of a specific landlord-tenant statute. *See, e.g., Javins v. First National Realty Corp.*, 428 F.2d 1071 (D.C. Cir. 1970).

Finally, low income and/or rural consumers are more likely to purchase manufactured housing or mobile homes than they are to purchase traditional real estate, because the cost of such housing is significantly lower. According to several studies, a large number of mobile home buyers experience major problems with the product itself or with the installation shortly after the purchase. Due to the fact that the manufacturer producing the product and the dealer who does the installation are typically separate entities, the consumer who complains about an issue is often caught in a type of limbo where the manufacturer blames the dealer and vice versa, but neither one is willing to address the problem.

Mobile homes are moved to the site, but they are often attached to real property in some way, making it unclear whether they are personal property or real property. Because these homes were not built on site but were moved there and not sufficiently attached to the land, mobile homes are often treated as personal property under the UCC. Cases are mixed as to whether a mobile home would be a "consumer product" under the MMWA, or whether it would be real property that is not covered. There are federal construction and safety standards for manufactured homes, but the law lacks a private remedy for consumers.

In response to consumer concerns and the gap in statutory protections, at least 22 states have enacted statutes that cover mobile home warranties.[17] These state laws typically require that the manufacturer issue an express warranty covering major defects. Enforcement of the warranties can still be an issue, however. The warranties can be enforced by the consumer and many statutes provide attorney's fees if the buyer prevails in a breach of warranty suit, which should be helpful to consumers who could not otherwise afford to litigate. On the other hand, mobile home contracts often contain mandatory arbitration clauses, which may pose an obstacle to the consumer seeking to enforce a warranty in court.

---

[17] *See* Dee Pridgen, Richard M. Alderman & Jolina Cuaresma, *Consumer Protection and the Law*, Appendix 17 for a summary of the state mobile home warranty laws (2019–2020 ed.).

CHAPTER ELEVEN
DEFAULT AND DEBT COLLECTION

A. LIMITS ON DEFAULT PROVISIONS IN CONSUMER CREDIT CONTRACTS— FTC CREDIT PRACTICES RULE

1. INTRODUCTION

A number of common clauses in consumer credit contracts are aimed at smoothing the way for creditors to collect in the event of default by the consumer. Six specific credit practices based on such clauses were considered unfair or deceptive, and are prohibited by the FTC Trade Regulation Rule Concerning Credit Practices (Credit Practices Rule), 16 C.F.R. Part 444, promulgated in 1985. Finance companies, retailers and other creditors within the jurisdiction of the FTC are subject to the Rule. The Consumer Financial Protection Bureau (CFPB) enforces the Credit Practices Rule, directly or indirectly, with regard to banks and other financial entities within its jurisdiction.

As noted previously in Chapter Two, there is generally no private right of action under the FTC Act for violation of an FTC Rule. However, state UDAP provisions that prohibit unfair or deceptive acts and practices could be used to challenge violations of the FTC Rule. A violation of an FTC Rule is treated as a *per se* violation of some state UDAP statutes.

Despite the relative clarity of the Credit Practices Rule and the enforcement alternatives available, many creditors continue to include prohibited provisions in their contracts. Spotting violations of the Credit Practices Rule, particularly among subprime lenders and credit sellers, is not uncommon. This is particularly true in the areas of confessions of judgments, waiver of exemptions and the taking of non-purchase money security interests in certain household goods.

2. PROHIBITED PRACTICES

The practices prohibited by the Credit Practices Rule that will be discussed below include: the use of cosigner provisions without providing the proper warning notice; pyramiding of late charges; confessions of judgment; non-purchase money security interests in household goods; waivers of exemptions; and assignments of wages.

a. Cosigner Provision

Many consumers, particularly those who are too young to have much of a credit record, or those who have built up a bad credit record, may not be able to get credit without getting a "cosigner" on their loan. A cosigner provides extra security for the creditor, who can look to the cosigner to pay the debt on the same basis as the principal debtor. Many cosigners are friends or relatives of the principal debtor who agree to cosigning without necessarily having full information on their obligations and the potential risks involved. Nonetheless, cosigning has its legitimate uses and can provide a way for a marginal borrower to receive a loan.

The FTC took the approach of requiring a plain English disclosure of cosigner liability prior to the transaction, rather than banning the practice. Thus, under 16 C.F.R. § 444.3, the failure to provide cosigners with the following warning, indicating the potential obligations of a cosigner, is prohibited by the Credit Practices Rule. The required notice is as follows:

NOTICE TO COSIGNER

You are being asked to guarantee this debt. Think carefully before you do. If the borrower doesn't pay the debt, you will have to. Be sure you can afford to pay if you have to, and that you want to accept this responsibility.

You may have to pay up to the full amount of the debt if the borrower does not pay. You may also have to pay late fees or collection costs, which increase this amount.

The creditor can collect this debt from you without first trying to collect from the borrower.

The creditor can use the same collection methods against you that can be used against the borrower, such as suing you, garnishing your wages, etc. If this debt is ever in default, that fact may become a part of *your* credit record.

This notice is not the contract that makes you liable for the debt.

This disclosure must be made on a separate document and be given to the cosigner prior to their becoming obligated. A person is not considered a cosigner if they are a joint applicant who is entitled to receive the proceeds or will be the co-owner of property purchased in the transaction.

b. Pyramiding Late Charges

Most consumer credit accounts, both open and closed end, impose a "late charge" if a scheduled payment is not made on time. Such charges, if reasonable in amount, are a legitimate charge to incentivize the borrower to pay on time and to cover the creditor's costs stemming from the late payment. When the creditor engages in a practice of stacking or pyramiding the late charges, however, the FTC considered there to be a potential unfair trade practice. "Pyramiding" occurs if the creditor assesses more than one delinquency charge for one late payment. Thus, under the Credit Practices Rule, if a debtor was late with a payment and was assessed a late fee on that payment, but failed to include the late fee in their next payment, a second late fee could not be added to the account if the next monthly payment arrived on time. It would be appropriate to add and carry the first late fee on the account, but not to add a second late fee unless the consumer was again late in making a subsequent payment. 16 C.F.R. § 444.4.

c. Confession of Judgment

Under the Credit Practices Rule, a consumer credit obligation must not contain a "cognovits" or confession of judgment, warrant of attorney or other waiver of the right to notice and the opportunity to be heard in the event of suit. 16 C.F.R. § 444.2(a)(1). Such a clause is an extremely harsh provision under which the borrower agrees in advance to allow the creditor's attorney to appear in court and enter a judgment against the debtor without any prior notice or right to contest. Most consumers did not understand the consequences of such provisions, which the FTC deemed to be unfair. While many state laws and individual court cases had already restricted or banned confession of judgment clauses, the Credit Practices Rule provides a comprehensive and absolute ban on their use.

d. Non-Purchase Money Security Interests in Certain Household Goods

In retail credit sales, the creditor will often take a security interest in the item being sold. This is known as a "purchase-money security interest." This type of security interest is expected by most consumers. Most people expect that the creditor could repossess the item (e.g., automobile or furniture) purchased on credit if they fail to make their required payments. Some lenders, however, required borrowers to offer as security for the loan not just the item purchased, but also all of their household goods. It is this type of "non-purchase" security interest in household goods that is limited by the Credit Practices Rule. 16 C.F.R. § 444.2(a)(4).

The futility and predatory nature of taking a security interest in existing household goods has long been attacked by consumer advocates. In many cases, creditors had no intention of foreclosing on this collateral, but merely took the security interest to exert leverage over the debtor, through the threat of repossession and the embarrassment it would cause. Most household goods have little resale value. It would cost more to repossess them than they would bring in resale. Thus, the unfairness of this type of security interest lies in its use as a psychological weapon to convince a defaulting consumer to possibly forego legitimate defenses or to take steps to pay they would not otherwise take, simply to protect his or her possessions that have more value to the consumer than they do to the creditor.

The Credit Practices Rule does not prohibit all non-purchase security interests, however. Recognizing that some household goods do have value and could appropriately serve a legitimate legal and economic interest as collateral for the credit transaction, the Rule allows for non-purchase money security interests in works of art, electronic entertainment equipment (except one television and one radio), items acquired as antiques and jewelry (except wedding rings). 16 C.F.R. § 444.1(i).

Through informal staff opinion letters, the FTC includes within the definition of "household goods," such items as vacuum cleaners, air conditioners, freezers, ovens, microwaves, fans, clocks and other items that are ordinary and essential items in daily living. Thus, through inclusion in the definition of "household goods," these items are intended to be protected from a non-purchase money security interest. But excluded from the definition of "household goods," and therefore subject to a security interest are such items as luggage, hot tubs, boats, snowmobiles, tape players, and barbeque grills. Since these excluded items of personal property also have low resale value and high personal value to the consumer, however, the FTC may have undermined the intent of its own regulation in the course of defining what is or is not covered.

e. Waiver of Exemptions

Every state has laws that exempt from seizure or attachment by creditors certain categories of property, such as a homestead, furniture and clothing, which are considered necessities of life. These so-called "exemption" laws were designed to allow debtors and their families to avoid destitution and to rehabilitate themselves to the extent that they could ultimately repay their debts. Some creditors sought to avoid the effects of the exemption laws by including in their contracts clauses under which the debtor "waived" the exemptions. As with non-purchase security interests in household goods, the exemption waivers were not well understood by consumers, and when they came into play, could be used by creditors as "in terrorem" weapons to pressure consumers into paying.

The FTC concluded that the waiver of exemption clauses were a different means to achieve the same effect as non-purchase money security interests in household goods. Thus, under the Credit Practices Rule, consumer credit contracts must not contain a waiver of exemptions concerning property exempt from attachment or execution, with some limited exceptions. 16 C.F.R. § 444.2(a)(2).

f. Assignment of Wages

A wage assignment is a contractual granting of a type of security interest in yet to be earned wages. Such a contract clause gives the creditor the right to receive wages directly from the consumer's employer, without any type of prior notice or judicial hearing. Wage "garnishment," by contrast, requires a court judgment and order, and is also subject to procedural and substantive safeguards. The FTC considered wage assignments to be unfair for the same reasons as the previously discussed non-purchase security interests in household goods and waiver of exemptions. These clauses can be used as a threat by the creditor to gain an unfair advantage. Also, consumers often do not understand the meaning of the clause or the grave consequences of losing one's salary without any recourse.

Thus, the Credit Practices Rule states it is an unfair act or practice for a consumer credit contract to include a provision for the assignment of wages, unless:

(1) the assignment by its terms is revocable at the will of the debtor, or

(2) the assignment is a payroll deduction plan or preauthorized payment plan, commencing at the time of the transaction, in which the consumer authorizes a series

of wage deductions as a method of making each payment, or

(3) the assignment applies only to wages or other earnings already earned at the time of the assignment.

16 C.F.R. § 444.2(a)(3).

"Earned wage advances," described *supra* Chapter Nine, are a relatively new phenomenon, in which a lender, an employee and an employer agree that earned wages can be advanced on request to the employee by the lender, and then automatically deducted from the upcoming paycheck to be paid back. This type of arrangement does not appear to run afoul of the Credit Practices Rule, and in fact is currently in a regulatory limbo.

Mandatory wage assignments are allowed in the context of pre-arranged payroll deduction plans of the type used to make regular payments in credit union loans, or to pay for insurance, healthcare, retirement and investment accounts, as long as only a part of the debtor's paycheck is taken or if the deductions are revocable. Employers do not violate the Rule by complying with a wage assignment, regardless of its legality under the Rule.

B. INFORMAL DEBT COLLECTION

1. INTRODUCTION

Debtors default on their credit obligations for many reasons, including job loss, medical bills, divorce, widowhood, etc. When debtors default, creditors will try to collect what is owed. Sometimes creditors collect their own debts "in-house," and at other times the creditor will place its unpaid debt with third party debt collectors. Such third-party debt collectors will be paid a portion of the amount collected. Ultimately, if all else fails, the creditor can sell accounts to debt buyers who acquire debts in large portfolios, for which they pay pennies on the dollar but keep whatever amount they can manage to collect.[1]

Because of the delay and expense involved in litigation, the creditor or other debt collector is likely initially to employ extra-judicial tactics to obtain payment. The extra-judicial collection method most generally used is the collection letter. This letter, containing a request for payment, can be either cordial or hostile depending on the policy of the debt collector and the length of time that the debt is outstanding. Debtors often do not respond to a polite request for payment. Consequently, creditors and debt collectors seek other methods to recover the money due and owing, including telephone calls, texts, emails, personal visits, threats of litigation, use of social media, and communications with the debtor's employer, family or friends. Occasionally the creditor or his agent becomes overzealous, particularly when the debtor is weak and vulnerable. Such practices may include late night or repeated telephone calls, false threats of lawsuits or arrest,

---

[1] Federal Trade Commission, COLLECTING CONSUMER DEBTS: THE CHALLENGES OF CHANGE 2–4 (2009), available at http://www.ftc.gov/.

threats to ruin a consumer's credit rating, and embarrassing communications with third parties, such as neighbors, friends or employers. Sometimes debt collectors will file en masse standardized lawsuits in small claims courts, often resulting in default judgments, which in turn enhances the leverage the collector has against the debtors.

2. COMMON LAW ACTIONS

Since 1977 there has been a federal statute, the Fair Debt Collection Practices Act (FDCPA), limiting debt collection practices by third party debt collectors. That law, however, does not apply to all debt collection, as will be explained below. As a result, overzealous extra-judicial collection efforts have also been subject to lawsuits based on common law actions, including defamation, invasion of the right to privacy, and intentional infliction of mental anguish. Recoveries on these theories, however, are relatively rare.

Defamation is aimed at publication of *false* material that results in injury to reputation. Truth is thus a defense—in most jurisdictions, an absolute defense. A statement truthfully disclosing that a debt is due, owing and unpaid is not actionable. A statement that falsely imputes a *general* unwillingness to pay debts or unworthiness to obtain credit may be the basis of a defamation action. To be subject to a defamation claim, the falsehood also must be publicized to other parties, not simply in direct communications with the debtor.

Another defense to defamation is privilege. A communication will be privileged if it pertains to a matter in which the recipient of the communication has a legitimate interest. Informing an employer that his employee has not paid his debts is a common collection tactic to induce payment through indirect pressure on the employee. Employers want to avoid the bother and costs of wage garnishment. Courts are divided as to whether employers have a sufficient interest to cause the communication to be privileged.

Debtors have also sued on invasion of privacy for injuries resulting from creditors' communications with employers—generally with little success. Public disclosure of private facts is one form of invasion of the right to privacy. However, as a general rule, reasonable oral or written communications to an employer have not been viewed as a sufficient disclosure of private facts; as with defamation, the communication is privileged based on the employer's interest in his employee's debts.

Some courts have granted recovery where the creditor has done more than inform the employer that a debt is overdue—for example, contacting the employer on numerous occasions. Additionally, there are cases finding an invasion of privacy by communications such as calls to the debtor's neighbors, publication of the debtor's name and amount of debt in a newspaper, and posting a notice of the indebtedness at the creditor's place of business. *See Jones v. U.S. Child Support Recovery*, 961 F. Supp. 1518 (D. Utah 1997).

A second form of violation of the right to privacy is a wrongful intrusion on the solitude of the debtor. Obviously, every creditor contact, every intrusion, is not actionable. The creditor has the right to contact the debtor—has the right to try and collect the debt. The problem is one of balancing the respective interests. Only unreasonable intrusions are actionable. In determining reasonableness, courts generally consider factors such as the content, nature, number and time of communications.

Where these communications are "extreme and outrageous" and result in severe emotional distress, the debtor may be able to recover on a theory of *intentional infliction* of mental distress. RESTATEMENT OF TORTS, Second, § 46. Several difficulties are inherent in such an action. As the "name" of the tort indicates, the debtor faces the problem of proving intent. The debtor must show that the collector intended the mental distress. The collector's actions must be beyond all bounds of decency. As one court put it, "the conduct must strike to the very core of one's being, threatening to shatter the frame upon which one's emotional fabric is hung." *Hamilton v. Ford Motor Credit Co.*, 502 A.2d 1057 (Md. App. 1986).

Another difficulty attending this cause of action is the requirement that the emotional stress be severe. The normal strain caused by contact with a collection agency is not sufficient. The debtor has to establish serious mental stress. *See, e.g., Caputo v. Professional Recovery Services, Inc.*, 261 F. Supp. 2d 1249 (D. Kan. 2003). Finally, a number of courts are still hesitant to impose liability for mental distress alone, and insist on some form of physical injury. Even if the debtor is able to establish all of the elements of one of the above-discussed common law causes of action, he or she still faces the problem of proving damages.

In addition to common law claims, many states have statutes which regulate debt collection activities. Some of the statutes are comprehensive, while others are weak tea.[2] Commonly found in the state laws are provisions for licensing of collection agencies, lists of prohibited practices, and the range of penalties provided for violation of the state law. In some states, statutory damages and attorney fees for successful consumers are available. Some states also cover practices of creditors collecting their own debts, whereas the federal statute does not. Nonetheless, it was the lack of meaningful legislation on the state level that led to the enactment of the Fair Debt Collection Practices Act of 1977 (FDCPA).

3. FAIR DEBT COLLECTION PRACTICES ACT

a. Introduction

The Fair Debt Collection Practices Act (FDCPA), in effect since 1978, is codified at 15 U.S.C. §§ 1692–1692*o*. It features a private right of action to enforce its provisions, as well as government enforcement. In

---

[2] For a summary of the state debt collection statutes, *see* Dee Pridgen, Richard M. Alderman & Jolina Cuaresma, *Consumer Credit and the Law*, Appendix 12 (2020 ed.); National Consumer Law Center, *Fair Debt Collection*, Appendix L (9th ed. 2018).

the early years, the Federal Trade Commission was the main enforcement agency, but did not have the authority to issue implementing regulations. The Consumer Financial Protection Bureau (CFPB) currently has sole rulemaking authority and concurrent enforcement authority with the FTC. The CFPB issued proposed regulations under the FDCPA in 2019, but they have not been finalized as of this writing. Both the FTC and the CFPB have been quite active in bringing cases against debt collectors who violate the FDCPA.

The purposes of the FDCPA are to eliminate abusive debt collection tactics and to ensure that ethical debt collectors are not competitively disadvantaged. The FDCPA prohibits debt collectors from using harassing or abusive conduct, false or misleading representations, or any unfair means to collect a consumer debt. Certain types of communications with debtors and third parties are also restricted.

b. Transactions and Persons Covered

Only consumer debts are covered by the FDCPA. A consumer debt is one in which a natural person is obligated to pay a debt arising out of a transaction that is primarily for personal, family or household purposes, whether or not such obligation has been reduced to judgment. 15 U.S.C. § 1692a(5). It also includes alleged debts and alleged debtors, in addition to valid debts and actual debtors. A consumer debt can include an obligation that is not the typical consumer loan or credit transaction. For example, in *Ladick v. Van Gemert*, 146 F.3d 1205 (10th Cir. 1998), an attempt to collect a condominium association assessment was held to trigger the provisions of the FDCPA. And in *Snow v. Jesse L. Riddle, P.C.*, 143 F.3d 1350 (10th Cir.1998), an attempt to collect on a dishonored check was held to be within the protections of the FDCPA. An FDCPA "debt" must arise out of a "transaction," and thus the term does not include the collection of unpaid taxes or fines, *see Gulley v. Markoff & Krasny*, 664 F.3d 1073 (7th Cir. 2011), nor does it include unpaid child support payments, *see Mabe v. G.C. Services Ltd. Partnership*, 32 F. 3d 86 (4th Cir. 1994).

Only debt collectors are covered by the Act. A debt collector is defined in 15 U.S.C. § 1692a(6) as:

> any person who uses any instrumentality of interstate commerce or the mails in any business the principal purpose of which is the collection of any debts, or who regularly collects or attempts to collect, directly or indirectly, debts owed or due or asserted to be owed or due another. (T)he term includes any creditor who, in the process of collecting his own debts, uses any name other than his own which would indicate that a third person is collecting or attempting to collect such debts.

Note that the definition refers to a person collecting debts "owed or due or asserted to be owed or due another." The definition of debt collector does not include a creditor collecting its own debt in the name of that creditor. 15 U.S.C. § 1692a(6)(A). As mentioned above, in that situation, an aggrieved debtor may have to fall back on common law tort actions or state debt collection laws for legal relief from harassing debt collection practices by creditors.

Debt buyers have become an increasingly important segment of the debt collection business within the last few decades, although they were not so prevalent when the FDCPA was passed in the late 1970s. Debt buyers purchase debts originally owed to others, but currently owed to them as the owners of these debts. In 2017, the U.S. Supreme Court considered whether or not a company that purchased debts already in default would be considered a "debt collector" as defined by the statute. Resolving a split in the federal circuit courts, and applying a strict textualist analysis, the Court in *Henson v. Santander Consumer USA, Inc.*, concluded that a debt buyer collecting debts owned by it was not an FDCPA "debt collector." 137 S. Ct. 1718 (2017). The Court noted that since the debt buyer in question owned the debts it was seeking to collect, it was not collecting or attempting to collect "debts owed or asserted to be owed or due another," which was the statutory definition of "debt collector." 15 U.S.C. § 1692a(6). Given the rise of debt buyers in the debt collection industry, this decision potentially exempts from the FDCPA a large portion of entities that are actually collecting debts. These exempt collectors may still be subject to regulation under state law, as noted above.

The *Henson* court did not rule on whether a debt buyer who owns the debts it collects might nonetheless be considered an FDCPA "debt collector" under the alternative part of the definition that includes any "business the principal purpose of which is the collection of any debts . . ." Subsequent Court of Appeals cases have held that any business, including one that buys debts, can be an FDCPA "debt collector" as long as the entity's most important aim is obtaining payment on the debts it acquires. *Barbato v. Greystone Alliance, LLC*, 916 F.3d 260 (3d Cir. 2019); *McAdory v. M.N.S. & Associates, LLC*, 952 F.3d 1089 (9th Cir. 2020).

The definition of "debt collector" also includes an attorney who regularly collects or attempts to collect, directly or indirectly, consumer debts. *Heintz v. Jenkins*, 514 U.S. 291, 115 S. Ct. 1489, 131 L.Ed.2d 395 (1995). Attorneys are frequent targets of FDCPA litigation, and many courts have grappled with the determination of what activities of an attorney constitute "regular" collection of debts. Law firms that specialize in debt collection are clearly subject to the FDCPA. The difficult cases arise when an attorney or a firm collects a debt for a client or clients only for a portion of their time. Many courts use a multi-factor test to determine whether or not an attorney or a firm is engaged in the regular collection of debt. Such factors include: the number of debt collection cases or activities; the frequency of such activities; the frequent use of particular debt collection documents; whether there is a steady relationship between the attorney or firm and a collection agency or creditor client; and the portion of the overall caseload that constitutes debt collection. *See Goldstein v. Hutton, Ingram, Yuzek, Gainen, Carroll & Bertolotti*, 374 F.3d 56 (2d Cir. 2004); *James v. Wadas*, 724 F.3d 1312 (10th Cir. 2013); and

Schroyer v. Frankel, 197 F.3d 1170 (6th Cir. 1999). Thus, attorneys who collect debts for clients on anything more than a minimal or isolated basis should be familiar with the provisions of the FDCPA lest they open themselves to liability. As will be seen in the discussion below, there are many technical provisions of the FDCPA that go beyond simply acting ethically.

In addition to the exclusion of creditors collecting their own debts, there are a number of other exclusions from the FDCPA's definition of "debt collector." Federal and state employees collecting debts in the performance of their official duties are exempt. 15 U.S.C. § 1692a(6)(C). There was an exemption from the Telephone Consumer Protection Act's ban on "robo calls" to mobile phones for persons collecting debts owed to or guaranteed by the federal government. That exemption was struck down by the U. S. Supreme Court, however, on the basis that it was in violation of the First Amendment because it was content-based and singled out a group of persons for special treatment. *Barr v. American Ass'n of Political Consultants,* 140 S. Ct. 2335 (2020). Also excluded are certain private entities that work with the local prosecutor to run pretrial diversion programs aimed at bad check writers. 15 U.S.C. § 1692p(a)(1). Nonprofit credit counseling programs that assist consumers in paying their debts are excluded from coverage as well. 15 U.S.C. § 1692a(6)(E).

Persons such as repossession companies or attorneys or others who engage in non-judicial foreclosures are specifically included in the definition of debt collector, at least with respect to the duty under 15 U.S.C. § 1692f(6), *i.e.,* not taking or threatening to take any nonjudicial action to effect dispossession or disablement of property if there is no present right to possession of the property claimed as collateral. 15 U.S.C. § 1692a(6). Thus, companies that do in fact have a right to repossess the collateral are often deemed to be excluded from the Act because they are only covered if they violate that particular provision. As to nonjudicial foreclosures, however, the Circuit Courts of Appeals had been divided, until the issue was resolved by the U.S. Supreme Court in 2019. In the case of *Obduskey v. McCarthy & Holthus, LLP*, 139 S. Ct. 1029 (2019), the Court held that a law firm whose collection activities were limited to nonjudicial foreclosures was not covered as a "debt collector" under the FDCPA outside of the narrow section cited above.

c. Validation of Debts

The FDCPA, under 15 U.S.C. § 1692g, requires a debt collector, either in the initial communication, or within five days after the initial communication, to send the debtor a written notice disclosing:

(1) the amount of the debt;

(2) the name of the creditor to whom the debt is owed;

(3) a statement that unless the consumer, within thirty days after receipt of the notice, disputes the validity of the debt, or

any portion thereof, the debt will be assumed to be valid by the debt collector;

(4) a statement that if the consumer notifies the debt collector in writing within the thirty-day period that the debt, or any portion thereof, is disputed, the debt collector will obtain verification of the debt or a copy of a judgment against the consumer and a copy of such verification or judgment will be mailed to the consumer by the debt collector; and

(5) a statement that, upon the consumer's written request within the thirty-day period, the debt collector will provide the consumer with the name and address of the original creditor, if different from the current creditor.

If within 30 days the consumer notifies the debt collector in writing that the debt is disputed, or requests the name and address of the original creditor, all collection activity must cease until written verification of the debt or the name and address of the original creditor is sent to the consumer. 15 U.S.C. § 1692g(b). Failure of the consumer to dispute the debt is not an admission of liability. 15 U.S.C. § 1692g(c).

The validation and verification requirement is intended to eliminate the problem of debt collectors dunning the wrong person or attempting to collect debts that have already been paid. At a minimum, this procedure can allow the debt collector and the consumer to exchange information about whether the consumer is disputing the debt or has hired an attorney.

The statutory duty for the debt collector to send the validation notice is triggered by the "initial communication." The Act was amended in 2006 to specify that a communication in the form of a formal pleading in a civil action is not to be treated as an initial communication for purposes of the validation notice. 15 U.S.C. § 1692g(d).

The Act provides that the consumer shall be notified that she or he has thirty days in which to notify the debt collector that the debt is disputed or to request the original creditor's contact information. However, the collector is allowed to continue collection activities and communications during the 30-day period unless the collector receives a notice from the consumer, as described. One major caveat to this right to continue collection is that "any collection activities and communication during the 30-day period may not overshadow or be inconsistent with the disclosure of the consumer's right[s]...." 15 U.S.C. § 1692g(b). This prohibition on overshadowing was added in 2006, but was based on a line of cases prohibiting overshadowing that preceded the statutory amendment.

Whether or not a particular debt collecting communication is "overshadowing" is a matter for case-by-case determination. For instance, one court held that a letter from an attorney debt collector to a debtor that appeared to state that suit was going to be filed unless immediate payment was received, would be confusing to an unsophisticated consumer and thus violated the statute even though the validation notice was contained below the signature block in legible print. *Pollard v. Law Office of Mandy L. Spaulding*, 766 F.3d 98 (1st Cir. 2014). On the other hand, a letter that requests payment but with no time period stated does not overshadow the validation notice. *Peter v. GC Services L.P.*, 310 F.3d 344 (5th Cir. 2002).

Although a written notice from the consumer is required to trigger the collector's obligation to obtain verification of the debt or the name and address of the original creditor, and to cease collection activities, oral notice is sufficient to notify the collector that the consumer is disputing the debt, thus eliminating the presumption of validity. 15 U.S.C. § 1692g(a)(3) and (4). Many courts have held that a validation notice that suggests the consumer must give written notice of disputing the debt in order to nullify the presumption of validity would be a violation. *See, e.g., Clark v. Absolute Collection Service, Inc.*, 741 F.3d 487 (4th Cir. 2014).

If a consumer requests verification of the debt, the Act does not specify what constitutes sufficient verification or what process must be employed to verify a debt.

The CFPB's proposed regulation of the validation notice allows for electronic disclosures and includes a model form that has a tear-off sheet for consumers to indicate they wish to dispute the debt and/or obtain the name and address of the original creditor. Collectors would also be allowed to provide the validation notice by means of a hyperlink to a website that might be supplied in an email. CFPB, Debt Collection Practices (Regulation F), Proposed Rule, 84 Fed. Reg. 23274 (May 21, 2019), to be codified at 12 C.F.R. 1006.34 & .42.

d. False or Misleading Information

15 U.S.C. § 1692e includes a general prohibition against the use of false, deceptive or misleading information in connection with the collection of any debt. The section also includes a list of sixteen specific representations or actions that are considered a violation of the FDCPA.

In determining whether or not a debt collector's communication is false, deceptive or misleading, most courts apply the "least sophisticated consumer" standard, *i.e.*, the court asks whether the representation at issue would be misleading from the point of view of the least sophisticated consumer. *Clomon v. Jackson*, 988 F.2d 1314 (2d Cir. 1993). At the same time, however, courts will not hold collectors liable for bizarre or idiosyncratic interpretations. The Seventh Circuit applies an "unsophisticated" consumer standard, rather than "least sophisticated." *Gammon v. GC Services Ltd. Partnership*, 27 F.3d 1254 (7th Cir. 1994).

The FDCPA prohibits a debt collector from threatening to "take any action that cannot legally be taken or that is not intended to be taken." 15 U.S.C. § 1692e(5). The most common violation in this category is the false threat or implied threat of a lawsuit. If a particular debt collector never actually

SEC. B INFORMAL DEBT COLLECTION

files lawsuits, then any such threat would be a violation. A letter that implies a suit will be filed by saying the matter would be "transferred to an attorney," could be a misleading statement if no suit was intended. *United States v. National Financial Services, Inc.*, 98 F.3d 131 (4th Cir. 1996). If the collector does in fact file suits, then a warning that suit could be filed may not be misleading.

Threatening to sue on a debt for which the statute of limitations has expired could be considered a false representation of the legal status of a debt, which would be illegal under 15 U.S.C. § 1692e(2). The topic of collecting on time-barred debts is considered in more detail in the next subsection. Other examples of misrepresenting the legal status of a debt include claiming a debt is owed by one individual, when it is actually owed by someone else, such as a relative. Threats to sue on debts already discharged in bankruptcy is another example of this type of false representation.

The addition of unauthorized charges by a debt collector, may violate the FDCPA prohibition on misrepresenting the amount of a debt.

It is also unlawful for the collector to misrepresent his or her identity in various ways. For example, a debt collector may not falsely state or imply a connection with the government, 15 U.S.C. § 1692e(1), nor may a debt collector use a written communication which simulates or is falsely represented to be a document authorized, issued, or approved by the United States or any individual state, 15 U.S.C. § 1692e(9). In a 2016 case, the U.S.

Supreme Court held that when a private attorney acting as "special counsel" to a state attorney general used the state AG letterhead in debt collection letters, there was no violation of this section. *Sheriff v. Gillie*, 136 S. Ct. 1594 (2016). The Court noted that in this case, the state AG required its special counsel to use the state letterhead in sending debt collection communications, and since the private counsel was indeed acting as the agent of the state, the use of the letterhead did not create any false impression. *Id.*

The Act also prohibits the "false representation or implication that any individual is an attorney or that any communication is from an attorney." 15 U.S.C. § 1692e(3). The implication that an attorney is involved in the debt collection often has a powerful *in terrorem* effect on an unsophisticated consumer. Thus an attorney may not authorize mass debt collection mailings under her signature if she has not been involved with the review of the file at least to some extent, although there is no set minimum amount of time that must be spent by an attorney to avoid liability. *See Boyd v. Wexler*, 275 F.3d 642 (7th Cir. 2001). In a related provision, the Act also prohibits the furnishing of form letters that create the false impression that the letter is coming from a person other than the creditor, *e.g.*, the supplying of attorney letterhead for use by a debt collector. This practice is known as "flat rating" and is prohibited under 15 U.S.C. § 1692j.

Debt collectors often use threats to adversely affect the debtor's credit rating, which need to be phrased carefully to avoid misrepresentation. A debt collector may not falsely represent or imply that it is itself a credit bureau (consumer reporting agency). 15 U.S.C. § 1692e(16).

A false threat of arrest, seizure or garnishment, or a statement that the consumer has committed a crime, can also be a violation of the FDCPA when employed by a debt collector. 15 U.S.C. § 1692e(4) & (7). This can occur when the collector states that the consumer has committed a crime by writing a check with insufficient funds if the statute requires intent to defraud for a crime to occur. A statement that the matter will be "referred" for criminal prosecution also falsely implies that the consumer will be arrested.

In conjunction with the general rule prohibiting false representations about the collector's identity, the Act also requires that the debt collector disclose the purpose of the communication in the initial communication with the debtor. Specifically, the debt collector must disclose that the debt collector is "attempting to collect a debt and that any information obtained will be used for that purpose." In subsequent contacts, the debt collector need only state that it is a debt collector attempting to collect a debt and does not have to repeat the statement that information obtained will be used for debt collection. 15 U.S.C. § 1692e(11).

e. Collection of Time-Barred Debts

With the rise of the debt buying industry, in which participants often sell or buy large portfolios of overdue consumer debts, there is an increasing problem of inclusion of debts that are too old to be sued on, under the relevant statute of limitations. If a debt collector were to threaten to sue on such a debt, it could well be a violation of the statutory prohibition against threatening to take an action that cannot legally be taken, or it could be a misrepresentation of the legal status of the debt. 15 U.S.C. § 1692e(2), (5). *See. e.g., Freyermuth v. Credit Bureau Services, Inc.,* 248 F.3d 767 (8th Cir. 2001). Even without a specific threat of litigation, a collection letter that seeks to "settle" or "resolve" a time-barred debt, without disclosing that suit is barred by the relevant statute of limitations, could mislead an unsophisticated consumer as to the legal status of the debt, and thus could violate the FDCPA. *See, e.g., Holzman v. Malcolm S. Gerald & Assoc., Inc.,* 920 F.3d 1264 (11th Cir. 2019). The CFPB's proposed debt collection regulation says a "debt collector must not bring or threaten to bring a legal action against a consumer to collect a debt that the debt collector knows or should know is a time-barred debt." Proposed Rule, 84 Fed. Reg. 23274 (May 21, 2019), to be codified at 12 C.F.R. § 1006.26.

The U.S. Supreme Court held in 2017 that filing a "proof of claim" in bankruptcy court when the claim is past the statute of limitations does not violate the FDCPA. *Midland Funding, LLC v. Johnson,* 137 S. Ct. 1407 (2017). The Court reasoned that in this situation, a bankruptcy trustee would review the claims to determine if they were valid.

A complicating factor with time-barred debts is that the statute of limitations (state law) typically bars the initiation of a lawsuit after a certain period of time has passed, but does not prohibit the collection or attempted collection of the underlying debt by means other than filing a lawsuit. This distinction could be confusing to the average consumer. Thus, several states require that any attempt to collect a time-barred debt be accompanied by a disclosure that the consumer cannot be sued and that, where relevant, a partial payment or written acknowledgement of the debt could revive it and effectively wipe out the protection of the statute of limitations. In a supplemental proposal, the CFPB also seeks to require a similar disclosure for time-barred debts and provides a model "safe harbor" form for collectors. Proposed by CFPB Feb., 2020, available at consumerfinance.gov.

f. Harassment or Abuse

15 U.S.C. § 1692d includes a prohibition on tactics that harass or abuse consumers. Without limiting the general ban, the following specified conduct would violate the section:

(1) The use or threat of violence or other criminal means to harm the person, reputation or property of the person.

(2) The use of obscene or profane language.

(3) The publication of lists of consumers who allegedly refuse to pay debts.

(4) Causing a telephone to ring or engaging any person in telephone conversation repeatedly or continuously with the intent to annoy, abuse or harass.

Use of repeated telephone calls to encourage payment of a debt is, of course, a common tactic of debt collectors, and is not of itself illegal. Prior to the CFPB's proposed regulation, there had been no bright line to determine when repeated phone calls become illegal harassment. For instance, calling five times in a 17-day period was *not* considered harassment in one case, whereas calling six times in a 24-minute period including two callbacks after the consumer hung up, was considered illegal in another case under the anti-harassment provision. *Compare Shuler v. Ingram & Associates*, 710 F. Supp. 2d 1213 (N.D. Ala. 2010) with *Kuhn v. Account Control Technology, Inc.*, 865 F. Supp. 1443 (D. Nev. 1994). Under the 2019 proposed regulation, a debt collector would be in violation if they called about the same debt more than seven times within seven consecutive days or within seven days after having had a conversation with the consumer. CFPB Proposed Rule, 84 Fed. Reg. 23274 (May 21, 2019), to be codified at 12 C.F.R. § 1006.14(b)(2). Critics point out that collectors could call many more times if a consumer had multiple debts. While frequent telephone calls may be considered illegal harassment under some circumstances, frequent communication by letter is usually not, because sending a letter is the least intrusive means of communicating by a debt collector.

g. Unfair or Unconscionable Practices

In addition to the prohibitions on the use of false or misleading representations, and harassment, the Act also prohibits the use of "unfair or unconscionable" means of collecting a debt. The statute contains a broad prohibition, together with a list of specific examples. 15 U.S.C. § 1692f.

There are three unfair practices listed that involve the use of postdated checks. The debt collector may not accept a check postdated by more than five days without giving prior written notice of when it intends to deposit the check. Collectors also may not deposit a postdated check prior to the date on the check, nor may the collector solicit a postdated check with the intent to use it to threaten or to institute a criminal action, such as prosecution under bad check laws. 15 U.S.C. § 1692f(2), (3) & (4).

The use of embarrassing publicity about a debt would be unfair to the consumer because it provides undue pressure. Thus, the Act specifies that it is an unfair practice to use a postcard to collect a debt, or to use any language or symbol on the envelope that indicates a debt collection purpose. 15 U.S.C. § 1692f(7) & (8). This provision is intended to protect the privacy of the debtor and limit the number of third parties who might learn of the debt. Even the display of the debtor's account number through the clear plastic window of the envelope was considered illegal under this section because the account number could be used to identify the recipient as a debtor. *See Douglass v. Convergent Outsourcing*, 765 F.3d 299 (3d Cir. 2014).

Imposing costs or fees that a consumer does not legally owe is an unfair practice, as well as a possible misrepresentation of the status of the debt, as discussed above. To be legal, costs must be expressly authorized by the underlying agreement creating the debt, or be permitted by law. 15 U.S.C. § 1692f(1). Thus, the attempt to collect a percentage collection charge when the agreement only authorized a charge for the actual cost of collection, was considered unfair and a violation of the Act. *Bradley v. Franklin Collection Service, Inc.*, 739 F.3d 606 (11th Cir. 2014).

It is also an unfair practice to dispossess property without having an enforceable security interest. 15 U.S.C. § 1692f(6). As discussed in the section on the definition of "debt collector," this section includes within the Act repossessors of personal property and persons who carry out non-judicial foreclosures, at least for purposes of this particular section.

Finally, forum abuse, i.e., filing a lawsuit in a jurisdiction far from the consumer's residence, is an illegal collection practice as defined in the Act. 15 U.S.C. § 1692i. The statute specifies that a debt collector bringing a legal action shall do so in the judicial district in which the secured real property is located, or in cases not involving real property, in the judicial district in which the consumer signed the contract or in which the consumer resides. Id. The Seventh Circuit dealt with a case where debt collectors were filing small claims actions in "township" districts far from the consumer's home and which historically had favored the debt collector. The court ruled that the small claims court township district would be considered its own "judicial district" for FDCPA purposes rather than being a part of the larger county judicial district. This case also held that, in general, a "judicial district" means the smallest geographic area relevant to venue in the court system in which the case is filed. *Suesz v. Med-1 Solutions, LLC*, 757 F.3d 636 (7th Cir. 2014).

h. Additional Restrictions on Communications with the Consumer and with Third Parties

The FDCPA contains several specific restrictions on communications with both the consumer and with third parties. These provisions aim to provide limits on both direct harassment as well as on the use of communication with third parties as a pressure point for the collector.

Without prior consent of the debtor or express permission by the court, a debt collector cannot communicate with a debtor "at any unusual time or place or a time or place known or which should be known to be inconvenient to the consumer." 15 U.S.C. § 1692c(a)(1). The FDCPA states the convenient time for communication is presumptively after 8:00 a.m. and before 9:00 p.m. local time at the consumer's location. In addition, the FDCPA prohibits communication with a consumer known to be represented by an attorney. 15 U.S.C. § 1692c(a)(2). No communication with the consumer by a collector is permitted at the consumer's place of employment "if the debt collector knows or has reason to know" the employer prohibits the communication. 15 U.S.C. § 1692c(a)(3). Finally, and significantly, the debt collector must also cease communication with the consumer for most purposes upon written notice from the consumer that the consumer either refuses to pay the debt or simply that the consumer wishes the debt collector to cease all further communication. 15 U.S.C. § 1692c(c). The triggering notice from the consumer, if it is in writing and reasonably clear, does not need to be in any particular form. *See, e.g., Cruz v. International Collection Corp.*, 673 F.3d 991 (9th Cir. 2012).

In order to protect the consumer's privacy, the FDCPA strictly limits the collector's communications with third parties. Under the statute, 15 U.S.C. § 1692c(b), no communication with third parties about a debt is allowed without prior consent of the consumer or a court order, with limited exceptions. Communication is specifically allowed with the consumer him or herself. The term "consumer" for purposes of this section is defined by the statute to include the consumer's spouse, parent (if the consumer is a minor), guardian, executor or administrator. The statute also allows the debt collector to communicate with the consumer's attorney; a consumer reporting agency; the creditor; the attorney for the creditor; and the attorney for the debt collector. 15 U.S.C. § 1692c(d). Thus, a debt collector may not contact the consumer's employer, even indirectly by sending a letter to the consumer "in care of" the employer at the employer's address. *Evon v. Law Offices of Sidney Mickell*, 688 F.3d 1015 (9th Cir. 2012).

When a debt collector tries to contact a consumer by telephone, and the call is routed to the consumer's voice mail, the issue is raised as to whether a message left by the debt collector could be an illegal communication to third parties in situations where persons other than the consumer have access to the voice mail on an answering machine. Collectors point out that they do not always know whether someone's voice mail is accessible to third parties. Also, they are required by the FDCPA itself to provide a meaningful disclosure of their identity as a debt collector in all communications with a consumer, so they could be violating the section if their voice mail does not identify the caller as a debt collector. Courts are split on this question, with at least one court concluding that a debt collector may leave a voice mail message if the collector gives only his/her name, phone number and the fact that it is a call from a debt collector. *See Zortman v. J.C. Christensen & Associates, Inc.,* 870 F. Supp. 3d 694 (D. Minn. 2012). On the other hand, another federal court ruled the opposite, stating that even if there is no possible voice mail message a debt collector could leave that wouldn't violate the FDCPA, "[t]he Act does not guarantee a debt collector the right to leave answering machine messages." *Edwards v. Niagara Credit Solutions, Inc.,* 584 F.3d 1350 (11th Cir. 2009).

The proposed CFPB regulation addresses the use of email and text messages for debt collection, allowing such means of communication under certain circumstances unless the consumer opts out. The use of social media platforms viewable by third parties would be prohibited. Proposed CFPB regulation, 84 Fed. Reg. 23274 (May 21, 2019).There is an exception to the ban on third party communication that allows debt collectors to contact third parties to obtain "location information" on the consumer. 15 U.S.C. § 1692b. The debt collector may not state that the consumer owes a debt during such a contact, and may not repeatedly communicate with the same person in this regard, unless requested to do so.

i. Government Enforcement, Civil Liability and Bona Fide Error Defense

Both the FTC and the CFPB have the authority to enforce the FDCPA, and both agencies have been active in this area. The FTC coordinates with state attorneys general nationwide and has successfully concluded cases against defendants allegedly selling fake payday loan portfolios, as well as other debt collectors attempting to collect debts from consumers who did not owe them. FTC Annual Debt Collection Report (2019), available at ftc.gov. The CFPB has also brought several actions against debt buyers and debt collection law firms charging them with abusive debt collection practices, including attempting to collect on debts not owed. These suits have led to millions of dollars of refunds to consumers. CFPB Annual Debt Collection Report (2019), available at consumerfinance.gov. The CFPB also has supervisory authority over debt collectors and has issued a "Bulletin" describing debt collection practices that may violate the statutory prohibition against unfair, deceptive or abusive practices, thus extending some protection for consumers against creditors and other entities not covered by the FDCPA. CFPB Bulletin 2013-07, available at consumerfinance.gov.

In addition to government enforcement, the FDCPA also provides a private right of action.

Violations of the FDCPA may result in civil liability for actual damages, additional statutory damages up to $1,000, attorney fees and costs. 15 U.S.C. § 1692k(a)(2)(A). Even without evidence of actual damages, statutory damages as well as attorney fees and costs may be awarded for a violation. Class actions are available and this tool can be useful where the violation is contained in form letters sent to large numbers of debtors. A class action can also be used to curb abuses by debt buyers who purchase large portfolios of overdue debts, and then file mass lawsuits to collect these debts through the default judgments. In one case, the Second Circuit affirmed class certification where the evidence showed the debt buyer was allegedly engaging in systematic fraud (*e.g.*, "sewer service," and "robo signing" of affidavits). *Sykes v. Mel S. Harris and Associates LLC*, 780 F.3d 70 (2d Cir. 2015).

The Act also provides that a debt collector will not be liable if it proves by a preponderance of the evidence that the violation was unintentional and resulted from a bona fide error, despite maintaining procedures to avoid the error. 15 U.S.C. § 1692k(c). The bona fide error defense is an affirmative defense that the debt collector has the burden to prove at trial. According to a 2010 U.S. Supreme Court ruling, the FDCPA's bona fide error defense does *not* include mistakes of law. *Jerman v. Carlisle, McNellie, Rini, Kramer & Ulrich LPA*, 559 U.S. 573 (2010).

As discussed in Chapter Five, *supra*, the U.S. Supreme Court in *Spokeo v. Robins*, 136 S. Ct. 1540 (2016), held that private plaintiffs in federal court must have Article III standing to sue, which means, in part, that the plaintiff must have suffered a concrete and particularized injury in order to collect statutory damages for a mere procedural violation of a federal consumer protection law. While *Spokeo* involved the Fair Credit Reporting Act, this holding can and will be applied in other contexts, such as the Fair Debt Collection Practices Act. The criteria for determining Article III standing in FDCPA cases is still evolving. For instance, a Second Circuit case held that certain disclosure violations of the FDCPA although "procedural" could still cause concrete injury, forming the basis for standing to sue in federal court. *Cohen v. Rosicki, Rosicki & Assoc., Inc.*, 897 F.3d 75 (2d Cir. 2018). On the other hand, a Sixth Circuit case held there was no standing to sue for a case alleging the plaintiff suffered anxiety from an implied threat to sue on a debt, where the implied threat was based solely on the use of attorney letterhead and signature. *Buchholz v. Meyer Njus Tanick, PA*, 946 F.3d 855 (6th Cir. 2020).

C. DEBT COLLECTION WITHIN THE JUDICIAL SYSTEM

The FDCPA, as summarized in the preceding section, deals mainly with curbing abuses by third party debt collectors who attempt to collect debts in informal ways prior to bringing an actual lawsuit. In this section, we will deal with selected aspects of debt collection within the judicial system.

There is little in the law of judicial collection that is peculiar to consumer credit transactions. All creditors have essentially the same collection remedies; the same statutes apply to commercial and consumer debts. In most jurisdictions, judicial collection remedies are conditioned on the filing of a law suit. There are several post-filing/*pre-judgment* creditor remedies that can be used *in certain statutorily prescribed situations*. Garnishment is perhaps the best known collection remedy available prior to judgment. It is also possible to reach property held by the debtor himself or herself prior to judgment through use of attachment and replevin or sequestration.

1. GARNISHMENT AND SEIZURE OF PROPERTY

Garnishment is a collection remedy directed not at the defendant/debtor but rather at some third person, the garnishee, who owes a debt to the principal debtor, has property of the principal debtor, or has property in which the principal debtor has an interest. Garnishment is a warning or notice to the garnishee that the plaintiff/creditor claims the right to have such debt or property applied in satisfaction of his claim, and that the garnishee should hold such property until the creditor's suit has been tried and any judgment satisfied. The most common examples of garnishees are the employer of the principal debtor and the bank in which the principal debtor has a savings or checking account.

Prejudgment remedies are of limited availability. If the creditor actually prevails in the lawsuit, however, then the creditor has a *right* to obtain a writ of execution directing the sheriff to seize and sell sufficient non-exempt property of the debtor to satisfy the judgment.

All states constitutionally or statutorily restrict creditor recourse to certain property. By allowing the debtor to retain certain property free from appropriation by creditors, exemption statutes extend to a debtor an opportunity for self-support so that he will not become a burden upon the public.

All states exempt certain personal property from creditor process. In some jurisdictions, the exempt property is identified by type (*e.g.*, the family bible, the family rifle); in others, by value (*e.g.*, personal property of a value of $500). In most states, some specific provision is made for the exemption of life insurance (both the proceeds of the policy and the cash surrender value thereof) and wages.

Almost all states also have legislative provisions, commonly referred to as homestead laws, designed to protect the family home from the reach of certain classes of creditors. Homestead laws only protect real property interests of the debtor and not all real property interests of the debtor may be the subject of a homestead claim. Common statutory limitations include the requirements that the debtor have a family, that the property be occupied and used as a residence (an almost universal limitation), that the owner have a specified interest (usually present, possessory) in the property, and (in a few states) that there be a formal declaration that the property is a homestead. By statute in most states, case law in others, purchase money mortgages and security interests are generally not affected by an exemption statute. Thus, the bank that finances the purchase of a home or car will be able to seize and sell the property notwithstanding the fact that the property is covered by an exemption statute.

There are also federal statutes that exempt property from the reach of creditors in either federal court or state court. Most of the federal provisions relate to the benefits of federal social legislation such as money paid under social security and veteran's benefits. The most significant federal exemption provision is found in the Consumer Credit Protection Act (CCPA), which provides a statutory minimum exemption of wages from garnishments. 15 U.S.C. §§ 1671–1677.

Under this law, creditors may only garnish in the aggregate only 25% of a person's weekly "disposable earnings" or the amount by which his disposable earnings exceed thirty times the minimum hourly wage, whichever is less. 15 U.S.C. § 1673(a). "Disposable earnings" is statutorily defined as salary less deductions "required by law." 15 U.S.C. § 1672(b). The following hypothetical illustrates how this works. X's salary is $10,800 a year, or $900 per month. X does not, however, receive $900 a month. Rather, X's "take-home pay" is only $700 a month because of the following deductions: $130 for taxes, $50 for social security, $20 for Blue Cross. Only the $130 for taxes and the $50 for social security are deductions "required by law." X's "disposable earning" is thus $720 a month or $180 a week and the maximum amount that X's creditors can garnish under the federal law is $45, which is 25% of disposable earnings.

Exceptions to the garnishment protection include money owed for state or federal taxes. And, if X also owes child support or alimony, less of his wages are protected. The federal law permits garnishment of up to 60% of disposable earnings to satisfy a support order. If the debtor is supporting either or both a spouse and a dependent child and the garnishment for support concerns someone else, *i.e.*, a former spouse or another dependent child, then only 50% of the disposable earnings is subject to garnishment.

The federal anti-garnishment law also protects debtors from being fired because of garnishment. The Act prohibits the discharge of any employee "by reason of the fact that his earnings have been subjected to garnishment for any *one* indebtedness." 15 U.S.C. § 1674(a). Thus if D is indebted to C, and C garnishes D's wages several times in an attempt to satisfy his claim, D's employer cannot discharge him because of these garnishments. On the other hand, if D is indebted to both C and E and both garnish D's wages, D's employer can discharge him because of the garnishments.

Where state restrictions are stronger, it will be state law which regulates because this federal restriction on garnishment does not preempt the stronger state restrictions. 15 U.S.C. § 1677. Most states currently have wage garnishment laws, but they are not uniform. Since many employers operate across state lines, and thus could face differing wage garnishment laws, the Uniform Law Commission in

2016 published a Uniform Wage Garnishment Act, endorsed by the American Payroll Association and the American Bar Association. It has not been passed in any state as of this writing. https://www.uniform laws.org/committees/community-home?community key=f12a323d-5b80-49bb-9d6a-d3a8046d8473&tab= groupdetails. This Uniform Act, if passed, would still allow states to exceed the minimum protections of the CCPA discussed above, and would also go beyond the CCPA by prohibiting termination of employment or other retaliation because of any garnishment, and would extend protections to independent contractors who do not meet the definition of "employee," but are functionally equivalent. It also "streamlines" state laws by providing for employer payments directly to creditors, rather than to the court or the sheriff, and by eliminating the requirement to renew garnishments and instead requiring only one filing that will last until the debt is fully paid.

There is no private remedy provision for this law but rather the provisions are to be enforced by the Secretary of Labor. There have been several reported cases that have considered implied private action contentions. The cases are split on the question. *E.g.*, *Stewart v. Travelers Corp.*, 503 F.2d 108 (9th Cir.1974) (private right of action for wrongful dismissal); *Smith v. Cotton Brothers Baking Co., Inc.*, 609 F.2d 738 (5th Cir.1980) (no private claim for wrongful dismissal).

2. OBTAINING JUDGMENTS

A creditor often wants to obtain the judgment as quickly and as inexpensively as possible. A default judgment is thus preferable to a judgment resulting from prolonged litigation. Most consumer collection actions do in fact result in a default judgment for the creditor. Some creditors increase their chances for judgment by default by never delivering the summons and complaint and executing a false and fraudulent affidavit of personal service. [This is commonly called "sewer service" to indicate the probable resting place of the process papers.]

A number of states permit service of process by private individuals. In such states, private process servers are generally paid only for completed service and this has resulted in widespread sewer service. Criminal prosecution for perjury and violation of civil rights under color of law has had a limited deterrent effect. More promising is the prospect of class actions instituted under the FDCPA, as discussed in the previous section. *See Sykes v. Mel S. Harris and Associates LLC*, 780 F.3d 70 (2d Cir. 2015).

Filing a collection action in a distant forum also significantly increases the chances of a default judgment. *Spiegel, Inc. v. FTC*, 540 F.2d 287 (7th Cir.1976), held that the Federal Trade Commission has the power to prevent creditors from suing consumers in inconvenient forums. As discussed in the previous section, the Fair Debt Collection Practices Act protects consumers from suits by *"debt collectors"* in inconvenient forums. 15 U.S.C. § 1692i.

3. SPECIAL RIGHTS OF LIEN CREDITORS

a. Repossession in General

Some creditors have rights in addition to those already discussed. There are two major sources of such additional rights: contracts and statutes. The debtor and the creditor may agree that the creditor is to have a *lien* on certain personal property (security interest) or real property (mortgage) of the debtor. Statutes are the other common source of liens: tax liens, artisans' liens, innkeepers' liens are but a few of the statutory liens that directly affect consumers.

A creditor with a consensual or statutory lien has special rights in the property subject to its liens, *i.e.*, collateral. These rights include a right of foreclosure—the right to proceed directly against the collateral (*e.g.*, an automobile purchased on credit) without resorting to the judicial process. Holders of consensual liens also enjoy this right to repossession of the collateral without recourse to the judicial process.

b. Actions Under UCC Article 9

Section 9–503 of the Uniform Commercial Code provides: "Unless otherwise agreed a secured party has on default the right to take possession of the collateral. In taking possession, a secured party may proceed without judicial process if this can be done without breach of the peace * * * ." This phrase, "breach of the peace," is nowhere defined in the Code or the Official Comments thereto.

The majority of cases takes the position that unauthorized entry into the debtor's home poses a danger of exciting a violent response. The courts apparently feel that trespassing on the driveway is not likely to produce the same response; courts have been virtually unanimous in upholding repossessions of cars from driveways, absent objection by the debtor.

Where the car is taken from the driveway over the debtor's protests, there is a breach of the peace. If the debtor is there and is objecting to the taking, this is a situation likely to produce violence. Remember the effect of so treating a debtor's protest is not to preclude repossession of the collateral; it merely precludes self-help repossession.

Repossession is generally followed by resale of the collateral. If the proceeds of the sale are not sufficient to satisfy the indebtedness, the debtor is liable for any deficiency, absent an agreement to the contrary. In seeking recovery of such deficiency, the creditor has all of the rights of a general creditor. In the unlikely event that the sale yields a sum greater than the amount owed by the debtor, the secured party must account to the debtor for any surplus.

c. Limitations on Deficiency Judgments

The theory underlying the secured party's right to recover deficiencies is simple. The debtor has undertaken an obligation to pay X dollars. The debtor should pay X dollars. If the sale of the repossessed collateral yields less than X dollars, the debtor should be required to make up this difference.

The problems commonly raised when deficiency judgments are pursued are that (1) the resale value of most consumer goods is considerably less than the original purchase price and (2) repossession sales do not always yield the fair value of the repossessed collateral.

The Uniform Commercial Code tries to require secured parties to conduct a sale that will yield the fair market value of the collateral. Section 9–504 requires that "reasonable notice" of the sale must be given to the debtor unless the collateral is perishable or threatens to decline in value or is of a "type customarily sold on a recognized market." More important, section 9–504 requires that every aspect of the sale be "commercially reasonable."

The Code does not have a definition of "commercially reasonable." The Code nowhere expressly states that a sale is not "commercially reasonable" because the price is too low. To the contrary, section 9–507 (2) states that the fact that a better price could have been obtained is not "of itself sufficient to establish that the sale was not made in a commercially reasonable manner." Nonetheless, the primary issue in most cases seems to be the sufficiency of the price. This is not to say that courts expressly reject section 9–507(2); rather, little more than an unusually low resale price is needed to establish that the sale was not commercially reasonable.

The fact that a higher price might have been obtained had the repossessed item been sold at retail, as opposed to a wholesale auction, does not mean that the auction price is not the "fair market" value. The Massachusetts Supreme Judicial Court held in 2018 that automobile finance companies that sell repossessed vehicles at a dealers' auction are obtaining a fair market value as set forth in the statute and need not use the higher retail market value to determine the deficiency amount to charge the debtor. *Williams v. American Honda Finance Corp.*, 98 N.E.3d 169 (Mass. 2018).

Section 9–507 imposes liability on a secured party who fails to give "reasonable notice" or hold a "commercially reasonable sale." The measure of damages is losses caused by the secured party's failure to comply with the requirements. Because of the difficulty of establishing such losses, a minimum recovery is guaranteed to consumers: an amount measured by the finance charge plus ten percent of the principal.

A number of states have statutorily restricted the right of a creditor with a security interest in consumer goods to repossess, resell *and* collect a deficiency judgment. Most of the statutes are modeled on the 1968 version of the Uniform Consumer Credit Code (UCCC). Under section 5.103, of the UCCC, the creditor must elect between repossessing the collateral and enforcing a personal judgment against the consumer in a consumer credit *sale* where the cash price was $1,000 or less [raised to $1,750 or less by the 1974 Official Text]. If the seller repossesses or voluntarily accepts surrender of the collateral, the buyer is not liable for the unpaid balance. If instead of repossessing, the seller sues on the debt and obtains a judgment he may not repossess the collateral, and the collateral is not subject to levy or sale on execution. Be sure you understand what the UCCC anti-deficiency judgment provision does and does not do. It does require *some* sellers to *choose* between pursuing the collateral and pursuing the debtor. It does not limit these sellers to the collateral. It does not in any way affect the sellers of new cars or other items costing more than $1,000 ($1,750, as amended). It does not in any way affect creditors who make secured *loans*.

CHAPTER TWELVE

CREDIT AND DEBIT CARDS AND OTHER MODERN CONSUMER PAYMENTS

A. SPECIAL PROTECTIONS FOR CREDIT CARD CONSUMERS

1. INTRODUCTION

Credit cards became an increasingly dominant form of consumer payment for goods and services in the second half of the twentieth century. Bank cards, such as Visa and Master card, came into common use beginning in the 1960s. Credit card debt has also exploded with the increasing availability and use of credit cards for everyday purchases. The Truth in Lending Act disclosure requirements for credit cards were discussed in Chapter Seven, *supra*. The ability of credit card holders to assert against the card issuer claims and defenses they might have against the seller is a variation of the holder in due course issue, and was discussed in Chapter Ten, *supra*. In this chapter, we will discuss some other special substantive protections for consumers using credit cards as a payment method, including limitations on liability for unauthorized use, and procedures for asserting billing errors. In the twenty-first century, credit card use may well be surpassed by debit cards, prepaid cards not associated with a bank account, and other forms of electronic payments such as Internet payments, digital wallets, mobile phone payments and even so-called crypto currency. We will

2. LIMITS ON RATES AND FEES

The Credit Card Accountability Responsibility and Disclosure Act (Credit CARD Act) of 2009 contained significant amendments to the Truth in Lending Act meant to provide some special substantive protections to credit card consumers. Many of these provisions go beyond changes to disclosures alone.

Because credit cards are open-end accounts that may last for many years, card issuers may legitimately wish to change some of the terms over the course of this relationship, due to market changes or changes in the status of the consumer. Nonetheless, unexpected rate increases posed some undue hardships on consumers, especially if an increased rate was applied retroactively to balances that were accumulated under a lower rate. In response to perceived unfairness to consumers, several reforms in credit card practices were mandated. As of 2010, introductory rates or fees may not be increased less than six months from their inception. 12 C.F.R. § 1026.55(b)(1). For other rates and fees, creditors must provide a 45 day notice of changes, rate increases may not be applied retroactively, and creditors must allow consumers to terminate their account if they wish to avoid the change. 12 C.F.R. §§ 1026.55(b)(3) and

1026.9(c)(2)(i).[1] If the consumer chooses to terminate an account because of a rate increase, the creditor shall not consider the account in default or accelerate the balance due, but rather, consumers should be given the option of a five-year amortization period to pay off the balance, or a minimum periodic payment that includes a percentage of the prior outstanding balance that is not more than twice the percentage required previously. 12 C.F.R. §§ 1026.55(c)(2) and .9(h).

In addition to rate increases, unexpected fees were also problematic for consumers, and some of these fee issues were addressed in the 2009 legislation. For instance, while most credit card accounts are subject to an upper limit of available credit and charge a fee to consumers who exceed the limit, many consumers were under the misimpression that if they attempted to make a charge that exceeded their credit limit, the card would be refused at the point of sale. The common practice of card issuers, however, was to let such over-limit charges go through and then later charge consumers an over-the-limit fee for such transactions. Under the current law, creditors may still impose an over-the-limit fee but only if the consumer has expressly elected, after receiving mandated disclosures, to permit the creditor to complete transactions that involve the extension of credit in excess of the amount of credit authorized. 15 U.S.C. § 1637(k)(1); 12 C.F.R. § 1026.56. If the consumer does not opt-in to the over-the-limit fee

---

[1] There is a limited exception for an APR increase based on the consumer's delinquency. 12 C.F.R. § 1026.55(b)(4).

after receiving proper notice, the charge will either be denied at the point of sale or the card issuer can extend the credit but cannot impose a fee on the non-consenting consumer.

Excessive fees are also limited under current law. Prior to the passage of the Credit CARD Act, some subprime credit card customers were charged fees that swallowed up a large percentage of their available credit. For instance, in a 2006 case involving allegedly improper use of prescreened lists, the credit card solicitation offered a minimum credit line of $250 if accepted, but the fees would have included a $9.00 processing fee (due on application), an acceptance fee of $119, an annual membership fee of $50, and a participation fee of $72 per year (charged at $6.00 per month), leaving the consumer with an effective amount of credit of $75.00 with an outstanding balance of $175.00. *Perry v. First National Bank*, 459 F.3d 816 (7th Cir. 2006). Under the current law, the aggregate of such fees during the first year in which an account is opened, may not exceed 25% of the total amount of credit authorized, with the exception of late fees, over-the-limit fees, or fees for returned payments. 12 C.F.R. § 1026.52(a).

In addition, fees such as late payment, over-the-limit, or other penalty fees may not be imposed unless they are reasonable and proportional to the omission or violation of the cardholder agreement. Furthermore, card issuers may not impose any fee for violating terms or other requirements where the violations do not impose any dollar cost on the creditor. 12 C.F.R. § 1026.52(b).

3. CREDIT CARDS AND YOUNG CONSUMERS

Over the years that credit cards have been popular as a means of payment, credit card consumers were at times offered far more credit than they could afford to repay, resulting in financial hardship in some cases. The current version of TILA imposes a general requirement that credit card issuers not open a credit card account or increase a credit limit unless it "considers the ability of the consumer to make the required payments." 15 U.S.C. § 1665e; 12 C.F.R. § 1026.51(a).

This concern for consumers being offered credit they cannot actually repay, which can result in dire consequences for that consumer, was also a theme underlying the special provisions in the Credit CARD Act restricting the offer of credit cards to young consumers, as discussed in this section.

During the 2000s, marketing of credit cards to younger consumers, especially to students on college campuses, raised concerns that credit cards were being issued to individuals who did not have the ability to repay or the maturity to handle excessive credit limits, and who would thus suffer untoward consequences from the overextension of credit. Credit card marketers appeared at times to promote the irresponsible acquisition of debt, by engaging in activities on campus involving free giveaways of tee shirts, pizza or other items in exchange for credit card applications. Some educational institutions were also allied with the credit card marketers by accepting financial support from the credit card companies in exchange for granting access to their students as potential customers.

Congress responded strongly to these concerns in the Credit CARD Act of 2009. When that law went into effect, credit cards could no longer be legally issued to consumers who had not attained the age of 21, unless one of two conditions applied. First, a credit card can be issued to a consumer under the age of 21 who submits financial information indicating that he or she has an independent means of repaying the debt arising from the proposed extension of credit. 15 U.S.C. § 1637(c)(8); 12 C.F.R. § 1026.51(b)(1)(i). The Official Staff Commentary states that the under-21 credit card applicant need only demonstrate the ability to make the minimum required periodic payments, not necessarily the ability to repay the full amount of the credit limit. Second, a credit card may be issued to an under-21 credit card applicant who applies with a financially capable cosigner who is at least 21 years old and who will be jointly liable for the debts incurred on the card. Such cosigners can include parents or guardians, but can also include any individual, even a fellow student, who is 21 or older and has the means to repay. The amount of credit authorized under a cosigner plan, however, cannot be increased without cosigner approval and assumption of joint liability for the increased credit limit. 12 C.F.R. § 1026.51(b)(1)(ii) and (b)(2).

In addition to the limitations on the issuance of cards, there are also provisions that limit the marketing of credit cards to younger consumers.

Consumer reporting agencies (credit bureaus) may not provide credit card issuers with prescreened lists of potential customers that include under-21 consumers, unless such consumers expressly consent to such inclusion. 15 U.S.C. § 1681b(c)(1)(B)(iv). This provision should diminish the number of "pre-approved" credit card applications received by young consumers. Furthermore, on-campus marketing of credit cards is subject to certain limits. Card issuers may not offer a college student any tangible item to induce a credit card application either on or near (within 1,000 feet of) the campus of an institution of higher learning, or at an event sponsored by such an institution. 12 C.F.R. § 1026.57(c).

In order to at least expose any connection between the college or university and the credit card issuers, the law requires all institutions of higher education to publicly disclose any marketing agreement made with a credit card issuer. Usually the disclosure is made via the school's web site. Card issuers must also submit an annual report to the CFPB regarding any marketing, promotional and college affinity card agreements with colleges or universities. 12 C.F.R. § 1026.57(b) & (d).

4. UNAUTHORIZED USE

From the outset, TILA has offered strong protection for consumers victimized by unauthorized use of a credit card. If a credit card holder notices a charge on their credit card statement that was not authorized, the Truth in Lending Act provides some protection from being charged for such use.

Specifically, 15 U.S.C. § 1643(a)(1) of TILA limits the liability of the cardholder for unauthorized use to $50 at most. That section provides that a cardholder is liable for the unauthorized use of a credit card *only if*:

(1) the card is an accepted card;

(2) the liability is not greater than $50;

(3) the card issuer gave adequate notice to the cardholder of the potential liability;

(4) the card issuer provided the cardholder with a description of a means by which the card issuer may be notified of loss or theft of the card;

(5) the unauthorized use occurred before the card issuer was notified of the unauthorized use; and

(6) the card issuer provided a method whereby the user of such card can be identified as the person authorized to use it.

This is basically a strict liability law because if these conditions are fulfilled, the consumer cannot be liable for more than $50 of unauthorized credit card use, even if the consumer was negligent in allowing the card to be lost or stolen, or is late giving notice of the disappearance of the card. If the conditions are *not* met, there is no consumer liability at all for unauthorized use. Congress apparently felt that card issuers were in a better position to protect themselves from unauthorized use than consumers because the card issuers can set up network-wide security systems or anti-fraud technology. Also, card issuers, mainly banks, can spread the loss from unauthorized use among all their customers, rather than imposing a potentially devastating loss on one customer.

Despite this very strong protection for consumers, many are not aware that they are protected from liability for unauthorized use by federal law, and most consumers usually will try to promptly notify the card issuer to avoid further loss, and some even buy insurance against liability for unauthorized use, despite the fact that $50 would be their maximum liability. Both Visa and MasterCard voluntarily waive even the $50 liability for unauthorized use if the cardholder reports the loss of the card within two business days. And under the statute itself, the cardholder is not liable for *any* loss if the card issuer is notified prior to any unauthorized use.

This protection from liability is only for "unauthorized use," however, which the statute defines as the use of the card by someone "other than the credit card holder who does not have actual, implied, or apparent authority for such use and from which the cardholder receives no benefit." 15 U.S.C. § 1602(p). Whether or not such authority exists is determined by the state law of agency. The burden falls upon the card issuer to show that the use was authorized. 15 U.S.C. § 1643(b). To meet its burden the card issuer must set forth facts that permit a reasonable person to conclude that the cardholder authorized the use of the card.

A consumer may be found to have authorized the use of his credit card even without actual intent to give such authorization because the statute considers the use to be "authorized" if someone uses a credit card with "apparent" authority. For example, in *Stieger v. Chevy Chase Sav. Bank*, 666 A.2d 479 (D.C.Ct.App.1995), the court had to answer the question of whether a credit cardholder who permitted a third person to use his credit card for a specific purpose was liable for other uses not specifically authorized. The court held that the card holder was liable for the extra charges where the signature on the sales slips matched the signature on the back of the card and where the holder voluntarily relinquished the card to the third party. Therefore, the court based its decision on a finding of "apparent authority."

In enacting this aspect of TILA, Congress contemplated and most courts have agreed they will defer to basic principles of agency law to determine the liability of cardholders where there is an alleged unauthorized use. As the statute indicates, this authority may be either implied, express or apparent. Implied or express authority can be ascertained by looking at the written or spoken words or the conduct of the principal. Apparent authority, however, is much harder to grasp because it is normally created through the words or conduct of the principal as they are interpreted by a third party.

The limitation on liability for unauthorized use of a credit card is specifically applicable to business credit cards, 15 U.S.C. § 1645, in contrast to most of the provisions of TILA which are limited to consumer credit transactions. As a result, there are a number of TILA cases involving allegedly unauthorized use of credit cards by dishonest employees. In *Minskoff v. American Express Travel Related Services Co.*, 98 F.3d 703 (2d Cir. 1996), the court found that apparent authority existed even where an administrative assistant had fraudulently obtained credit cards in the name of her boss without either implied or express authority. "Apparent" authority was created because the cardholder negligently failed to examine the credit card statements sent by the issuer itemizing the charges made by the employee, which were paid by the employee with forged checks. The court held that by his negligent acts or omissions the cardholder created an appearance of authority vis-à-vis the card issuer for the fraudulent use of the card by the embezzling employee. Therefore, the card holder was not limited to the $50 amount as provided for in § 1643, but was held liable for all the charges made by the embezzler after the credit card statements were issued because the use was deemed "authorized" as defined by the statute.

Quite often, the "authorized" use will be carried out by a friend or relative to whom the cardholder has given the card, but with certain limitations. Or a card may be provided for a spouse but then once the couple becomes estranged or divorced, one of the spouses may want to terminate the authority of the other. Merely notifying the bank that a party who was furnished the card no longer has authority to use it may not be sufficient, at least according to some older cases. *See, e.g., Walker Bank & Trust Co. v. Jones*,

672 P.2d 73 (Utah 1983). The cardholder may need to physically retrieve the card or close the account to terminate liability for authorized use.

If a card issuer intends to impose liability on the cardholder for unauthorized use, it must investigate the claim in a reasonable manner. This duty is reciprocal on the cardholder, however, because the cardholder must cooperate with the card issuer in conducting its investigation or the issuer may terminate its investigation. Steps which may be taken in conducting a reasonable investigation include:

(1) reviewing the types or amounts of purchases made in relation to the cardholder's previous purchasing pattern;

(2) reviewing where the purchases were delivered in relation to the cardholder's residence or place of business; and

(3) reviewing where the purchases were made in relation to where the cardholder resides or normally has shopped. *See* 12 C.F.R. § 1026.12(b), Official Staff Commentary.

If the card issuer continues to seek payment for unauthorized use of a credit card, despite having been so notified by the card holder and having reason to know that the charge may be unauthorized, the card holder can sue for violation of this provision of TILA and seek to be repaid for the amount of unauthorized charges already paid. *Krieger v. Bank of America, N.A.*, 890 F.3d 429 (3d Cir. 2018). To disallow suit by the consumer simply because the disputed charges had been paid would undermine the consumer protection purpose of the statute.

5. BILLING ERRORS

Trying to correct credit card billing errors can be troublesome to consumers due to the prevalence of automated systems and the lack of personal customer service. Indeed, the scourge of the unresponsive computer has been an issue for credit card customers from the early days of credit card use. In response to consumers' frustration, Congress passed the Fair Credit Billing Act (FCBA) in 1974, codified as part of the Truth in Lending Act. 15 U.S.C. §§ 1666 to 1666a. This law provides some procedural protection for consumers by requiring that open-end creditors, upon receipt of the consumer's written notice, conduct a reasonably speedy investigation of billing errors, and halt all collection efforts and adverse credit reports for the disputed amount pending resolution. The Act applies only to open-end credit accounts *e.g.*, credit card accounts, revolving charge accounts and overdraft checking accounts. But, the FCBA does not encompass loans or credit sales which are paid according to a fixed schedule until the entire amount is paid back.

If the consumer sees a billing error, then the consumer who wishes to trigger an investigation by the card issuer must provide a written notice of the error within 60 days after the statement was transmitted showing the error. If the error was first corrected by the card issuer and then reappears on the credit card statement some time later, the 60-day period runs from the date the consumer received the statement reinstating the charge. *Krieger v. Bank of America, N.A.*, 890 F.3d 429 (3d Cir. 2018). The notice sent by the consumer must be fairly detailed, *i.e.*, it must enable the creditor to identify the consumer's name and account number, and indicate the consumer's belief and the reasons for the belief that a billing error exists, and the type, date and amount of the error. 12 C.F.R. § 1026.13(b). Creditors can provide a specific address for such notices which must be disclosed on each periodic statement, and a notice of the relevant billing error procedures must be disclosed to the consumer both in the account-opening disclosure and at least once a year thereafter.

Once the creditor/card issuer receives a billing error notice from the consumer, a series of duties arises. First, the card issuer must mail an acknowledgement within 30 days of receiving the notice, and then conduct a reasonable investigation within two billing cycles, but no longer than 90 days. While the investigation is pending, the consumer need not pay the disputed amount and the creditor may not charge a finance charge on the disputed amount, nor can the creditor report it as a delinquency, accelerate the debt, or restrict or close the consumer's account due to the assertion of a billing error. 12 C.F.R. § 1026.13(c) & (d). The consumer's rights under the FCBA cannot be waived in the credit card contract. *Gray v. American Express Co.*, 743 F.2d 10 (D.C. Cir. 1984).

The definition of billing error for credit cards includes unauthorized use, failure to properly credit a payment, computational errors, and failure to deliver charged-for merchandise, among other things. 12 C.F.R. § 1026.13(a). Although the definition of billing error includes unauthorized use, and the billing error procedures could certainly be used by a victim of unauthorized use, the limitation on liability for unauthorized use is separate and distinct, as is the provision for raising claims and defenses against the seller (discussed previously in Chapter 10). Thus, a consumer could still assert a claim of unauthorized use against the card issuer and/or a claim or defense of undelivered merchandise (which is also a "billing error" as defined), even though the consumer did not comply with the 60-day notice provision to trigger the billing error procedures. *See, e.g., Crestar Bank, N.A. v. Cheevers*, 744 A.2d 1043 (D.C. Cir. 2000) (unauthorized use); and *Citibank (South Dakota) v. Mincks*, 135 S.W.3d 545 (Mo. Ct. App. 2004) (claim of undelivered merchandise).

Once the creditor receives a billing error notice in proper form and in a timely manner from the consumer, it must conduct a reasonable investigation. If the creditor concludes that a billing error occurred as asserted, then it must correct the billing error and credit the consumer's account with any disputed amount and related finance charges, and mail or deliver a correction notice to the consumer. 12 C.F.R. § 1026.13(e). If the creditor concludes that a billing error did not occur, then the creditor must mail or deliver to the consumer a notice and explanation of the reasons for the creditor's belief that the billing error did not occur as alleged, and furnish copies of relevant documents if the consumer requests. If after the investigation, the creditor concludes that the consumer still owes all or part of the disputed amount, the consumer can be billed for that but must be given a notice of when and how much is due, and shall allow the same amount of time to pay after receiving the notice as the consumer would normally have to pay an undisputed amount, but not less than 10 days. 12 C.F.R. § 1026.13(g). If the consumer sends a further written notice that he or she still disputes the amount, then the creditor must report the amount as disputed. *Id.*

The FCBA does not itself guarantee any particular result but only requires the creditor to conduct a reasonable investigation and comply with the other duties outlined above. The consumer could still in theory litigate the disputed amount if the billing error resolution is not favorable. The consumer could also litigate noncompliance with the procedures mandated by the FCBA.

6. BILLING PERIODS AND PAYMENTS

Many credit card agreements provide for a "grace period" during which the consumer may avoid paying finance charges if he pays the full amount of the bill within that period of time. Although credit card companies do not have to provide consumers with a "grace period," TILA requires that any such period be disclosed. 12 C.F.R. § 1026.7(a)(8).

Prior to the enactment of certain TILA reforms, very few consumers were actually able to take advantage of this "grace period" due to timing issues with the periodic statement. Assume the following information: (1) the buyer could avoid all finance charge by paying the entire balance within 20 days after the date ending the billing cycle, (2) the billing cycle ends on the last day of the month and (3) the creditor does not mail out statements until the 10th of the month. That means that the grace period was largely illusory because few consumers would have been able to act quickly enough to take advantage of it. In essence, rather than a 20-day grace period the consumer only had about a five day grace period. Consumer advocate groups labeled this practice as the "shrinking billing period" problem.

TILA deals with this issue in 15 U.S.C. § 1666b. It requires that bills be mailed early enough to permit consumers to take advantage of any "grace periods" offered by the creditor. Specifically, if the creditor wants to offer a "grace period," the creditor must adopt reasonable procedures designed to ensure that billing statements are mailed or delivered at least "21 days before the date specified in the statement by which payment must be made in order to avoid imposition of that finance charge." In addition, card issuers must adopt reasonable procedures to ensure that periodic statements (regardless of grace period being offered) are mailed or delivered at least 21 days prior to the payment due date, and, in order to treat a payment as late for any purpose, must show that the periodic statements are mailed or delivered at least 14 days prior to the date on which the required minimum periodic payment must be received. 12 C.F.R. § 1026.5(b)(2)(ii).

The following is a hypothetical which illustrates the application of Section 1666b. A credit plan provides for a finance charge based on an APR of 18%. It further provides that no finance charge will be imposed if the debtor pays the full amount of the balance within 25 days after the end of the billing cycle, which is the last day of the month. The debtor makes the following purchases and payments:

February 10—$100 purchase of clothes

March 10—creditor sends statement

March 30—debtor pays $10 minimum payment

Even though the debtor did not pay the debt in full within the grace period, Section 1666b of TILA will prevent the creditor from collecting any finance charge since the creditor mailed the bill too late. The creditor should have mailed the bill by March 4th—twenty-one days prior to the date specified in the statement by which the payment must be made in order to avoid imposition of that finance charge if it wanted to collect a finance charge.

Other bill-paying protections instituted by the 2009 Credit CARD Act include a requirement that cut-off times for timely receipt of payments should be no earlier than 5:00 PM on the due date. 15 U.S.C. § 1666c(a). Prior to this requirement, consumer advocates noted that some creditors had specified a cut-off time earlier than 5:00 PM, such as noon, which meant that if the creditor received its mail at

1:00 PM on the due date, that payment would be considered late, contrary to reasonable consumer expectations. Due dates must also fall on the same date each month, and if a payment due date falls on a weekend or holiday when the creditor does not accept payments, then any payment received on the next business day after the weekend or holiday due date must not be treated as late. 12 C.F.R. §§ 1026.7(b)(11)(i)(A) and .10(d).

Credit card accounts typically feature different rates for different types of balances, such as purchases, cash advances, balance transfers, etc. As of 2010, card issuers must apply payment amounts in excess of the minimum payment first to the card balance bearing the highest rate of interest, and then to each successive balance bearing the next highest rate of interest, until the payment is exhausted. 12 C.F.R. § 1026.53. This method of applying payments is more favorable to the consumer and will result in a lower accumulation of finance charges in most cases.

B. DEBIT CARDS AND OTHER ELECTRONIC FUND TRANSFERS

1. OVERVIEW

In the 21st century American consumer economy, plastic has replaced cash or paper checks as the preferred payment methods. The term "Plastic" in this context usually refers to either credit cards or debit cards. The special consumer protections applicable to credit cards were discussed above. Debit cards, also known as ATM cards or bank cards, are quickly outpacing credit cards as the preferred method of payment for most consumer transactions. The consumer protection law applicable to this type of payment will be discussed in this section. Stored value cards, as well as prepaid replenishable cards, are a third type of "plastic" that is increasing in importance and will be discussed in a subsequent section. Ultimately, payments may become totally electronic, either internet based or mobile device based, thus eliminating the "plastic" altogether.

The Electronic Fund Transfer Act (EFTA), enacted in 1978, was Congress's response to provide rights for consumers in the new electronic age of banking. 15 U.S.C. §§ 1693–1693r. The accompanying set of regulations is known as Regulation E, 12 C.F.R. Part 1005. The regulations were originally under the jurisdiction of the Federal Reserve Board and are now issued by the Consumer Financial Protection Bureau (CFPB).

The term "electronic fund transfer" or EFT is defined as "any transfer of funds that is initiated through an electronic terminal, telephone, computer, or magnetic tape for the purpose of ordering, instructing, or authorizing a financial institution to debit or credit a consumer's account." 12 C.F.R. § 1005.3(b)(1); 15 U.S.C. § 1693a(7). EFTs do not involve an extension of credit, but rather funds are transferred directly from one account to another.

Electronic fund transfers occur in many different ways. Customers deposit and make withdrawals during all hours of the day and night via automated teller machines. Employees have their pay checks directly deposited into their accounts and insurance companies automatically draw on a consumer's account for payment of monthly premiums. Consumers can transfer money from one account to another, pay for utilities and other bills through their home computer or telephone. Consumers can use their debit cards for point-of-sale or online purchases. These transactions are conducted through electronic debits and credits without the consumer ever writing a check. Although there is some usage overlap with credit cards, particularly in the area of purchases, the regulation of EFTs is governed by a different federal regulatory regime.

The EFTA provides a "basic framework establishing the rights, liabilities and responsibilities" of EFT participants in a number of areas. 15 U.S.C. § 1693(b). These areas include: disclosure of the terms and conditions with respect to EFT consumer accounts; documentation of EFT transactions; error resolution; consumer liability for unauthorized withdrawals and liability for failing to make transfers ordered by consumers and to comply with orders to stop payment of preauthorized transfers; and the suspension of a consumer's obligation when an EFT system malfunctions.

The scope of the EFTA is determined by looking at the definition of an electronic fund transfer, as quoted above. The Act only applies to electronic fund transfers. As defined, an EFT is tied to a consumer's "account." That term means "a demand deposit (checking), savings, or other consumer asset account held directly or indirectly by a financial institution and established primarily for personal, family or household purposes. 12 C.F.R. § 1005.2(b)(1). As of 2019, an amended version of Regulation E defines "account" to also include prepaid accounts, meaning payroll cards, government benefit accounts, and prepaid reloadable cards that are not drawn on a checking account. 12 C.F.R. § 1005.2(b)(3). The EFTA does not cover so-called "wire transfers," which are a form of electronic fund transfer used primarily for large business transactions. UCC § 4A–108.

Financial institutions that handle EFTs for consumers are required to send a monthly statement to each consumer having an account that may be accessed by means of an electronic fund transfer. 15 U.S.C. § 1693d(c); 12 C.F.R. § 1005.9(b). The statement must set forth, with regard to each EFT during the period, identifying information about each transfer, the amount of any fee assessed during the period, the balances in the consumer's account at the beginning and close of the period and the address and telephone number to be used by the consumer to contact the financial institution about errors. *Id.* Such statements are typically combined with the consumer's monthly checking account statement that shows checks, EFTs, and other transactions affecting their bank account. Additionally, for each transfer initiated by the consumer from an electronic terminal, the financial institution must make available to the consumer, at the time of the transfer, written documentation (receipt) of the transfer. 15 U.S.C. § 1693d(a); 12 C.F.R. § 1005.9(a). Alternatives to the traditional paper/mailed periodic statement, *i.e.*, account information by telephone, website or in paper on request, may be provided for government benefit accounts, 12 C.F.R. § 1005.15(d), payroll card accounts, 12 C.F.R. § 1005.18(c) and other types of prepaid accounts.

2. UNAUTHORIZED USE

The consumer's liability in the event of unauthorized use of the consumer's credit card account was discussed in the preceding section. Similarly, the EFTA has a provision governing the consumer's liability for unauthorized use of a debit card or other forms of unauthorized EFTs. The general rule is that the consumer incurs no liability for such unauthorized use except as provided for in 15 U.S.C. § 1693g. That section imposes three requirements for a consumer to be liable. First, the access card must have been "accepted" by the consumer. That means that the consumer must have requested the card, received the card, signed the card and used the card or authorized someone else to use it. Secondly, the card issuer must have provided a means to identify the user of the card as the person authorized to use it, *e.g.*, provided the consumer with a personal identification number (PIN). Third, the financial institution must have provided required disclosures regarding the potential liability of the consumer, contact information for the consumer to notify the financial institution of possible unauthorized use, and the financial institution's business days. 12 C.F.R. § 1005.6(a). The burden is on the financial institution to establish the above preconditions for consumer liability for unauthorized transfers.

As was the case with consumer liability for unauthorized use of credit cards, under the EFTA consumers are protected by the liability limits in the Act regardless of consumer negligence, such as keeping a written notation of the PIN number with the card. If the consumer notifies the financial institution of the loss or theft of the "access device" within two business days of the loss, the consumer's liability, provided the disclosure conditions are met, is limited to $50 for losses occurring before notice to the financial institution. 12 C.F.R. § 1005.7(b)(1). Unlike the situation with credit cards, however, consumers can be liable for much more than $50 if they do not promptly notify the financial institution once they learn of the loss of the debit or ATM card. Where timely notice is *not* given, the consumer is liable for losses up to $50 or the amount of unauthorized transfers that occurred within two business days, whichever is less, plus the losses which occur between the close of the 2nd business day after the consumer learns about the theft or loss and the day he or she finally notifies the financial institution, up to a total of $500. 12 C.F.R. § 1005.6(b)(2). Thus, if $500 in losses occurred on day one, but no losses occurred thereafter until the consumer finally reported the loss of the access device more than two days later, the consumer's liability is limited to $50. But if $450 or more in losses occurred more than two business days after the consumer learned of the loss of the device, the consumer could be liable for up to $500 under this provision.

Additionally, the consumer is liable for all losses resulting from his failure to notify the financial institution within 60 days after he receives his account statement, of unauthorized transfers which appear in that statement. In this case the consumer bears unlimited liability for losses occurring after the 60-day period (but before the bank is finally notified) which the financial institution can prove would have been avoided had the consumer given timely notice. 12 C.F.R. § 1005.6(b)(3). Thus, some California consumers were liable for over $9,000 of unauthorized transfers because they had failed to report a $20 unauthorized use of the same card that had appeared on their bank statement over six months earlier. *Kruser v. Bank of America*, 230 Cal. App. 3d 741, 748, 281 Cal. Rptr. 463, 466 (5th Dist. 1991).

All three tiers of liability ($50, $500 and unlimited) can apply to a series of unauthorized transfers. For example, a consumer could be liable for $50 for transfers that occurred before the close of two business days after the consumer learned of the loss or theft of his card; for another $450 for transfers occurring after the close of the 2 business days and before the lapse of the 60 day period following the transmittal of a periodic statement; and for an unlimited amount of liability for transfers occurring after the close of the 60 day period, if the financial institution can prove when the consumer learned of the loss or theft, and that the losses occurring after the close of 2 business days and after the close of the 60 days would not have occurred but for the failure of the consumer to notify the financial institution.

The EFTA definition of unauthorized transfers, unlike that of TILA, is based on lack of "actual" authority rather than on the concept of "apparent" authority. However, the statutory definition of "unauthorized" transfers under EFTA does not include a situation in which the consumer entrusted his access card to a person who uses it to effect transfers beyond those actually authorized by the consumer. 15 U.S.C. § 1693a(12); 12 C.F.R. § 1005.2(m). Where such is the case, the consumer is liable for all the transfers made by that third party. Significantly, however, the consumer's liability for use by a third party to whom the access device was furnished ends when the consumer notifies the financial institution that the use is no longer authorized. Also, if the consumer is tricked into furnishing his or her card to a third party who surreptitiously learns the PIN number, the EFT may still be "unauthorized" under the statutory definition because the consumer did not furnish the full "means of access," which would include both the card and the PIN number. *Ognibene v. Citibank, N.A.*, 112 Misc. 2d 219, 446 N.Y.S.2d 845 (N.Y. City Civ. Ct. 1981).

3. BILLING ERRORS

The EFTA, like the Fair Credit Billing Act for credit cards, mandates that certain error resolution procedures be followed by the relevant financial institution. Such a procedure is particularly important for EFT errors because typically funds have already been withdrawn from the consumer's account when the error is first discovered. An erroneously debited amount could result in the dishonoring of outstanding checks, or depending on the circumstances, the consumer might be left without enough funds to pay for necessary expenses. Thus, the EFTA error resolution procedures are a bit more stringent than those of the FCBA. The time period for investigation and resolution is shorter, and in some instances, the consumer's account must be re-credited pending the results of the investigation.

EFTA billing errors include an unauthorized electronic fund transfer, an incorrect electronic fund transfer, computational errors, and receipt of an incorrect amount of money from an ATM, among other things. 15 U.S.C. § 1693f(f) and 12 C.F.R. § 1005.11(a).

If the consumer believes, based on documentation (usually a periodic statement) received from the bank, that an error involving an EFT has been made, the consumer should follow the error resolution procedure specified in the statute. These procedures are required to be disclosed to consumers as well. 12 C.F.R. § 1005.8(b). The consumer is to notify the financial institution of such error within 60 days of receiving the documentation showing the error. The notice can be either written or oral and must enable the institution to identify the consumer's name and account number, indicate why the consumer believes an error exists, and include to the extent possible the type, date and amount of the error. The financial institution may require the consumer to give written confirmation of an error within 10 business days of an oral notice. 12 C.F.R. § 1005.11(b).

If the notice is received by the financial institution within 60 days of sending the documentation to the consumer, the financial institution must conduct an investigation concerning the error. If, however, the consumer fails to notify the creditor within the 60-day period, the creditor is under no obligation to conduct any investigation. The investigation must be completed within 10 business days of receiving the notice and a report must be sent to the consumer within three days after completion of the investigation. 12 C.F.R. § 1005.11(c)(1).

The financial institution may extend its investigation period beyond the 10 day period up to 45 days from receipt of the notice of error if the institution provisionally re-credits the consumer's account for the amount alleged to be in error. 12 C.F.R. § 1005.11(c)(2). The provisional credit must be at the disposal of the consumer until the investigation is concluded. If the institution discovers that an error did in fact occur, then the institution must "promptly" re-credit the consumer's account. The institution can take no longer than one business day to make such a correction. Should, however, the institution learn that no error has been made, the institution must supply the consumer with an explanation of its findings within 3 business days after the conclusion of its investigation. The explanation must include a notice that the consumer can request copies of any documents the financial institution relied upon to reach its determination. 12 C.F.R. § 1005.11(d).

If the consumer has given oral notice of the error but does not comply with a written confirmation requirement within 10 days, then the financial institution does not have to provisionally re-credit the consumer's account. If the account has been provisionally re-credited and the financial institution concludes after investigation that no error has occurred, the amount provisionally re-credited may be debited at that time, but the bank must notify the consumer of the debit, and agree to honor checks using those provisionally re-credited funds for five business days after transmittal of the notice. 12 C.F.R. § 1005.11(d)(2)(ii).

The section prescribing the error resolution procedures, 15 U.S.C. § 1693f(e), provides that in certain cases the consumer can recover treble his actual damages. Treble damages are recoverable if the financial institution did not provisionally credit the amount of the alleged error to the consumer's account as required and either failed to make a good faith investigation of the alleged error or did not have a reasonable basis for believing that the consumer's account was not in error.

4. OVERDRAFT PROTECTION AND DEBIT CARD/ATM TRANSACTIONS

Based on consumer complaints about excessive "overdraft protection" fees associated with debit card use, Regulation E was amended effective in 2010 to require that consumers must "opt-in" to receive fee-based overdraft protection from their financial institutions. 12 C.F.R. § 1005.17. This issue came to a head when, during the early 2000s, consumers began using their debit cards as a cash substitute to make numerous small purchases or cash withdrawals during a short time period, such as a single day. At the same time, banks offering debit/ATM cards were routinely enrolling these customers into their "overdraft protection" plan, under which the bank would cover the purchase or cash withdrawal even if the consumer had insufficient funds in their account, but would charge a fee for each such transaction. As consumers used their debit cards for a series of relatively small purchases, such as a $3.00 cup of coffee, or a $10 meal, the fees of around $30 or more per transaction could far exceed the amount by which their accounts were overdrawn. Most consumers, until they incurred such fees themselves, assumed that their debit or ATM transactions would simply be declined if they had insufficient funds in their accounts. Thus, there was a huge consumer outcry against the use of relatively large overdraft protection fees for these small transactions.

The problem was exacerbated by the practice of some banks who were using "high to low" posting order for accounts that had debit/ATM cards associated with them. Using this posting order, if a consumer had $100 in her account, and purchased ten small items totaling $99 followed by a $100 item, all on the same day, but with the $100 item being the last transaction of the day, then under low-to-high, or even chronological posting, there would be only one overdraft transaction and one overdraft fee. If the bank used "high to low" posting, however, the bank would wait until the end of the day and then post the highest item, for $100, first, followed by the other smaller items, so that there would be ten transactions that overdrafted instead of one, and each of the ten would incur a separate overdraft fee. If the fee for each overdraft was in the $30 range, then the customer would end up paying some $300 in fees for a $99 overdraft. The Ninth Circuit Court of Appeals held that this practice could be misleading to consumers, who were led to believe by the bank's own marketing that items would be taken out of their account in chronological order, not high to low. *Guitierrez v. Wells Fargo Bank, N.A.*, 704 F.3d 712 (9th Cir. 2012).

The response by the Federal Reserve Board was to issue a new regulation requiring financial institutions to give consumers the right to "opt-in" or affirmatively consent to overdraft protection, along with its concomitant fees, rather than making this part of their standard form contract. The regulation does not ban either overdraft protection or high-to-low posting, however. 12 C.F.R. § 1005.17. The regulation applies to ATM and one-time debit card transactions, but does not apply to check transactions or recurring debits. The regulation provides safeguards designed to inform consumers of the nature of the "overdraft protection service," as well as the fees involved, prior to the opt-in decision. The consumer must be allowed to opt out or revoke their consent at any later time even after they have chosen to opt in.

The CFPB, which is currently charged with enforcing this regulation, has settled or brought charges in several cases. For instance, Regions Bank agreed to pay up to $49 million in refunds for charging overdraft fees to consumers who had not opted in. *In re Regions Bank*, Consent Order, CFPB File No. 2-15-CFPB-0009, filed April 28, 2005. In two other cases, financial service providers were charged with deceptive or abusive marketing of their overdraft protection plans. *In re Santander Bank*, File No. 2016-CFPB-0012, Consent Order (97/14/2016); *CFPB v. TCF National Bank*, 2017 WL 6211033 (D. Minn. 2017).

If the consumer does not opt for overdraft protection, and then attempts to carry out a transaction that would result in an overdraft of their account, the bank can refuse to honor the debit card or ATM withdrawal on the spot.

5. PREAUTHORIZED EFT

Assume that a consumer has authorized his bank in writing to transfer monthly payments from his account to the account of GMAC to pay for an automobile he purchased pursuant to a retail installment sales contract. This is considered as a "preauthorized electronic fund transfer" and is permitted under the Act. 15 U.S.C. § 1693a(10). What is the bank's liability if the bank's EFT system malfunctions and it fails to make the transfer for one month? The consumer may have suffered damages as a result, because under the terms of the retail installment contract, the non-payment could be considered as a default and GMAC could repossess the car.

The bank's liability in this situation is covered by 15 U.S.C. § 1693h, which makes the bank "liable to a consumer for all damages proximately caused by ... the financial institution's failure to make an electronic fund transfer, in accordance with the terms and conditions of an account, in the correct amount or in a timely manner when properly instructed to do so by a consumer." There are some exceptions, however. A financial institution's liability will be limited to "actual damages proved" when the failure to make the transfer was unintentional and resulted from a bona fide error despite the existence of procedures designed to avert such errors. 15 U.S.C. § 1693h(c). A financial institution will have a complete defense to liability if it can show that the failure to make the transfer resulted from either "(1) an act of God or other circumstance beyond its control, that it exercised reasonable care to prevent such an occurrence, and that it exercised such diligence as the circumstances required; or (2) a technical malfunction which was known to the consumer at the time he attempted to initiate an electronic fund transfer or, in the case of a preauthorized transfer, at the time such transfer would have occurred." 15 U.S.C. § 1693h(b).

In the example, the most significant damage to the consumer would be the repossession of his car. However, the creditor may not have the right to repossess the car, regardless of the terms of the retail installment contract, where the failure to make the transfer is caused by an EFT system malfunction. 15 U.S.C. § 1693j provides that "if a system malfunction prevents the effectuation of an electronic fund transfer initiated by the consumer to another person, and such person has agreed to accept payment by such means, the consumer's obligation to the other person shall be suspended until the malfunction is corrected and the electronic fund transfer may be completed." In this situation, the creditor cannot lawfully repossess because there has been no default in payment since the consumer's obligation is suspended. Rather, the creditor must wait until the EFT system is fixed, unless he subsequently makes in writing a demand for payment by some other means.

Similar to the UCC provision for stopping payment, a stop payment for a preauthorized transfer may be issued by a consumer under the EFTA. The stop payment provision, however, is very limited. A stop payment may be made on preauthorized transfers such as a payment to an insurance company if the consumer notifies the bank at least three business days before the scheduled transfer. The notification can be given orally and is non-waivable even if the agreement with the bank provides that written notification must be given. 15 U.S.C. § 1693e.

Preauthorized electronic fund transfers from a consumer's account must be authorized by the consumer in writing, and a copy of such authorization must be provided to the consumer. 15 U.S.C. § 1693e. Also, a potential creditor cannot condition the extension of credit on repayment by preauthorized electronic fund transfers. 15 U.S.C. § 1693k.

These EFTA provisions have been applied in government enforcement cases. One example is the failure of internet-based companies who receive recurring payments from consumers via electronic fund transfer to obtain the consumer's written authorization in advance and failure to notify the consumers in advance if the amount of a particular transfer will vary from the pre-authorized amount or range of amounts.[2] For example, AOL, an internet service provider, was targeted by an FTC investigation because they would debit a consumer's account $9.95 one month and $38.95 another month for miscellaneous fees without proper authorization. Some online payday lenders have been accused by the Consumer Financial Protection Bureau of violating this section of the EFTA by putting money into consumers' accounts without authorization, and then deducting fees by preauthorized EFTs, also without prior written authorization. Such lenders have also been accused of illegally requiring preauthorized electronic fund transfers as a condition of receiving credit. *See Consumer Financial Protection Bureau v. Hydra Group,* Complaint (W.D. Mo. Sept. 2014), available at http://files.consumer finance.gov/f/201409_cfpb_complaint_hydra-group .pdf.

---

[2] *See* Roscoe B. Starek, III and Lynda M. Rozell, *A Cyberspace Perspective: The Federal Trade Commission's Commitment to On-line Consumer Protection*, 15 J. Marshall J. Computer & Info. L. 679 (1997).

6. CIVIL AND CRIMINAL LIABILITY

The EFTA provides substantial incentive for a financial institution to comply with the provisions of the Act. A financial institution which fails to comply with an EFTA provision with respect to a consumer is liable under 15 U.S.C. § 1693m (the general civil liability provision) for actual damages suffered by the consumer, a minimum penalty (from $100 to $1,000 in an individual action), and the costs of the action plus a reasonable fee for the consumer's attorney.

The EFTA also imposes criminal liability for a number of offenses, including knowing and willful failure to comply with any of its provisions. 15 U.S.C. § 1693n. Another criminal offense is knowingly and willfully giving false information or failing to provide information which the EFTA requires to be disclosed. The maximum penalties for these offenses are a $5,000 fine or imprisonment for one year, or both.

C. GIFT CARDS, STORED VALUE/PREPAID CARDS AND INTERNATIONAL REMITTANCES

In addition to credit and debit cards, many Americans are now using so-called "stored value" or prepaid cards to make purchases, withdraw funds, pay bills or receive deposits. These cards include gift cards, payroll cards, electronic benefit transfer (EBT) cards and "general purpose reloadable" (GPR) cards. They are not credit cards because these cards involve prepaid accounts, with the value either stored on the card itself or accessed from the card. Thus, they are not covered by TILA or Regulation Z.[3] These types of cards are very useful to the "unbanked" population who wish to have the convenience of plastic but without having to maintain a bank account. Most aspects of these cards are covered by an amended Regulation E. Some of the stored value cards have their own specific regulatory provisions within Regulation E, such as gift cards, payroll cards and EBT cards. The general purpose reloadable prepaid cards are also now under the wing of Regulation E, due to a revised regulation issued by the Consumer Financial Protection Bureau (CFPB) that became effective in April 2019. Each of these types of cards will be discussed below.

1. GIFT CARDS

Gift cards and gift certificates have been very popular for many years with both retailers and their customers. Such cards are prepaid, typically by a donor, and can be "spent" by the recipient either at a single merchant or group of merchants. There are general purpose gift cards that are part of the VISA or MasterCard networks as well. The amount that can be redeemed is preset, and is usually not renewable or subject to increase. There is no requirement for the issuer of such cards to send out periodic statements, and the balance remaining on the card is usually available at the cash register of the retail outlet where it is honored. If there is not

---

[3] Some prepaid cards, known as "hybrid prepaid-credit cards," are permitted to include credit features but those credit features are subject to Regulation Z safeguards. 12 C.F.R. § 1026.61.

enough money available on the card to cover a purchase, the customer will simply make up the difference with cash, check or a different card. These cards basically are a cash substitute, with no identification or PIN number required for use, and no protection against unauthorized use.

Since gift cards are prepaid and widely viewed as equivalent to cash, there was some controversy over the undisclosed imposition by some issuers of dormancy fees or inactivity charges, as well as relatively early expiration dates, such that consumers may have felt that their "cash" was unfairly losing its value. A provision of the Credit CARD Act, effective 2010, responded to these concerns by requiring special disclosures and some restrictions, but without including gift cards within the EFTA for all purposes. 15 U.S.C. § 1693*l*–1; 12 C.F.R. § 1005.20. Under current law, any dormancy fee, inactivity charge, service or other fees, as well as any expiration date, with respect to gift certificates, store gift cards, and general-use prepaid gift cards, must be disclosed to the buyer prior to sale, and on the card or certificate itself. Dormancy fees may not be charged prior to a 12-month period of inactivity, and not more than one fee may be charged in any single month. Expiration dates cannot be earlier than five years after the date of purchase or the date on which funds were last loaded. *Id.*

2. STORED VALUE/PREPAID CARDS

Government benefits such as food stamps as well as other types of benefits, are often distributed via special stored-value cards that can be reloaded remotely and can be used as a substitute for paper checks. This system is more cost efficient for the government than mailing paper checks or issuing food stamps. It is also helpful to recipients who receive their benefits more quickly and, because many of the recipients do not have bank accounts, the cards allow the benefits to be spent or cashed without having to use a check cashing service. Some employers also choose to use so-called "payroll cards," in a somewhat similar way and for similar reasons.

Such prepaid EBT and payroll cards are covered by the protections of EFTA and Regulation E, including limited liability for unauthorized use and error resolution, but with some variations. The financial institution involved with these particular cards are excused from issuing periodic statements, as long as they make the information available through alternative means such as by telephone, internet or in paper form on request. 12 C.F.R. § 1005.18 (payroll card accounts); 12 C.F.R. § 1005.15 (government benefits card). The statute contains an important caveat, however, that no one may "require a consumer to establish an account for receipt of electronic fund transfers with a particular financial institution as a condition of employment or receipt of a government benefit." 15 U.S.C. § 1693k(2).

The category of General Purpose Reloadable (GPR) cards is probably the most rapidly growing type of consumer plastic payment card. It is offered by nonbank entities such as large retailers, as well as by some banks, and can be part of the VISA or

MasterCard networks, but are prepaid and fully reloadable. This type of card is a substitute for a credit or debit card for the unbanked or underbanked segment of the population who may not qualify for a credit card and who do not have a bank account but wish to have a convenient way to pay for items with a card either in stores or online. These cards can be loaded with cash or by direct deposit of a paycheck or other means. They can also be used at ATMs for cash withdrawal or deposits.

As of April 1, 2019, prepaid cards or "prepaid accounts," have been swept under the wing of Regulation E without the need to be associated with a bank account or depositary institution. Now general purpose reloadable prepaid cards, payroll cards, government benefit cards and "campus cards" used by colleges and universities to disburse financial aid to students, are all under the purview of Regulation E. 12 C.F.R. § 1005.2(b)(3). Under this regulation, these cards will receive the benefits of Regulation E's billing error resolution and unauthorized use protections, provided the consumer registers and verifies their identification with the issuer. 12 C.F.R. § 1005.18(e)(3). As with payroll and government benefit cards, the prepaid general purpose cards are also permitted to use electronic and telephonic alternatives to periodic statements. 12 C.F.R. § 1005.18(c).

Prior to the issuance of the amended regulation, some consumers were vexed by unexpected fees associated with the prepaid cards. Now, customers will receive a "short form" disclosure prior to acquiring the card, which highlights the most pertinent fees that may be applicable, such as those for account maintenance, transaction fees, fees charged for ATM withdrawals, and cash-reloading fees. The "long form" discloses more details about fees, as well other fees that are not as common but are possible under certain circumstances. 12 C.F.R. § 1005.18(b).

Some prepaid cards, known as "hybrid prepaid-credit cards," are permitted to include credit features but those features are subject to Regulation Z safeguards. 12 C.F.R. § 1026.61. The hybrid cards must comply with the normal consumer protection requirements for credit cards, including ability to pay analysis, providing periodic statements, allowing at least 21 days to pay prior to assessing late fees, as well as other fee-limiting provisions applicable to other credit cards. To avoid consumer confusion, the issuer must wait at least 30 days after a prepaid account is registered to solicit a consumer to add a credit feature. 12 C.F.R. § 1026.61(c).

Prepaid cards, often set up as debit cards associated with a bank, may be used by colleges and universities to disburse financial aid to their students. These so-called "campus cards" are regulated by the Department of Education. 34 C.F.R. §§ 668.161–.167. Safeguards include a ban on charging students fees for account opening or receipt of access devices, a requirement that students be informed of their choices of financial institutions to hold this type of account, assurance that students will have reasonable access to surcharge-free ATMs, ban on requiring students to open an account with a particular financial institution to receive financial aid, and a requirement to obtain student consent before opening an account with a third party servicer. In 2015, bank affiliate Higher One entered a consent order with the Federal Reserve Board to settle charges that it misled students receiving financial aid disbursements regarding fees, choices of financial institutions, and affiliation with the sponsoring school. Higher One agreed to pay millions in restitution and civil penalties. www.federalreserve.gov/newsevents/pressreleases/files/enf20151223a1.pdf.

There have been some enforcement actions taken by the relevant government agencies regarding prepaid cards. For instance, in 2017 the FTC settled a case with NetSpend, which had advertised its prepaid cards as providing immediate access to loaded funds, whereas many consumers experienced delays. The company agreed to pay up to $53 million in refunds to consumers. *FTC v. NetSpend Corp.*, Case No. 1:16-CV-4203, Stipulated Order for Permanent Injunction (N.D. Ga. 2017), available at FTC.gov. The CFPB settled a case involving "RushCard" accounts. Rush Card experienced technical difficulties that left thousands of consumers without access to their prepaid funds, including some directly deposited paychecks, for undue periods of time. The company agreed to pay $10 million in consumer redress and $3 million in civil penalties. *In re UniRush, LLC*, No. 2017-CFPB-0010 (Jan. 31, 2017), available at consumerfinance.gov.

3. INTERNATIONAL REMITTANCES

There is another important type of electronic fund transfer, international remittances, that are used by consumers but do not usually involve any type of plastic card. International remittances are money transfers sent by individuals in the United States to friends, relatives and businesses abroad, typically using the services of non-bank "money transmitters." International remittances involve relatively small individual transactions but cumulatively amount to billions of dollars per year. The money is delivered abroad in the local currency through convenience stores or banks. They were not regulated under the EFTA until 2010, when the statute was amended specifically to include them. 15 U.S.C. § 1693o–1; 12 C.F.R. §§ 1005.30–1005.36.

The law requires that a remittance transfer provider issue a pre-payment disclosure stating the transfer amount in the currency transferred, all transfer fees, the total amount of the transaction, the exchange rate and the transfer amount in the currency of the recipient. 12 C.F.R. § 1005.31(b)(1). In addition, the consumer must be provided with a receipt and a statement regarding error resolution procedures and cancellation rights. In recognition of the fact that many international remittance users may actually be using their mobile phones to make these transfers, the disclosures can be made available to consumers in a variety of ways, including orally, by email, mobile application, or by text message. 12 C.F.R. § 1005.31(a).

Error resolution procedures require that consumers send a notice of error within 180 days. The remittance provider then has up to 90 days to investigate, and one to three days after completion of the investigation to correct the error or send a notice and explanation of the results. 12 C.F.R. § 1005.33. Errors include payment of an incorrect amount, computational errors, and failure to make available the disclosed amount to the designated recipient, *i.e.,* releasing the funds to the wrong person. The list of "errors" does *not* include sending the money to the wrong person if the sender provided the wrong account information and the remittance provider has given notice beforehand that the sender could lose the funds if he/she provides the wrong account number. 12 C.F.R. § 1005.33(h). In a unique provision, the sender of an international remittance has up to 30 minutes to cancel the transaction if sufficient identifying information is provided and the transferred funds have not yet been picked up or deposited. 12 C.F.R. § 1005.34.

D. INTERNET, MOBILE PAYMENTS, AND CRYPTOCURRENCY

Beyond the various types of "plastic" payment systems discussed in the preceding sections, consumers are increasingly using the internet, mobile devices and even so-called "cryptocurrency" such as Bitcoin, to finance transactions. This new frontier of consumer payments is partly regulated under current law, and partly operates in an unregulated environment.

1. INTERNET-BASED AND MOBILE DEVICE PAYMENTS

In the early 2000s, services such as that offered by PayPal, allowed consumers to transfer payments directly to other persons or companies, using an account funded by cash, credit card or a bank account. This could be considered an early type of "digital wallet" that allows a consumer to access various other accounts to pay for items as they choose. Accounts like this that are funded by a credit or debit card would be regulated by TILA or EFTA. Usually these types of internet-based payment systems can be accessed on a mobile phone, personal computer or tablet device. A true mobile payment uses the mobile phone provider as a go-between, with the charge appearing on the phone bill. Other mobile phone apps allow payment from preloaded accounts with particular merchants by simply waving a bar code at the register. Consumer issues such as errors, fraud and fees can occur with these types of payments, but the regulatory landscape is fragmented. The FTC sued PayPal, which owns a P2P (peer-to-peer) service called Venmo, for failure to tell consumers that holds were sometimes placed on their payments, despite notifications that a Venmo payment had been received, leaving consumers who were relying on the use of such payments high and dry. *In re PayPal*, FTC Consent Order C-4651 (May 24, 2018), available at ftc.gov.

2. CRYPTO- AND VIRTUAL CURRENCY

Cryptocurrencies are the newest innovation in consumer payments. The most popular and most familiar one is Bitcoin, although there are many others. These currencies can be used to buy and sell products and services among willing participants, but they are not recognized as legal tender by any government. These currencies are created and maintained by computer systems and encryption, such as "block chain," a type of public ledger used to process and verify transactions. They are typically used for P2P payments and eliminate the intermediary functions of financial institutions and governments. The participants also use pseudonyms or are anonymous. Transactions resemble the use of paper currency in that payment is final and usually untraceable. Cryptocurrency is not regulated by either TILA (no consumer credit involved) or EFTA (no consumer account).

For less adventurous or independent users, a new type of business has sprung up that works as a third party on behalf of others to exchange virtual currency (a subset of cryptocurrency) for money or other things of value, to transfer virtual currency from one party to another, store it for later use, etc. A new uniform law, entitled "Uniform Regulation of Virtual-Currency Businesses Act," was drafted by the National Conference of Commissioners on Uniform State Laws and approved by the American Bar Association as a model statute in 2018. This model law is meant to provide the states with a statutory framework for licensing and supervising virtual currency businesses. In addition to licensing, the Act provides some modest consumer protection by requiring disclosures of applicable fees, insurance, liability, and the risk involved in using virtual currency (*i.e.*, irrevocability of transfers, not legal tender). This uniform law has been enacted in Rhode Island, and introduced in California, Oklahoma and Hawaii. www.uniformlaws.org.

INDEX

References are to Pages

Add-on interest, 69–70, 163–164, 186, 198
Adjustable rate mortgages (ARMs), 228, 233–34, 236
Adverse action, *see* Fair Credit Reporting Act and Equal Credit Opportunity Act
Advertiser, 61, 64, 71
Advertising substantiation doctrine, 60, 61–62
American Law Institute
   Restatement of the Law of Consumer Contracts (proposed), 92
Annual percentage rate (APR), *see* Truth in Lending Act
Arbitration, 49–56, 88, 91–92, 146–147, 151, 242, 246–247, 272–273, 351
   American Arbitration Association, 53
   CFPB regulation of arbitration clauses with class action waivers, Congressional veto, 55–56
   Consumer Due Process Protocol for Mediation and Arbitration of Consumer Disputes, 53–54
   Federal Arbitration Act & U.S. Supreme Court decisions, 50–53
   MMWA informal dispute resolution mechanisms, 54–55, 339–341
Assignee liability
   HOEPA, 175, 241
   Holder in due course rule, 313–315
   TILA, 264–266
Assignment of wages, 360–361
ATM transactions, 431–434
Attorney general, 30–32, 377–378
Attorney's fees
   ECOA, 162
   FCRA & CROA, 146, 151
   Holder in Due Course, 320–321
   MMWA & Lemon Laws, 338, 346, 351
   State UDAPs, 34, 38–40, 42–43, 47–48, 52

Truth in Lending Act, 270
Auto leases
    Consumer Leasing Act, 71, 280–283
Automobile title pawn, 304, 308
Bait and switch advertising, 37, 64–65, 217
Billing systems (credit cards)
    Average daily balance method, 215–216
    Previous balance method, 216
    Two-cycle average daily balance method, 216
Breach of the peace, 397–398
Buried finance charges, 192–195
CAN-SPAM Act, 86–87
Celebrity endorsements, 66
Children's Online Privacy Protection Act (COPPA), 94–95, 105–108
Class actions, 42–48
    Abuse in class actions, 46–48
    Certification requirements, 44–45
    Class Action Fairness Act (CAFA), 47–48
    Class action waivers, 48
    FCRA, 146
    National Association of Consumer Advocates' Standards and Guidelines for Litigating and Settling Class Actions, 46–47
Closed-end credit
    TILA disclosures, 180–208
        Format, 200–203
        Timing, 180–183
Common law remedies
    Credit reports, 121–123
    Debt collection, 363–366
    Fraud and misrepresentation, 57–59
    Privacy, 95–97
Confession of judgment, 356–357
Consumer Credit Protection Act, 168
Consumer Financial Protection Bureau, 26–30
    Constitutionality, 26–27
Consumer Leasing Act, 280–283
Consumer Review Fairness Act, 67
Consumer transaction, definition of, 1–3

INDEX

Cooling-off periods
   Door-to-door sales, 76
   HOEPA, 240
   Right to rescind under TILA, 76–77, 273–278
Corrective advertising, 63–64
Cosigner, 354–356
Credit advertising, 69–75, 258
Credit bureaus/Consumer Reporting Agencies (CRAs), 119–120, 128–132
Credit CARD Act, 167, 211, 404–406, 420–421, 440
Credit cards
   Billing errors, 415–418
   Defenses against credit card issuer based on merchant dealings, 322–326
   Grace periods, 418–420
   Rates and fees, limits on, 404–406
   Unauthorized use, 409–415
   Young consumers, 407–409
Credit insurance
   Truth in Lending disclosures, 185–187, 189–191
   Voluntariness, 191
Credit Repair Organizations Act (CROA), 149–152
Credit reports/consumer reports, 119–121, 123–127
   Security freeze, 143–144
Credit sales
   Time-price doctrine, 298–299
Credit scoring, 155–156
Creditor, *see* Truth in Lending Act
Cryptocurrencies, 448
Data security, 108–114
Dealer-arranged financing
   Home improvement dealers, 241
   Lender liability, 241
Debit cards, 421–434
   Billing errors, 428–431
   Electronic Fund Transfer Act, 422
   Unauthorized use, 425–428
Debt collection, 361–401
   Breach of the peace, 397–398
   Common law remedies, 363–366

INDEX

Fair Debt Collection Practices Act, 366–390
Debt collector, *see* Fair Debt Collection Practices Act
Deceptive trade practices, 18–19, 27–28, 30–31, 33
    FTC policy statement, 19
Defamation, 122
Deficiency judgment
    Exempt property, 393
    Garnishment, 391–395
    Judicial collection efforts, 390–391
    Redeeming collateral, 397–398
    Repossession, 397–398
Depositary Institutions Deregulation and Monetary Control Act (DIDMCA), 301–302
Discrimination in access to credit, *see* Equal Credit Opportunity Act
Dodd Frank Wall Street Reform and Consumer Protection Act, 303
Do-Not-Call Registry (FTC), 25, 79–80
Door-to-door sales, 75–77
Earned wage advances, 307–308
Education loans, private, *see* Truth in Lending Act
Electronic Funds Transfer Act, 422–424
Equal Credit Opportunity Act, 153–162
    Adverse action notification, 133–134
    Discrimination in evaluating credit applications, 153
    Discrimination in obtaining information, 154–155
    Effect on state law, 161
    Notification, 159–161
    Remedies, 161–162
    Scope, 153–154
    Spousal signature rule, 154
Fair Credit and Charge Card Disclosure Act, 211
Fair Credit Billing Act, 415–418
Fair Credit Reporting Act, 123–148
    Administrative remedies, 145–146
    Adverse action, 133–134
    Civil liability, 146–148
    Consumer credit reporting agencies, requirements, 128–132
    Furnishers of information, requirements, 135–137
    Prescreened lists, 125–126

Rights of consumers, 137–142
Scope, 123–127
Users of consumer reports, requirements, 132–135
Fair Debt Collection Practices Act, 366–390
Attorney as debt collector, 370–371
Bona fide error defense, 389
Civil liability, 389
Debt, defined, 367–368
Debt buyers, 369–370
Debt collector, defined, 368–372
Electronic disclosures & other communications in collection, 375–376, 387
False or misleading information, 376–379
Harassment or abuse, 381–382
Persons and transactions covered, 367–372
Regulation, CFPB proposed, 367
Restrictions on communications, 385–388
Standing to sue in federal court, 389–390
Telephone calls, harassing, 382
Time-barred debts, 379–381
Validation of debts, 372–376
False advertising, 57–61
Federal Reserve Board, 26–27
Federal Trade Commission
Advertising substantiation doctrine, 61–63
Cooling-Off Rule, 76
Credit Practices Rule, 353–361
History, 17–26
Industry guides, 23–24
Native advertising in social media, 66
Telemarketing Sales Rule, 79
Trade Regulation Rule Concerning Preservation of Consumers' Claims and Defenses (Holder in Due Course Rule), 315–322
Trade regulation rules, 24–25
Federal Trade Commission Improvement Act, 24–25
Finance charge, *see* Truth in Lending Act
FinTech (financial technology), 157, 304–305
Fraud, *see* Common law remedies

Garnishment
  Restrictions on garnishment, 391–395
General Purpose Reloadable cards, 441–442
Gift cards, 439–440
Gramm-Leach-Bliley Act, 114–117
Hidden contract terms, 87–92
Hidden finance charges, *see* Truth in Lending Act, Buried finance charges
Holder in Due Course Doctrine, 312–314
  FTC Holder Rule, 315–322
  Limitations on affirmative recovery under FTC rule, 318–321
  UCC, 312
Home Equity Lines of Credit (HELOC), 223–226
Home improvement dealers
  Deceptive practices, 241
Home Ownership and Equity Protection Act (HOEPA), 236–241
Household goods, non-purchase security interest in, 357–359
HUD, 250, 287
Identity theft
  Fair Credit Reporting Act provisions, 142–145
  Identity Theft and Assumption Deterrence Act, 142
Infomercials, 65
Interest rate
  Add-on, 163–164
  Discounted, 164
International remittances, 445–446
Interstate Land Sales Full Disclosure Act, 283–286
Invasion of privacy, 96, 122, 148, 364
Kickbacks, *see* Real Estate Settlement Procedures Act, Anti-kickback provisions
Late charges, 356
Leasing
  Consumer Leasing Act, 280–283
Lemon Laws, 342–346
"Little FTC Acts," *see* UDAP statutes
Magnuson-Moss Warranty Act, 332–341
  Disclosures, 334–336
  Informal dispute resolution mechanisms & arbitration, 339–341
Mail, Internet or Telephone Order Merchandise Rule, 81–82

Military Lending Act, 305–306
Mortgage Reform and Anti-Predatory Lending Act, 167, 227, 242, 267
Motor Vehicle Information and Cost Savings Act, 347–348
Nader's raiders, 21–22
National Association of Consumer Advocates (NACA), 46–47
National Bank Act, 299–300
Negative option plans, 82–84
Non-purchase money security interest in household goods, 357–359
Odometer Act, 347–348
Official Staff Commentary, Regulation Z, 168–169
Online sales, 87
    Shrinkwrap, clickwrap, and browsewrap, 88–91
Open-end credit, 210–226
    Defined, 176
    Fair Credit Billing Act, 415–418
    Spurious open-end credit, 176–177, 212–213
    Unauthorized transactions, 409–415
Overdraft protection, 431–434
Pawnshops, 304
Payday loans, 172, 304
    Pullback of proposed CFPB regulation, 308–309
    State laws, 306–307
Peer-to-peer payments, 447
Phishing, *see* Privacy
Preauthorized electronic fund transfers, 434–437
Prepaid cards, 440–444
    Campus cards, 443–444
    CFPB regulation, 442–443
    Hybrid prepaid cards, 443
Prepayment penalties, 238, 240–241, 246
Prescreened lists, *see* Fair Credit Reporting Act
Pretexting, *see* Privacy, Financial privacy
Privacy
    California privacy law, 104–105
    Children's online privacy, 105–108
    Common law privacy torts, 95–97
    Data security, 108–114

INDEX

Financial privacy
    Gramm-Leach-Bliley Act, 114–117
    Online privacy, 98–105
    Pretexting, 117
Phishing, 117
Puffing, deceptive advertising defense, 57–58, 327
Pyramid schemes, 84–86
Pyramiding late charges, 356
Racketeer Influenced and Corrupt Organizations Act (RICO)
    Civil suits by consumers, 40–42
Rate ceilings, *see* Usury laws
Real Estate Settlements Procedures Act (RESPA), 227, 286–289
    Anti-kickback provisions, 248
Real estate transactions and TILA, 226–251
    Ability to repay requirement, 242–243
    Appraisal independence, 248–249
    High cost or HOEPA loans, 236–241
    Integrated TILA/RESPA disclosures, 230–232
    Mortgage servicing regulation, 248
    "Qualified" mortgage loans, 244–245
    Rescission, 240, 273–278
    Special early disclosures, 229–233
Referral sales, 84
Regulation E, 422, 431–432, 441–442
Regulation Z, 164–165, 168–169, 175–177, 213, 223, 250, 256–257, 439, 443
Reliance, as requirement for common law fraud, 57
Rent-to-own, 172, 281
Repossession, 371–372, 397–398
Rescission, *see* Real estate transactions and TILA
Residential mortgage transactions, *see* Real estate transactions and TILA
Restore Online Shoppers' Confidence Act (ROSCA), 83
Reverse mortgages, 249–251
Security freeze, credit reports, 143–144
Security interests, 203–204
    Household goods, 357–359
SPAM (unsolicited commercial e-mails), 86–87
Spousal signature rule, *see* Equal Credit Opportunity Act
Spurious open-end credit, 176–177, 212–213

Standing to sue in federal court, Article III
    FCRA, 147–148
    FDCPA, 389–390
    TILA, 258–259
State agency enforcement, 30–32
State Attorney General
    Enforcement of state UDAP statutes, 230–232
State credit reporting statutes, 148–149
Stored value cards, 438, 440–444
Subprime credit market
    Abusive lending practices, 236–237
    Discount financing, 192
Telemarketing, 25, 77
Telemarketing and Consumer Fraud and Abuse Prevention Act, 78–79
Telemarketing Sales Rule (FTC), 79–80
Telephone Consumer Protection Act, 78
Telephone Disclosure and Dispute Resolution Act, 80
Time-price doctrine, 298
Title pawn, 304
Truth in Lending Act
    Advertising provisions, 69–75
    Annual Percentage Rate (APR), 178–79, 183, 198–199, 218
    Buried finance charges, 192–197
    Closed-end credit, 180–208
    Consumer Leasing Act, 280–283
    Consumer remedies, 256–264
    Credit insurance, 189–191
    Creditor, defined, 173–175
    Damages, 184, 259, 262
    Defenses, 264–269
    Federal enforcement of TILA, 253–256
    Finance charge, 183–197
    General disclosure requirements, 177–180
    Location of disclosures, 207–208
    Official Staff Commentary, 168–169
    Open-end credit, 210–226
    Private education loans, 204–207
    Private enforcement, 256–264

INDEX

Real estate transactions, *see* Real estate transactions and TILA
Regulation Z, 168–169
Residential mortgage transactions, *see* Real estate transactions and TILA
Security interests, 203–204, 357–59
Standing to sue, 257–259
Truth in Lending Simplification and Reform Act of 1980, 165
Truth in Savings Act, 278–280
UDAP (Unfair or deceptive acts and practices) statutes, 30–31, 33
    Attorney's fees, 38–40
    Deceptive advertising, 60–64, 67–69
    "Little FTC Acts," 33
    Remedies, 37–40
    State Attorney General enforcement, 30–32
Unconscionability, 52, 91–92, 302
Unfairness, 18–19, 24–25, 101–102, 358
    FTC policy statement, 18–19
Uniform Commercial Code
    Breach of the peace, 397–398
    Holder in due course doctrine, 312–313, 321–22
    Limitations on deficiency judgments, 398–400
    Repossession, 397
    Warranties, 326–331
        Disclaimers, 330–331
        Express, 327
        Implied, 327–328
Uniform Consumer Credit Code, 84, 315, 400–401
Uniform Small Loan Law, 293
United Nations Guidelines for Consumer Protection, 10
Unordered merchandise, 82
Unsolicited commercial e-mails (SPAM), 86–87
Used Car Rule (FTC), 346–347
    Buyer's Guide, 346–347
Usury laws, 163, 185, 190, 291–92
    Federal preemption, 299–304
    Proving usury, 296–299
    Rate ceilings, 294–296
    State laws on payday lending, 306–307